www.bm

MRCS Practice Papers Part A: Paper 1 SBAs

Second edition

MRCS Practice Papers Part A: Paper 1 SBAs

Second edition

Irfan Halim
MBBS MRCS MSc
Specialist Registrar in General Surgery
SW Thames
SpR Rotation

Egerton Court
Parkgate Estate
Knutsford
Cheshire
WA16 8DX

Telephone: 01565 752000

First published 2006, Second edition 2009

ISBN: 1 905635 613
ISBN: 978 1 905635 610

A catalogue record for this book is available from the British Library.

Text prepared by Carnegie Book Production, Lancaster

Printed and bound in the UK by CPI Antony Rowe

Contents

Foreword

This book is intended primarily for candidates sitting the new MRCS Part A examination (SBAs). The four practice papers included in this book each provide 135 questions in the SBA or 'single best answer' format. Each of the papers has been specifically structured and the contents aim to reflect the syllabus as set by the Royal College of Surgeons.

The written component of the new MRCS Intercollegiate examination is set in two papers in Part A (SBAs and EMQs), covering the applied basic sciences and principles of surgery in general. The new Part B is now the clinical component of the examination which is conducted via OSCEs (Objective Structured Clinical Examination).

This book aims to help you to pass the Part A MRCS examination: you will learn to assess your knowledge and also be alerted to those areas that may require further revision.

This book alone is not a substitute for the necessary reading required before sitting the exam. It should be used in conjunction with a good background of reading materials that aim to cover the syllabus and other practice question books. The questions covered within these practice papers represent a good range of 'hot-topics' that are found year to year within the MRCS examination. The questions are also set in levels of varying difficulty just as in the real exam. The answers include a paragraph justifying themselves as well as commenting on the relevant surgical topics.

As with most MRCS MCQ exams throughout the past years, candidates may find that there is a particular bias with an excess of questions from one or more specialties. Previous sittings have had a greater emphasis on head and neck anatomy in one year or endocrine/paediatrics/statistics questions in another. Some exams will have had many (>5) questions on blood gas interpretations and other years may have had none. This is purely a random selection of questions with no intentional weighting on any particular subjects. The best advice that still remains is to read the MRCS syllabus in its entirety and then practice as many questions as possible from question banks in books and online. All candidates are in the same boat and face the same stresses as each other so do not worry too much about a particularly difficult or unusual paper. Much of passing the examination is about technique and reading the question properly rather than pure knowledge itself and these principles can only be gained through practising MCQs and reading around subjects that are unclear.

I hope that you find this book helpful in guiding you in your future examinations. I hope also that this book will not be restricted to MRCS candidates, but be useful for Final Year medical students and other students of surgery.

Irfan Halim

Acknowledgements

I should like to make special mention of the following contributors who provided question materials and advice for the new edition of the book:

Mr Rory McGoldrick
Mr Fahir Khiard
Dr Juan Rodriguez
Dr Vishal Patel
Mr Fady Yanni

I would also like to mention the contributors who assisted in the previous edition of this book from which questions have been updated:

Mr Scott Maskell
Mr Nirooshun Rajendran
Mr Naveed Shaikh
Mr Rene Chang
Dr Kamal Halim
Mr Mumtazudeen Haider
Miss Kimberly Lammin
Dr Mehnaz Tawhid
Dr Akash Sharma
Dr Amir Halim
Miss Lorna Cook

Also, A very special thanks to Cathy Dickens and her team at PasTest. They have been a great source of encouragement for this book as well as previously completed projects. This book could not have been completed without their support and guidance.

This book is dedicated to my parents, my wife Saila and my babies Zara and Adam; who provide me with all the love and inspiration to do great things.

Irfan Halim
December 2009

Examination Technique

This is a brief guide which I hope you find helpful for the SBA paper of the MRCS.

Most of the points mentioned below are fairly obvious, but during the stress of the exam it is easy to forget some of them.

Revision

- Start revising early – you never have as much time as you thought you did
- Try and revise with someone else sitting the same exam
- Do plenty of practice questions so that you are familiar with the format

In the exam itself

- Read the instructions carefully
- Allow enough time to complete the paper
- If you are initially writing the answers on the question paper, make sure you allow time to transfer them to the answer sheet
- Always turn over the last page – you wouldn't be the first person to miss the last few questions
- Read the questions thoroughly, paying particular attention to questions asking which of the following is correct/INcorrect
- If the question seems too simple, it probably is that straightforward – there should not be any trick questions in the exam

Good luck

Abbreviations

AAA	abdominal aortic aneurysm
ACE	angiotensin-converting enzyme
ACTH	adrenocorticotropic hormone
ADH	antidiuretic hormone
AFP	alpha-fetoprotein
ALT	alanine aminotransferase
ANP	atrial natriuretic peptide
APTT	activated partial thromboplastin time
ARDS	acute respiratory distress syndrome
ASA	American Society of Anesthesiologists
ATLS	advanced trauma life support
AXR	abdominal X-ray
BMI	body mass index
BP	blood pressure
BPH	benign prostatic hypertrophy
BRCA1 and *2*	familial breast cancer genes
CABG	coronary artery bypass graft
cAMP	cyclic adenosine monophosphate
CEA	carcinoembryonic antigen
CIN	cervical intraepithelial neoplasia
CMV	cytomegalovirus
CN	cranial nerve
COPD	chronic obstructive pulmonary disease
CSF	cerebrospinal fluid
CT	computed tomography
CVA	cerebrovascular accident
CVP	central venous pressure
CXR	chest X-ray
DIC	disseminated intravascular coagulation
2,3-DPG	2, 3-diphosphoglycerate
DPL	diagnostic peritoneal lavage
EBV	Epstein–Barr virus

ECF	extracellular fluid
ECG	electrocardiogram
ERCP	endoscopic retrograde cholangiopancreatography
ESR	erythrocyte sedimentation rate
FAP	familial adenomatous polyposis
FFP	fresh frozen plasma
Fio_2	concentration of inspired oxygen
FNA	fine-needle aspiration
FSH	follicle-stimulating hormone
5-FU	5-fluorouracil
GCS	Glasgow Coma Scale
GFR	glomerular filtration rate
GGT	γ-glutamyltransferase
GH	growth hormone
Hb	haemoglobin
HbF	fetal haemoglobin
HBV	hepatitis B virus
hCG	human chorionic gonadotropin
HIV	human immunodeficiency virus
HLA	human lymphocyte antigens
HNPCC	hereditary non-polyposis colon cancer
HR	heart rate
Ig	immunoglobulin
ITU	intensive therapy unit
IV	intravenous
IVC	inferior vena cava
JVP	jugular venous pressure
KUB	kidney, ureter and bladder
LDH	lactate dehydrogenase
LH	luteinising hormone
LH-RH	luteinising hormone-releasing hormone
MEN	multiple endocrine neoplasia syndromes
MI	myocardial infarction
MRI	magnetic resonance imaging
NADPH	[reduced form of] nicotinamide-adenine dinucleotide phosphate

NSGCT	non-seminomatous germ-cell tumour
NICE	National Institute for Health and Clinical Excellence
NK	natural killer
NSAID	non-steroidal anti-inflammatory drug
Pao_2	partial pressure of oxygen
PAS	periodic acid–Schiff
PT	prothrombin time
Pco_2	partial pressure of carbon dioxide
PCWP	pulmonary capillary wedge pressure
PDS	polyglecapone polydioxanone sulphate
PPH	prolapse and haemorrhoidopexy
PPI	proton-pump inhibitor
PR	per rectum
PSA	prostate-specific antigen
PTH	parathyroid hormone
PTFE	polytetrafluoroethylene (polytef)
PUJ	pelvi-ureteric junction
PUVA	psoralen plus ultraviolet A
Rh	rhesus
RR	respiration rate
SCC	squamous cell carcinoma
SIRS	systemic inflammatory response syndrome
SLE	systemic lupus erytheromatosus
SVC	superior vena cava
T_3	tri–iodothyronine
T_4	thyroxine
TIA	transient ischaemic attack
TNM (stages)	tumour-node-metastasis staging system
TPN	total parenteral nutrition
TSH	thyroid-stimulating hormone
TT	thrombin time
TUR	transurethral resection
TURP	transurethral resection of prostate
UTI	urinary tract infection
VMA	vanillyl-mandelic acid
WCC	white cell count

PRACTICE PAPER 1: QUESTIONS

PRACTICE PAPER 1: QUESTIONS

1 The superior vena cava is formed by the union of the right and left brachiocephalic veins behind the:

- A Right sternoclavicular joint
- B Left sternoclavicular joint
- C Right first costal cartilage junction
- D Left first costal cartilage junction
- E Manubriosternal joint

2 The oblique sinus of the heart:

- A Is bounded by the pulmonary arteries
- B Forms a recess between the pericardium and the left atrium
- C Lies posteriorly between the aorta and pulmonary trunk anteriorly
- D Lies anteriorly between the superior vena cava (SVC) and left atrium
- E Is smaller than the transverse sinus

3 Which of the following statements regarding core temperature is TRUE?

- A Axillary temperature is normally 0.5 °C higher than the core temperature
- B Hypothermia is defined as core temperature <35 °C
- C Diurnal variation is seen, with core temperature higher in the morning than in the evening
- D Autonomic termperature control is regulated by the parasympathetic system
- E The core temperature rises minimally during sleep

4 Which statement is true of the brachial plexus?

- A The medial cord continues as the musculocutaneous nerve
- B The posterior cord continues as the axillary nerve
- C The lateral cord continues as the axillary nerve
- D The nerve to subclavius is a branch of the C8 nerve root
- E The suprascapular nerve is a branch of the lower trunk

5 Structures NOT at risk of being damaged during carotid endarterectomy include the:

- A Hypoglossal nerve
- B Greater auricular nerve
- C Vagus nerve
- D Recurrent laryngeal nerve
- E Accessory nerve

6 For a 70-kg man, the volume of intracellular water in the body in litres (l) is approximately:

- A 11 l
- B 14 l
- C 28 l
- D 35 l
- E 42 l

7 A 72-year-old man underwent an emergency operation for a strangulated inguinal hernia, during which he also had a small-bowel resection for infarcted bowel. He is noted on post-operative bloods to have a potassium of 6.5 mmol/l. In looking at his past medical history, he suffers from hypertension, adrenal problems, and a recently diagnosed oesophageal stricture. Hyperkalaemia in this patient is most likely to result from:

- A Hyperaldosteronism
- B Metabolic acidosis
- C Steroid therapy
- D Loop diuretics
- E Dysphagia

8 Causes of hyponatraemia include all of the following, EXCEPT:

- A Heart failure
- B Hypoalbuminaemia
- C Diabetes insipidus
- D Addison's disease
- E Post-operative excess intravenous 5% dextrose prescribing

9 The correct composition of 'Hartmann's solution' is as follows (all in mmol/l):

	Na^+	Cl^-	Dextrose	K^+	PO_4^{3-}	Ca^{2+}	HCO_3^-
A	154	154	–	20	–	2	18
B	131	111	–	5	–	2	29
C	129	109	–	4	1.5	–	29
D	30	30	222	2	–	2	–
E	147	156	–	4	–	2.2	–

10 The abdominal aorta lies on the:

- A Left of the sympathetic trunk
- B Left of the inferior mesenteric vessels
- C Left of the azygos vein
- D Right of the cisterna chyli
- E Right of the IVC

11 You ask your surgical house officer to prescribe a 1-litre bag of normal saline for a patient who is suffering from small-bowel obstruction and appears dehydrated. The sodium content of 0.9% normal saline is:

- A 30 mmol/l
- B 131 mmol/l
- C 147 mmol/l
- D 154 mmol/l
- E 308 mmol/l

12 Which of the following antiemetics is correctly classed as a 5-HT_3 antagonist:

- A Prochlorperazine
- B Metoclopramide
- C Ondansetron
- D Hyoscine
- E Cyclizine

13 Which of the following parenteral analgesics would be the most appropriate in a severely injured, haemodynamically unstable patient following a road traffic accident?

- A Paracetamol
- B Morphine
- C Midazolam
- D Propofol
- E Fentanyl

14 The right ureter in females:

- A Lies beneath the third part of the duodenum at its origin
- B Runs over the ovarian artery
- C Crosses the uterine artery
- D Is crossed by the right colic artery
- E Lies beneath the bifurcation of the iliac vessels

15 Passing through the lesser sciatic foramen are the:

- A Inferior gluteal artery
- B Pudendal nerve
- C Posterior cutaneous nerve of the thigh
- D Inferior gluteal nerve
- E Nerve to quadratus femoris

16 All of the following functions are mediated by the α adrenoreceptors within the sympathetic nervous system, EXCEPT:

- A Inhibition of detrusor contraction
- B Bronchodilation
- C Ejaculation
- D Pupillary dilation
- E Secretion of thick saliva

17 Stimulation of the parasympathetic nervous system:

- A Increases the heart rate
- B Decreases the rate of gastric emptying
- C Dilates the pupil
- D Causes vasoconstriction
- E Causes contraction of the detrusor muscle in the bladder

18 Which of the following statements regarding pulmonary physiology is CORRECT?

- A Pulmonary airways are all collapsible
- B An increased systemic P_{CO_2} causes a respiratory alkalosis
- C The Haldane effect promotes the transport of O_2 in systemic arterial blood
- D Respiratory chemoreceptors in the carotid and aortic bodies are the most important in the ventilatory response to an elevated P_{O_2}
- E Ventilation can be increased in respiratory failure

19 Which statement is true of the compartments of the leg?

- A The anterior compartment contains the superficial peroneal nerve
- B The lateral compartment contains the deep peroneal nerve
- C The lateral compartment contains peroneus tertius
- D The deep posterior compartment contains plantaris
- E The posterior compartment contains the peroneal artery

20 The brachial artery:

- A Commences at the upper border of teres major
- B Initially lies anterior to the humerus
- C Lies medial to the median nerve proximally
- D Lies medial to the ulnar nerve proximally
- E Lies lateral to biceps distally

21 During the surgical ward round, you note that two of your patients are on the ITU following complicated emergency abdominal surgery. The ITU nurse mentions that both of your patients are still requiring inotropes. Which of the following inotropes are commonly used in the management of sepsis in an ITU setting?

- A Dobutamine
- B Adrenaline (epinephrine)
- C Dopamine
- D Noradrenaline (norepinephrine)
- E Isoprenaline

22 The following statements regarding the absolute refractory period in the ventricles are correct, EXCEPT:

- A This is the period when the ventricles are completely inexcitable
- B It corresponds to the period of ventricular depolarisation
- C It corresponds to the period of ventricular contraction
- D It is shorter than the corresponding period in atrial muscle
- E It decreases during sympathetic stimulation of the heart

23 **The role of coronary angioplasty and coronary artery bypass surgery is to improve coronary blood flow. In a normal, healthy 70-kg man, which of the following statements regarding myocardial blood flow is correct?**

- A It is approximately 125 ml/min at rest
- B It is increased by pain
- C The right coronary artery typically a third of the blood to the right ventricular muscle
- D Occurs during systole and diastole
- E It is independent of arterial pressure

24 **Which of the following medications is NOT known to cause renal failure?**

- A Diclofenac
- B Ciprofloxacin
- C Simvastatin
- D Furosemide
- E Mannitol

25 **Which statement is true of diaphragmatic openings?**

- A The thoracic duct passes through the opening at T12
- B The aorta passes through the opening at T10
- C The left phrenic nerve passes through the opening at T8
- D The right gastric artery passes through the opening at T10
- E The azygos vein passes through the opening at T10

26 Regarding shock, which one of the following associations is most correct?

- A Cardiogenic shock is associated with a high cardiac output and low systemic vascular resistance (SVR)
- B Septic shock is characterised by a low SVR and a high cardiac output
- C Cardiogenic shock is best treated with noradrenaline (norepinephrine)
- D Septic shock is characterised by a high SVR and a low cardiac output
- E Noradrenaline is a vasodilator

27 Your medical student has just performed her first arterial blood gas procedure and runs to the ITU to process the sample. She returns promptly with the results below and asks you to explain them. You outline the clinical picture and then describe the blood gas results.

pH	7.39
Po_2	14.6 kPa
Pco_2	2.6 kPa
Bicarbonate	10 mmol/l
Base excess	−13

Which statement best describes this arterial blood gas profile?

- A Uncompensated respiratory acidosis
- B Compensated respiratory acidosis
- C Compensated metabolic acidosis
- D Uncompensated metabolic acidosis
- E Compensated respiratory alkalosis

28 Regarding inotropes and circulatory support, which one of the following statements is correct?

- A Dobutamine acts mainly on α-adrenergic receptors
- B Salbutamol has maximal effect on β1-adrenergic receptors
- C Noradrenaline has maximal effect on α-adrenergic receptors
- D All inotropic agents are vasocontrictors
- E Milrinone acts via adrenergic receptors

29 The muscle divided in the Hardinge approach to the hip is the:

- A Obturator internus
- B Piriformis
- C Gluteus maximus
- D Superior gemellus
- E Vastus lateralis

30 Which statement is TRUE regarding the rotator cuff?

- A Teres minor is attached to the lesser tuberosity
- B The muscles attach at the level of the surgical neck of the humerus
- C The tendon of infraspinatus is fused with the capsule of the shoulder joint
- D Subscapularis runs through a tunnel formed by the acromion and the coraco-acromial ligament
- E It supports the shoulder joint but is deficient inferiorly

31 **A 74-year-old immunosuppressed patient presents with recurrent pneumonia. He is quite unwell and showing signs of a swinging pyrexia. A chest CT scan reveals that he has an empyema in his right chest cavity. Complications of an empyema within the pleural cavity include all of the following, EXCEPT:**

- A Chronic scarring
- B Bronchiectasis
- C Systemic sepsis
- D Bronchopleural fistula
- E Lung collapse

32 **A 61-year old man is referred to your surgical clinic with right calf pain which occurs on walking 300 yards and is relieved by rest. He has a past history of hypertension, diabetes and hypercholesterolaemia and smokes 15 cigarettes a day. On examination, he has weak groin pulses and absent distal pulses on the right side and weak pulses distal to a normal femoral pulse on the left side. Which of the following is the correct next step in managing this patient?**

- A Arrange a duplex scan of his vessels
- B Arrange a digital subtraction angiogram
- C Lifestyle advice and tightening of risk factor control
- D Prescribe warfarin to prevent thrombus formation
- E Elective admission for a left femoro-popliteal bypass graft

33 **An 81-year-old patient is noted to be in atrial fibrillation but she states that she has never been on anticoagulation therapy. You consider that to lessen the risk of future emboli, she would benefit from starting on long-term warfarin and that this would reduce her risk of developing acute strokes, visceral or limb ischaemia. Arterial emboli leading to acute limb ischaemia most commonly lodge at which one of the following sites?**

- A Brachial artery
- B Common femoral artery
- C Popliteal artery
- D Aortic bifurcation
- E Common iliac bifurcation

34 **Sites of ulnar nerve entrapment include the:**

- A Arcade of Frohse
- B Carpal tunnel
- C Lateral triangular space
- D Arcade of Struthers
- E Cubital fossa

35 Which statement is true of the inguinal region?

- A The midpoint of the inguinal ligament lies halfway between the anterior superior iliac spine and the pubic symphysis
- B The midinguinal point lies halfway between the anterior superior iliac spine and the pubic tubercle
- C The deep inguinal ring lies at the midinguinal point
- D The femoral artery lies at the midpoint of the inguinal ligament
- E The femoral nerve lies halfway between the anterior superior iliac spine and the pubic tubercle

36 A pregnant 41-year-old woman with tortuous varicose veins in the right thigh and leg attends the Vascular Clinic. A Doppler scan shows incompetence at the right sapheno-femoral junction, with multiple perforators. Which one of the following treatment options is best in this case?

- A Multiple avulsions
- B Endovenous laser therapy (EVLT)
- C Compression hosiery and review in clinic at a later date
- D Multiple avulsions plus high tie at the sapheno-femoral junction
- E Compression bandaging and injection of sclerosant

37 An elderly man is admitted to the Surgical Assessment Unit with diverticulitis. On clerking him, you note that he appears to have bibasal crepitations and bronchial breathing in the right lower zone, with dullness to percussion. A blood gas taken shows the following:

pH	7.54
Po_2	9.1 kPa
Pco_2	5.5 kPa
Bicarbonate	34.7 mmol/l

Which of the following best describes the blood gas results?

- A Uncompensated respiratory alkalosis
- B Compensated respiratory alkalosis
- C Uncompensated metabolic alkalosis
- D Compensated metabolic alkalosis
- E Compensated respiratory acidosis

38 The boundaries of the inguinal canal include:

- A The lacunar ligament as part of the roof
- B The inguinal ligament as part of the roof
- C External oblique as part of the roof
- D The conjoint tendon as part of the roof
- E The transversalis fascia as part of the roof

39 Which of these structures does NOT pass posterior to the medial malleolus?

- A Tibialis posterior tendon
- B Saphenous vein
- C Flexor digitorum longus tendon
- D Flexor hallucis longus tendon
- E Posterior tibial artery

40 Which of the following statements about hernias is TRUE?

- A Paraumbilical hernias are usually congenital
- B Lumbar hernias usually present as an emergency with strangulation
- C A hernia containing a strangulated Meckel's diverticulum is a Littre's hernia
- D Femoral hernias appear below and medial to the pubic tubercle
- E Spigelian hernias generally occur through the epiploic foramen of Winslow

41 Which of these nerves does NOT lie in the lateral wall of the cavernous sinus?

- A Trochlear nerve
- B Oculomotor nerve
- C Mandibular branch of the trigeminal nerve
- D Maxillary branch of the trigeminal nerve
- E Ophthalmic branch of the trigeminal nerve

42 Which of the following muscles does NOT attach to the common flexor origin of the forearm?

- A Pronator teres
- B Palmaris longus
- C Flexor carpi ulnaris
- D Flexor carpi radialis
- E Flexor pollicis longus

43 Which of these statements is TRUE regarding the femoral triangle?

- A The lateral border of sartorius forms the lateral border
- B The lateral border of adductor magnus forms the medial border
- C Adductor brevis forms part of the floor
- D Adductor magnus forms part of the floor
- E Pectineus forms part of the floor

44 All of the following statements about radiotherapy are true, EXCEPT:

- A It can be administered via X-rays
- B The nature of the surrounding tissue influences how much radiotherapy is administered
- C Multiple fractions are required for palliation of bone pain
- D Seminomas are very sensitive to radiotherapy
- E Ulceration is a recognised complication

45 The rectus sheath does NOT contain the:

- A Rectus abdominis
- B Inferior epigastric vein
- C Superior epigastric artery
- D Lower eight thoracic nerves
- E Pyramidalis

46 Which statement is correct regarding respiratory volumes?

- A The tidal volume in males is 1000 ml
- B The inspiratory reserve volume is 2000 ml
- C The vital capacity is 2000 ml
- D The residual volume is 1900 ml
- E The total lung capacity is 4000 ml

47 The following statements regarding lung function tests are true, EXCEPT:

- A The functional residual capacity is made up of the residual volume and expiratory reserve volume
- B In an average 20-year-old male, tidal volume is approximately 0.5 litres
- C The residual volume is the amount of air remaining in the lungs after maximum expiration
- D Total lung capacity is the sum of residual volume and tidal volume
- E Vital capacity can be measured by spirometry

48 Which of these is NOT part of the medial longitudinal arch of the foot?

- A Talus
- B Navicular
- C Cuboid
- D Calcaneus
- E Medial cuneiform

49 The plane of Louis is NOT the:

- A Level of the aortic arch
- B Level of the third costal cartilage
- C Level of the lower border of T4
- D Level of the bifurcation of the trachea
- E Level at which the azygos vein enters the SVC

50 Which of the following regarding the duodenum is INCORRECT?

- A The duodenum is composed of four parts
- B The first part lies at the level of L1
- C The second part lies at the level of L2
- D The third part lies at the level of L3
- E The fourth part lies at the level of L4

51 The sciatic nerve does NOT supply which of the following muscles:

- A Obturator externus
- B Semimembranosus
- C Superior gemellus
- D Quadratus femoris
- E Biceps femoris

52 The branches of the posterior cord of the brachial plexus do NOT include the

- A Upper subscapular nerve
- B Lower subscapular nerve
- C Axillary nerve
- D Musculocutaneous nerve
- E Thoracodorsal nerve

53 Which of the following statements about arterial ulcers is NOT true?

- A They are often found at the tips of the toes
- B The foot can show venous guttering
- C They are associated with lipodermatosclerosis
- D They are painful
- E They have a 'punched out' appearance

54 Which of the following is NOT risk factors for bladder cancer?

- A β-Naphthylamine
- B *Schistosoma*
- C Catheterisation
- D Alcohol
- E Smoking

55 The criteria for brainstem death do NOT include:

- A Apnoeic coma requiring ventilation
- B Absence of sedative medications
- C Absence of gag reflex
- D Lack of response to painful stimulus
- E Normal body temperature

56 Risks associated with carotid endarterectomy include all of the following, EXCEPT:

- A Stroke
- B Myocardial infarction (MI)
- C Wound infection
- D Damage to the accessory nerve
- E Damage to the glossopharyngeal nerve

57 Which statement is correct regarding the oxygen haemoglobin (Hb) transport curve?

- A Each gram of haemoglobin binds 1 ml of oxygen when fully saturated
- B At a PaO_2 of 40 mmHg the saturation of Hb is 50%
- C Fetal haemoglobin moves the curve to the right
- D Alkaline pH moves the curve to the right
- E Increased temperature moves the curve to the right

58 Which statement is correct regarding carbon dioxide transport?

- A 10% is transported as carbaminohaemoglobin
- B The carbaminohaemoglobin dissociation curve readily saturates
- C 20% is transported dissolved in the plasma
- D 50% is transported as sodium bicarbonate
- E Carbonic anhydrase catalyses the reaction of CO_2 and plasma

59 The carpal tunnel does NOT contain:

- A Flexor digitorum superficialis
- B Flexor digitorum profundus
- C Median nerve
- D Flexor pollicis longus
- E Flexor carpi ulnaris

60 Which statement is correct regarding cerebrospinal fluid (CSF)?

- A The normal total volume is 250 ml
- B It passes from the lateral to the third ventricles via the foramen of Monro
- C It is reabsorbed by the choroid plexuses
- D The rate of production is proportional to the systemic blood pressure (BP)
- E It passes from the third to the fourth ventricles via the foramen of Magendie

61 The maximum safe dose of 1% lidocaine without adrenaline for a 70-kg male is:

- A 14 ml
- B 21 ml
- C 28 ml
- D 35 ml
- E 40 ml

62 Parathyroid hormone (PTH) secretion is decreased by:

- A An increase in serum phosphate
- B A decrease in free Ca^{2+}
- C A large decrease in serum magnesium
- D An increase in serum potassium
- E A decrease in $1,25(OH)_2$ vitamin D

63 Structures passing through the foramen magnum do NOT include the:

- A Vagus nerve
- B Accessory nerve
- C Medulla
- D Meninges
- E Vertebral arteries

64 Calot's triangle:

- A Is bounded laterally by the common hepatic duct
- B Is bounded medially by the right hepatic duct
- C Is bounded laterally by the cystic duct
- D Contains the left hepatic duct
- E Contains the hepatic artery

65 The epiploic foramen:

- A Is the opening of the lesser sac on the left side of the abdomen
- B Lies anterior to the SVC
- C Lies inferior to the quadrate lobe of the liver
- D Is superior to the third part of the duodenum
- E Contains the hepatic artery lying on the left of the common bile duct in the anterior border

66 A 60-year-old man presents with a history of claudication pain in his left leg after walking 20 yards, which is impacting significantly on his lifestyle. He is investigated by arteriography, which shows an 2-cm stenosis in the proximal superficial femoral artery. The most appropriate management is:

- A Below-knee amputation
- B Correction of risk factors only
- C Percutaneous balloon angioplasty
- D Femoro-popliteal bypass
- E Femoro-distal bypass

67 Types of tumour markers do NOT include:

- A Enzymes
- B Hormones
- C Ectopic hormones
- D Oncofetal antibodies
- E Oncofetal antigens

68 The transpyloric plane of Addison:

- A Passes through the inferior border of L2
- B Encompasses the tail of the pancreas
- C Is at the same level as the 8th costal cartilages
- D Is the level at which the inferior mesenteric artery commences
- E Lies halfway between the jugular notch and the pubic symphysis

69 A man presents with left buttock, thigh and calf claudication pain. Which of the following is the most likely site of arterial disease?

- A Left superficial femoral artery
- B Left common iliac artery
- C Left external iliac artery
- D Left internal iliac artery
- E Lower aorta

70 The stomach bed does NOT include the:

- A Splenic artery
- B Coeliac trunk
- C Transverse mesocolon
- D Left adrenal gland
- E Neck of the pancreas

71 Which of the following statements is true regarding the planes of the abdomen?

- A The subcostal plane runs through the inferior border of L3
- B The transtubercular plane runs through the body of L5
- C The sagittal planes run through the midpoints of the inguinal ligaments
- D The transpyloric plane runs through the superior border of L2
- E The transumbilical plane runs through the L2/3 intervertebral disc

72 The facial nerve passes through:

- A The superior orbital fissure
- B The foramen ovale
- C The foramen rotundum
- D The stylomastoid foramen
- E The petrosquamous fissure

73 Which of the following statements about abdominal aortic aneurysms is TRUE?

- A They can can be stented if above the renal arteries
- B They are operated on when <5.5 cm in diameter
- C They can cause emboli
- D They are not identified on ultrasound scan
- E They are more common in females

74 Extensor compartment II of the wrist contains:

- A Abductor pollicis longus
- B Extensor pollicis brevis
- C Extensor carpi radialis
- D Extensor pollicis longus
- E Extensor digitorum

75 Which of the following is NOT a Gram-negative rod?

- A *Escherichia coli*
- B *Clostridium tetani*
- C *Proteus* species
- D *Legionella*
- E *Pseudomonas*

76 The quadrilateral space:

- A Is bounded inferiorly by teres minor
- B Is bounded inferiorly by subscapularis
- C Is bounded laterally by the long head of triceps
- D Is bounded inferiorly by teres major
- E Contains the radial nerve

77 All of these statements about lymphoedema are correct, EXCEPT:

- A It can be a primary problem
- B Malignant infiltration of lymphatics is a common cause of secondary lymphoedema
- C It can occur secondary to radiotherapy
- D Ulceration in primary lymphoedema is common
- E Operative treatment is rarely used

78 Which statement is correct regarding secretions from the adrenal glands?

- A Aldosterone is produced by the zona glomerulosa
- B Progesterone is produced by the zona fasciculata
- C Testosterone is produced by the zona reticularis
- D Adrenaline is produced by the zona reticularis
- E Cortisol is produced by the zona glomerulosa

79 Which of the following statements is true regarding the pharyngeal arches and pouches?

- A The superior parathyroid glands are derived from the fourth pharyngeal pouch
- B The mandible is derived from the second pharyngeal arch
- C The third pharyngeal arch is supplied by the vagus nerve
- D The pharyngeal arches consist of endoderm and ectoderm only
- E The inferior parathyroid glands are derived from the fifth pharyngeal pouch

80 Epstein–Barr virus (EBV) is known to be a carcinogen for:

- A T-cell lymphoma
- B Non-Hodgkin's lymphoma
- C Leukaemia
- D B-cell lymphoma
- E Hepatocellular carcinoma

81 One litre of Hartmann's solution contains

- A 154 mmol/l of sodium
- B 5 mmol/l of glucose
- C 130 mmol/l of chloride
- D 10 mmol/l of calcium
- E 5 mmol/l of potassium

82 A 4-year-old girl falls from her bike, landing on her left leg, which becomes tender and swollen. X-ray shows a fracture of the proximal tibia, which goes through a radiolucent area with a well-defined sclerotic edge. The most likely diagnosis is:

- A Osteosarcoma
- B Chondrosarcoma
- C Bone cyst
- D Bone metastasis
- E Ewing's sarcoma

83 Which of the following statements is true regarding the adrenal glands?

- A The right adrenal is more medial than the left
- B The right adrenal lies lateral to the superior phrenic vessels
- C The left adrenal lies posterior to the splenic artery
- D The right adrenal vein drains into the right renal vein
- E Cortisol is secreted by the zona glomerulosa

84 Volumes of gastrointestinal secretions per day are:

- A 3000 ml of saliva
- B 2000 ml of pancreatic juices
- C 2000 ml of bile
- D 3500 ml of small-bowel secretions
- E 1500 ml of large-bowel secretions

85 A 40-year-old diabetic man presents with pain in the upper lumbar spine. X-ray at the time showed soft-tissue swelling only and he was discharged home with anti-inflammatories. He returns 10 days later as his symptoms are no better and he has been suffering from a constant fever. X-ray at this time shows sclerotic changes and periosteal reaction. His symptoms are most likely to be due to infection with:

- A *Salmonella*
- B *Haemophilus influenzae*
- C *Gonococcus*
- D Tuberculosis
- E *Staphylococcus aureus*

86 Which of the following is NOT true regarding gastric secretions?

- A Gastrin is produced by the G cells of the pyloric glands
- B Pepsinogen is produced by the chief cells
- C Mucus is produced by the surface epithelial cells
- D Intrinsic factor is produced by the parietal cells
- E Hydrochloric acid is produced by the chief cells

87 Which of the following factors is part of the extrinsic pathway in the coagulation cascade?

- A Factor XII
- B Factor XI
- C Factor IX
- D Factor VII
- E Factor XIII

88 The following are all features of carpal tunnel syndrome, EXCEPT:

- A Pain often worse at night
- B Positive Tinel's test
- C Positive Phalen's test
- D Wasting of the hypothenar muscles
- E Paraesthesia over thumb and lateral two fingers

89 Functions of the terminal ileum do NOT include:

- A Folate reuptake
- B Bile salt reuptake
- C Vitamin B_{12} uptake
- D Water reabsorption
- E Gamma-globulin uptake

90 Which of the following statements is NOT true regarding vitamin B_{12}?

- A It is necessary for maturation of red cells
- B It is stored in the liver
- C Intrinsic factor is required for its absorption
- D Stores can last for up to a year
- E There is a small amount in bile

91 Which of the following is an exocrine secretion of the pancreas?

- A Pancreatic polypeptide
- B Somatostatin
- C Trypsinogen
- D Glucagon
- E Insulin

92 All of the following may be radiological features of osteoarthritis, EXCEPT:

- A Bone cysts
- B Subchondral sclerosis
- C Osteophytes
- D Increased joint space
- E Joint effusion

93 Lung compliance is increased by:

- A Alveolar oedema
- B Pulmonary hypertension
- C Atelectasis
- D Pulmonary fibrosis
- E Emphysema

94 The posterior pituitary releases:

- A Adrenocorticotropic hormone (ACTH)
- B Follicle-stimulating hormone (FSH)
- C Antidiuretic hormone (ADH)
- D Thyroid-stimulating hormone (TSH)
- E Growth hormone (GH)

95 Which of the following statements about the popliteal fossa is TRUE?

- A The lateral edge is bounded by semimembranosus and gastrocnemius
- B The deep fascia forms the roof and is pierced by the long saphenous vein
- C The popliteal artery is the deepest structure within the fossa
- D The common peroneal nerve lies medially within the fossa
- E Soleus forms the medial lower edge

96 **Which of the following is NOT the correct daily requirement for an average 70-kg male?**

- A 150 mmol sodium
- B 2500 ml water
- C 70 mmol calcium
- D 70 mmol potassium
- E 70 mmol chloride

97 **Which of the following statements about the brachial plexus is FALSE?**

- A The thoracodorsal nerve arises from the posterior cord
- B The medial and lateral cords join to form the median nerve
- C The trunks of the plexus are found in the posterior triangle of the neck
- D The long thoracic nerve originates from trunks C5, C6 and C7
- E The nerve that supplies subscapularis is a branch from the posterior cord

98 **Causes of metabolic acidosis with a normal anion gap include:**

- A Diarrhoea
- B Diabetic ketoacidosis
- C Salicylate overdose
- D Renal tubular acidosis
- E Lactic acidosis

99 Which statement is true of pleomorphic adenoma:

- A It is the second commonest salivary gland tumour
- B It usually affects the submandibular gland
- C It is more common in females
- D Approximately 10% are bilateral
- E It is commonest in the fourth and fifth decades

100 Which of the following are NOT normally found in bile?

- A Sodium chloride
- B Unconjugated bilirubin
- C Cholesterol
- D Water
- E Bile salts

101 A 26-year-old woman is involved in a road traffic accident. On arrival in the Emegency Department she has a painful, deformed-looking left leg, which is shortened and internally rotated. She is unable to dorsiflex or plantar-flex her foot and there is sensory loss below the knee apart from the medial leg and foot and upper back of the calf. The nerve most likely to have been affected is:

- A Obturator nerve
- B Sciatic nerve
- C Femoral nerve
- D Tibial nerve
- E Common peroneal nerve

102 Reed–Sternberg cells are characteristic of:

- A Hodgkin's lymphoma
- B Non-Hodgkin's lymphoma
- C Burkitt's lymphoma
- D B-cell lymphoma
- E T-cell lymphoma

103 Risk factors for hepatocellular carcinoma do NOT include:

- A Hepatitis B
- B Hepatitis C
- C Hepatitis E
- D Aflatoxin
- E Anabolic steroids

104 A 35-year-old tennis player finds herself unable to play because of a painful left shoulder. Pain is worse on lifting the arm, particularly when elevated between 60–120 degrees. On examination there is tenderness just lateral to the acromium process. The diagnosis is:

- A Supraspinatus rupture
- B Frozen shoulder
- C Acromioclavicular joint dislocation
- D Supraspinatus tendonitis
- E Biceps tendon rupture

105 Infantile hypertrophic pyloric stenosis:

- A Is more common in females
- B Is more common in second-born and subsequent children
- C Usually presents at approximately 3 months old
- D Causes a metabolic acidosis
- E Occurs in 1 in 31 000 live births

106 Tumour markers for testicular cancer do NOT include:

- A Gamma-glutamyltransferase (GGT) for seminoma and non-seminomatous germ-cell tumour (NSGCT)
- B Human chorionic gonadotropin (γ-hCG) for seminoma and NSGCT
- C Lactate dehydrogenase (LDH) for NSGCT
- D Carcinoembryonic antigen (CEA) for NSGCT
- E Alpha-fetoprotein (AFP) for NSGCT

107 All of the following statements about a fractured neck of femur are true, EXCEPT:

- A The affected leg is shortened and externally rotated
- B Associated mortality is in the region of >30% at 6 months
- C Intertrochanteric fractures are usually fixed using a dynamic hip screw
- D Intracapsular fractures can result in avascular necrosis of the femoral head
- E Femoral nerve injury is common

108 The following viruses are NOT known to be carcinogenic:

- A Epstein–Barr virus
- B Hepatitis B
- C Human immunodeficiency virus (HIV)
- D Hepatitis A
- E Human papilloma virus (HPV)

109 Swan–Ganz catheters CANNOT be used to directly measure:

- A Pulmonary artery wedge pressure
- B Mean arterial pressure
- C Cardiac output
- D Systemic vascular resistance (SVR)
- E Central venous pressure (CVP)

110 A 67-year-old man presents extremely unwell with left-sided abdominal pain, fever and shock. At emergency laparotomy he is found to have a large tumour of the sigmoid colon, which has perforated, causing faecal contamination. What is the most appropriate operation?

- A Left hemicolectomy and primary anastomosis
- B Sigmoid colectomy
- C Hartmann's procedure
- D Anterior resection
- E Abdominoperineal resection

111 Multiple endocrine neoplasia type I (MEN I)

- A Has an autosomal recessive inheritance
- B Has its gene located on chromosome 10
- C Is known as Sipple syndrome
- D Commonly includes phaeochromocytoma
- E Commonly includes hyperparathyroidism

112 Which of the following is NOT true regarding malignant hyperpyrexia?

- A It can be caused by suxamethonium
- B It can be caused by isoflurane
- C It can be caused by nitrous oxide
- D Dantrolene is the treatment
- E It occurs in 1 in 150 000

113 The liver does NOT synthesise:

- A Prothrombin
- B Pro-accelerin
- C Plasminogen
- D Antithrombin
- E Fibrinogen

114 Local factors that affect wound healing do NOT include:

- A Foreign bodies
- B Haematoma
- C Malnutrition
- D Infection
- E Decreased blood supply

115 Which statement is correct regarding the renin–angiotensin system?

- A Antidiuretic hormone (ADH) is released from the anterior pituitary
- B Renin is secreted by the granular cells of the juxtaglomerular apparatus
- C Angiotensinogen is released into the plasma only when required
- D Antidiuretic hormone is produced by the anterior pituitary
- E Angiotensin I is converted to angiotensin II by angiotensin-converting enzyme (ACE) in the liver

116 Which statement is correct regarding transport in the proximal tubule of the kidney?

- A Sodium is passively reabsorbed
- B Glucose is passively reabsorbed
- C Amino acids are actively reabsorbed
- D Urea is actively reabsorbed
- E Potassium is secreted

117 The chemoreceptors involved in maintenance of blood pressure are:

- A Located in the pulmonary arteries
- B Stimulated by high oxygen levels
- C Stimulated by alkaline pH
- D Stimulated by high carbon dioxide levels
- E Stimulated by stretching of the vessel walls

118 Which of the following is NOT part of the flight or fight response?

- A Constriction of blood vessels
- B Constriction of the pupils
- C Sweating
- D Increased heart rate
- E Decreased GI activity

119 Which of the following is an anion?

- A Sodium
- B Magnesium
- C Phosphate
- D Calcium
- E Potassium

120 Which is NOT a common feature of MEN IIB?

- A Medullary thyroid carcinoma
- B Multiple mucosal neuromas
- C Phaeochromocytoma
- D Marfanoid appearance
- E Gastrinoma

121 Which of the following is an accessory muscle of expiration?

- A Sternocleidomastoid
- B Pectoralis major
- C Scalenus anterior
- D Latissimus dorsi
- E Rectus abdominis

122 Characteristic signs of acute inflammation include all of the following, EXCEPT:

- A Dolor
- B Palor
- C Rubor
- D Tumor
- E Calor

123 Apoptosis:

- A Is a process which results from energy deprivation
- B Is initially reversible and becomes irreversible
- C Is initiated by an injury
- D Causes swelling of the cell
- E Results in orderly vesicle formation

124 Tumours that commonly metastasise to bone do NOT include:

- A Breast
- B Lung
- C Prostate
- D Adrenal
- E Thyroid

125 Meckel's diverticulum:

- A Is more common in females
- B Is usually 2-cm long
- C Can contain hepatic mucosa
- D Contains only the mucosa and submucosa of the intestinal wall
- E Is a remnant of the omphalomesenteric duct

126 Granulomas are NOT found in:

- A Tuberculosis (TB)
- B Sarcoidosis
- C Ulcerative colitis
- D Crohn's disease
- E Leprosy

127 Dysplasia does NOT cause:

- A Increased cell growth
- B Cellular atypia
- C Abnormal differentiation
- D A low nuclear-to-cytoplasmic ratio
- E Pleomorphism

128 Psammoma bodies are characteristic of:

- A Follicular thyroid carcinoma
- B Anaplastic thyroid carcinoma
- C Papillary thyroid carcinoma
- D Medullary thyroid carcinoma
- E Thyroid lymphoma

129 Risk factors for malignant melanoma include:

- A Fair skin
- B Family history
- C Continuous sun exposure
- D Xeroderma pigmentosa
- E Albinism

130 Which of the following is NOT a benign skin lesion?

- A Pott's peculiar tumour
- B Seborrhoeic keratosis
- C Hamartoma
- D Merkel cell tumour
- E Turban tumour

131 Which of the following is NOT a nutritional factor involved in wound healing?

- A Vitamin A
- B Vitamin B_3
- C Vitamin B_6
- D Zinc
- E Copper

132 For which of the following is blood for transfusion NOT screened?

- A EBV
- B Hepatitis B
- C Syphilis
- D Hepatitis C
- E HIV

133 Which of the following statements is correct regarding cells involved in wound healing?

- A Platelets take 1 day to appear
- B Neutrophils take 2 days to appear
- C Macrophages appear immediately
- D Fibroblasts take 3 days to appear
- E Endothelial cells take 1 day to appear

134 Which of the following statements regarding cell growth is NOT true?

- A Hypertrophy is an increase in cell size
- B Hyperplasia is an increase in cell number
- C Metaplasia is the conversion of one tissue type to another
- D Teratoma is a growth of cells originating from more than one germ-cell line
- E Hamartoma is an overgrowth of a cell not normally found in that tissue

135 The most common type of lung cancer is:

- A Squamous cell carcinoma
- B Small-cell carcinoma
- C Large-cell carcinoma
- D Adenocarcinoma
- E Adenosquamous carcinoma

PRACTICE PAPER 1: ANSWERS AND TEACHING NOTES

PRACTICE PAPER 1: ANSWERS AND TEACHING NOTES

1 C: Right first costal cartilage junction

The right brachiocephalic vein is formed by the union of the right internal jugular and right subclavian veins behind the right sternoclavicular joint. In a similar manner, the left brachiocephalic vein forms behind the left sternoclavicular joint with the union of the left internal jugular and left subclavian veins. The two brachiocephalic veins join to form the superior vena cava (SVC) behind the right first costal cartilage and descend to enter the right atrium.

2 B: Forms a recess between the pericardium and the left atrium

The two **pericardial sinuses** are formed by the reflection of the pericardium on the heart and great vessels. The **transverse sinus** lies posteriorly between the aorta and pulmonary trunk and anteriorly between the superior vena cava and left atrium. The **oblique sinus** forms a recess between the pericardium and the left atrium and is bounded by the four pulmonary veins and the inferior vena cava (IVC). It is larger, more J-shaped, and lies inferior to the transverse sinus.

3 B: Hypothermia is defined as core temperature <35 °C

Temperature control is regulated by the hypothalamus as well as by the sympathetic nervous system. The core temperature is generally about 0.5 °C higher than the axillary temperature, with the normal range being between 36 °C and 37.5 °C. Temperatures <35 °C are regarded as hypothermia and can often be fatal at levels under 30 °C.

Temperature variation can be seen throughout the day, with core temperatures being lower in the morning and higher in the evening.

Variations might also be seen over the menstrual cycle, with the temperature being about 0.5 °C higher in the latter half of the cycle. During sleep, the core temperature falls slightly.

Cardiac arrhythmias occur at core temperatures below 32 °C and asystole can supervene below 28 °C; re-warming of the patient can reactivate the heart. It is therefore essential to re-warm the patient before confirming cardiac arrest. Hypothermia is associated with pulmonary hypertension and left heart failure and can lead to electromechanical dissociation with absent pulses. The line of demarcation between viable and non-viable tissue usually regresses following re-warming.

4 B: The posterior cord continues as the axillary nerve

The lateral cord continues as the musculocutaneous nerve.

The medial cord continues as the ulnar nerve.

The posterior cord continues as the radial nerve and the axillary nerve.

The nerve to subclavius is a branch of the C6 root.

The suprascapular nerve is a branch from the upper trunk.

5 E: Accessory nerve

The hypoglossal, greater auricular, vagus and recurrent laryngeal nerves are all at risk during carotid endarterectomy. The superior laryngeal and accessory nerves are not.

6 C: 28 l

The volume of water in an average 70-kg male is approximately 60% of the body weight or about 42 kg (42 l). Approximately two-thirds of this is intracellular (28 l) and the remaining third is extracellular (14 l). The extracellular compartment can be further divided into plasma (3 l) and interstitial fluid (11 l). Transcellular fluid (1 l), such as that in cerebrospinal fluid, peritoneal and intraocular fluids, makes up part of the interstitial fluid.

7 B: Metabolic acidosis

Hyperkalaemia can result from decreased excretion, increased extraneous load, or release from cells. In this gentleman, cell lysis from the infarcted bowel is the most likely cause and he would also have a metabolic (lactic) acidosis, which would also result in hyperkalaemia. In the post-operative period, secretion of ADH in response to the operation also tends to raise serum potassium levels. The *best* answer from the choices given is therefore metabolic acidosis.

Decreased excretion of potassium:

- Renal failure
- Potassium-sparing diuretics
- Adrenocortical insufficiency
- Metabolic acidosis.

Increased extraneous load of potassium:

- Potassium chloride
- Blood transfusion
- Potassium citrate.

Release of potassium from cells:

- Acidosis
- Rhabdomyolysis
- Tumour lysis
- Succinylcholine
- Digoxin poisoning
- Vigorous exercise.

8 C: Diabetes insipidus

Hyponatraemia is defined as a serum sodium concentration of less than 135 mmol/l.

Dehydration	No dehydration or oedema	Oedema
Renal losses:	**Artefact:**	Congestive heart failure
Diuretics	Sample taken intravenously from the arm	Nephrotic syndrome
Adrenal insufficiency		Cirrhosis
Osmotic diuresis (glucose, urea, mannitol)	**Pseudohyponatraemia:**	Renal failure
Renal tubular acidosis	Hyperglycaemia	
	Hypertriglyceridaemia	
Fluid loss:	Hyperproteinaemia	
Vomiting	**Acute onset:**	
Diarrhoea	Excess intravenous intake post-operatively	
Sweating	Psychogenic polydipsia	
	Chronic onset:	
	Syndrome of inappropriate ADH secretion (SIADH)	
	Hypothyroidism	
	Glucocorticoid deficiency	
	Pain, emotion or drugs	

9	B: Na^+	Cl^-	Dextrose	K^+	PO_4^{3-}	Ca^{2+}	HCO_3^-
	131	111	–	5	–	2	29

Hartmann's solution is a crystalloid solution composed of Na^+ 131 mmol/l; K^+ 5 mmol/l; HCO_3^- 29 mmol/l; Cl^- 111 mmol/l and Ca^{2+} 2 mmol/l, which is isotonic with body fluid. As its composition is near-physiological, it is commonly used intraoperatively to replace fluid losses.

10 C: Left of the azygos vein

The aorta lies on the right of the sympathetic trunk, inferior mesenteric vessels, left crus of the diaphragm and coeliac ganglion. It lies on the left of the azygos vein, cisterna chyli, thoracic duct, IVC and right crus of the diaphragm.

11 D: 154 mmol/l

The sodium content of the following commonly prescribed fluids are as follows:

- 0.18% saline contains 30 mmol/l
- Hartmann's solution contains 131 mmol/l
- Ringer's lactate contains 147 mmol/l
- 0.9% normal saline contains 154 mmol/l
- 1.8% twice-normal (hypertonic) saline contains 308 mmol/l.

12 C: Ondansetron

Ondansetron is an example of a 5-HT_3 antagonist. The main mechanism of action lies in the blockage of the receptors, which are located in the chemoreceptor trigger zone (CTZ). The CTZ is found within the area postrema of the brainstem and is a direct stimulator of the vomiting centre in the medulla oblongata. The CTZ also contains D2 receptors, which can be blocked by the use of dopamine antagonists such as prochlorperazine and metoclopramide. Hyoscine works as an antimuscarinic agent and cyclizine as an antihistamine. Both muscarinic and histamine receptors are present directly on the vomiting centre, and blockage of these is used to reduce motion sickness-induced nausea.

13 E: Fentanyl

Paracetamol is a weak analgesic in the setting of severe trauma. Morphine administration should be avoided as it is associated with histamine release, which can result in vasodilatation and worsening hypotension in the unstable patient. Propofol and midazolam have no analgesic properties. Fentanyl is ideal for use in haemodynamically unstable patients with severe injuries as it is a very strong analgesic with a rapid onset of action and short half-life, with no resultant metabolites.

14 D: Is crossed by the right colic artery

The right ureter lies beneath the second part of the duodenum at its origin. It is crossed by the ovarian, uterine, right colic and ileocolic arteries. It crosses the bifurcation of the iliac arteries.

15 B: Pudendal nerve

The structures that pass through the lesser sciatic foramen are the pudendal nerve, nerve to obturator internus, internal pudendal artery and tendon of obturator internus.

16 B: Bronchodilation

Sympathetic functions can be classified by the class of adrenoreceptor that is stimulated by noradrenaline (norepinephrine).

Alpha functions include:

- Pupillary dilation
- Secretion of thick saliva
- Peripheral blood vessel constriction
- Increase in gut sphincter tone
- Splenic capsular contraction
- Gluconeogenesis ($\beta 2/\alpha$)
- Relaxation of the detrusor muscle (also $\beta 2$)
- Contraction of the bladder neck
- Ejaculation
- Piloerection.

Beta functions include:

- Increase in heart rate and force of contraction (β1)
- Vasodilatation in vessels supplying the muscles (β2)
- Bronchodilatation (β2)
- Glycogenolysis (β2)
- Gluconeogenesis (β2/α)
- Relaxation of the detrusor muscle (β2/α)
- Uterine relaxation (β2).

17 E: Causes contraction of the detrusor muscle in the bladder

Parasympathetic functions include:

- Pupil dilation
- Salivary and lacrimal secretion
- Reduction of heart rate and contractility
- Bronchoconstriction
- Gastrointestinal enzyme secretion
- Increased gastrointestinal motility and gastric emptying
- Bladder contraction and micturition
- Penile erection.

18 E: Ventilation can be increased in respiratory failure

Not all pulmonary airways are collapsible because bronchi contain cartilage and therefore do not collapse. An increased systemic P_{CO_2} causes an acidosis due to increased carbonic acid formation. The function of central chemoreceptors (medullary neurones) is to detect changes in P_{O_2} levels. Chemoreceptors in the carotid and aortic bodies are peripheral chemoreceptors which respond to changes in blood P_{CO_2} and pH, as well as P_{O_2}. During respiratory failure a patient might hyperventilate in an attempt to correct abnormal arterial gases. Hyperventialtion can also occur with an emotional upset, in response to a metabolic acidosis (in this instance the P_{CO_2} concentration drops, helping the pH to return to normal), and with marked falls in arterial pressure (this effect is mediated via chemoreceptor stimulation in conditions of very low blood flow, when the tissue P_{O_2} falls).

The Haldane effect relates to CO_2 transport – it is the Bohr effect that relates to O_2 transport. The Haldane effect promotes CO_2 release in the pulmonary capillaries as the Po_2 rises, thereby almost doubling the amount of CO_2 which is taken up by blood as it passes through the systemic capillaries.

19 E: The posterior compartment contains the peroneal artery

The anterior compartment contains the deep peroneal nerve and anterior tibial artery. The lateral compartment contains the superficial peroneal nerve and no artery. Peroneus tertius is in the anterior compartment; peroneus brevis and longus are in the lateral compartment. The superficial posterior compartment contains gastrocnemius, soleus and plantaris. The posterior compartment contains the posterior tibial nerve, posterior tibial artery and peroneal artery.

20 D: Lies medial to the ulnar nerve proximally

The artery commences at the lower border of teres major. It initially lies medial to the humerus and then moves anteriorly. Proximally the ulnar nerve is medial to it, and the musculocutaneous and median nerves lie laterally. It lies medial to biceps and its tendon.

21 D: Noradrenaline (norepinephrine)

Sepsis induces systemic vasodilatation. Adrenaline works on $\alpha1$, $\beta1$ and $\beta2$ receptors and while it does have a role in sepsis it is not frequently used because of the β-agonist effect (more likely to cause tachycardia). Dobutamine also works primarily on β receptors. Dopamine has a dose-dependent effect on β, α and δ receptors. Noradrenaline increases blood pressure and cardiac output by a vasocontrictive $\alpha1$ effect. Isoprenaline is a β-selective agonist.

22 D: It is shorter than the corresponding period in atrial muscle

The state in which the ventricles are completely inexcitable defines an 'absolute refractory period' during a heartbeat. During this absolute refractory period the ventricles are in a state of contraction where all the cells are completely depolarised and cannot be excited, ie it is impossible to generate another action potential. The refractory period limits the frequency at which action potentials can be generated to <1000/s and ensures that, once initiated, an action potential can only travel in one direction. Sympathetic stimulation results in a decreased refractory period, thereby permitting higher heart rates.

23 C: The right coronary artery typically supplies a third of the blood to the right ventricular muscle

Myocardial blood flow is approx 250 ml/min at rest. This represents 5% of the cardiac output and is dependent on arterial pressure. Flow is seen in diastole and pain reduces myocardial blood flow.

24 C: Simvastatin

Drugs can cause renal failure through a variety of mechanisms. Those that have a direct tubular effect include aminoglycosides, mannitol, NSAIDs, ACE inhibitors and ciclosporin. Sulphonamides and aciclovir can cause tubular obstruction, and beta lactam antibiotics, vancomycin, ciprofloxacin and furosemide can cause acute interstitial nephritis. Acute glomerulonephritis is a recognised complication of penacillamine use. Simvastatin is not known to cause renal impairment.

25 A: The thoracic duct passes through the opening at T12

The openings are:

- T8 – the opening for the inferior vena cava; also passing through is the right phrenic nerve
- T10 – the opening for the oesophagus; also passing through are the left gastric artery and vein
- T12 – the opening for the aorta; also passing through are the thoracic duct and azygos vein

26 B: Septic shock is characterised by a low SVR and a high cardiac output

Shock is the inability of the body to maintain tissue perfusion and oxygen delivery to its tissues. Septic shock is characterised by vasodilatation (low SVR) and a hyperdynamic circulation / high cardiac output. Cardiogenic shock, on the other hand, generally results in a low cardiac output state with a high SVR to try to maintain tissue perfusion. Noradrenaline is a potent vasoconstrictor used in the treatment of septic shock. It is not used generally in the treatment of cardiogenic shock.

27 C: Compensated metabolic acidosis

The blood gas profile given in the question is a compensated metabolic acidosis as the pH is within the normal range, but the low bicarbonate has been compensated for by hyperventilation (which has caused a low $P\text{CO}_2$.) A base excess of –13 (or base deficit of 13) indicates that there is loss of bicarbonate, which must be replenished, in addition to the removal of the cause of metabolic acidosis, in order to achieve acid–base correction.

28 C: Noradrenaline has maximal effect on α-adrenergic receptors

Noradrenaline is a vasoconstrictor and acts mainly via α-adrenergic receptors. Dopexamine acts via β1 and β2 receptors and has no α-adrenergic action. It is therefore an vasodilator. Inotropic agents can be vasodilators or vasocontrictors. Salbutamol acts via β2-adrenergic receptors. Milrinone is a type III phosphodiesterase inhibitor and acts by inhibiting the degradation of intracellular cyclic AMP, causing an increase in intracellular calcium concentration.

29 E: Vastus lateralis

The Hardinge (lateral) approach to the hip splits tensor fascia lata, vastus lateralis and gluteus medius. Piriformis, obturator internus and the gemellae are detached from the greater trochanter in the posterior approach to the hip.

30 E: It supports the shoulder joint but is deficient inferiorly

The rotator cuff is a ring of muscles that surrounds and strengthens the shoulder joint, but is deficient inferiorly. They attach at the level of the anatomical neck of the humerus. Specifically, the attachments are: subscapularis to the lesser tuberosity; supraspinatus, teres minor and infraspinatus to the greater tuberosity (in that order from above down). As well as moving the shoulder joint they also act as a muscular support. Supraspinatus runs thorough a tunnel formed by the acromion and the coraco-acromial ligament and its tendon is fused to the capsule of the shoulder joint.

31 B: Bronchiectasis

An empyema is defined as pus within the pleural cavity or gallbladder. Organisms causing empyema include *Streptococcus pneumoniae*, *Staphylococcus aureus* and other organisms arising from the specific cause. Gram-negative organisms can cause empyema in trauma and in oesophageal surgery or disease.

Causes of empyema include the following:

- Pulmonary infections:
  - Pneumonia
  - TB
  - Lung abscess
- Other infections:
  - Subphrenic abscess
  - Mediastinitis
  - Distant foci
- Complications of thoracic surgery
- Penetrating chest trauma.

Complications of empyema include:

- Lung collapse
- Bronchopleural fistula
- Pleural scarring
- Systemic sepsis.

Bronchiectasis is a *cause* of empyema, not a complication of the disease.

32 C: Lifestyle advice and tightening of risk factor control

This patient has multiple vascular risk factors and a history which suggests a stenosis of the left superficial femoral artery. As he is able to walk 300 yards at present, most of his daily activities are not limited by this claudication. He needs an initial modification and tighter control of his hypertension, diabetes and hypercholesterolaemia, which will prevent progression of his vascular disease. He also needs lifestyle advice – he should stop smoking altogether, eat a healthy diet and take regular exercise. He should be encouraged to walk through the pain. These initial measures might very well improve his symptoms of claudication but in a few people the disease can progress to a point where intervention is required. A duplex scan initially or angiogram might be worthwhile if any intervention is being considered at a later stage. He certainly should not be taken for surgery in the immediate instance and this can be undertaken should the disease or symptoms progress.

33 B: Common femoral artery

The common femoral artery is the commonest site of arterial emboli causing acute limb ischaemia. The treatment of choice is urgent femoral embolectomy.

34 D: Arcade of Struthers

The ulnar nerve can get trapped in the arcade of Struthers, which is the proximal end of the cubital tunnel. The median and radial nerves pass through the cubital fossa, but not the ulnar. The radial nerve passes through the lateral triangular space and the median nerve through the carpal tunnel. The arcade of Frohse is a site of possible posterior interosseus nerve entrapment.

35 E: The femoral nerve lies halfway between the anterior superior iliac spine and the pubic tubercle

The midpoint of the inguinal ligament is halfway between the anterior superior iliac spine and the pubic tubercle. The deep inguinal ring and femoral nerve lie at this point. The midinguinal point is halfway between the anterior superior iliac spine and the pubic symphysis. The femoral artery lies at this point.

36 C: Compression hosiery and review in clinic at a later date

Pregnancy is a risk factor for the development of varicose veins. During pregnancy, however, compression stockings alone are used to treat the symptoms of varicose veins. Surgical options might be considered post-partum if the veins are persistent and symptomatic.

37 C: Uncompensated metabolic alkalosis

The high pH indicates that he is in a state of alkalosis. As the PCO_2 is normal and he has a raised bicarbonate, the correct choice is uncompensated metabolic alkalosis. This could be due to gastrointestinal losses from vomiting, hypercalcaemia, bicarbonate ingestion or hypokalaemia (eg due to diuretics, hyperaldosteronism).

38 D: The conjoint tendon as part of the roof

The boundaries of the inguinal canal are:

- Roof – transversus abdominis, internal oblique and the conjoint tendon
- Floor – inguinal ligament and lacunar ligament
- Anterior – external oblique and internal oblique
- Posterior – transversalis fascia and the conjoint tendon.

39 B: Saphenous vein

The saphenous vein passes anterior to the medial malleolus. The structures passing posterior, from nearest back are: tibia, posterior tendon, flexor digitorum longus tendon, posterior tibial artery, posterior tibial vein, posterior tibial nerve and the flexor hallucis longus tendon.

40 C: A hernia containing a strangulated Meckel's diverticulum is a Littre's hernia

Paraumbilical hernias occur just above and just below the umbilicus and are more commonly seen in women. They are acquired, and predisposing factors are obesity and multiple pregnancies. They are at high risk of strangulation as the neck is usually narrow. A hernia that contains a strangulated Meckel's diverticulum is known as a Littre's hernia and can progress to gangrene, suppuration and formation of a local fistula. Hernias that present below and lateral to the pubic tubercle are femoral hernias as opposed to inguinal hernias, which present above and medial to the pubic tubercle. Hernias that appear spontaneously just superior to the iliac crest are most likely to be lumbar hernias. They occur through the lumbar triangle of Petit, formed by the iliac crest, posterior external oblique and anterior latissimus dorsi. Spigelian hernias present through the linea semilunaris at the lateral border of the rectus sheath. They occur at the point where the posterior rectus sheath becomes deficient posteriorly.

41 C: Mandibular branch of the trigeminal nerve

The nerves lying in the lateral wall of the cavernous sinus are the oculomotor, the trochlear and the ophthalmic and maxillary branches of the trigeminal.

42 E: Flexor pollicis longus

The muscles attached to the common flexor origin are pronator teres, flexor carpi radialis, palmaris longus, flexor digitorum superficialis and flexor carpi ulnaris. The deep muscles of the forearm do not attach, and they are pronator quadratus, flexor digitorum profundus and flexor pollicis longus.

43 E: Pectineus forms part of the floor

The boundaries are:

- Superiorly (base) – inguinal ligament
- Medially – medial border of adductor longus
- Laterally – medial border of sartorius
- Floor – adductor longus, pectineus, iliac and psoas
- Roof – fascia and skin.

44 C: Multiple fractions are required for palliation of bone pain

Radiotherapy uses ionising radiation to kill cells. Doses are given at intervals, allowing the normal tissues to recover, but preventing the malignant cells, which take longer to regenerate, from growing. It works by damaging DNA through release of kinetic energy and can be administered through a variety of methods, including electrons, protons, neutrons, X-rays and gamma rays. The success of radiotherapy treatment is dependent on the radiosensitivity of the tumour (for example seminoma is very radiosensitive) and the tolerance of the surrounding tissue, as this can limit the amount of radiotherapy administered. It can be given as a primary treatment, adjuvant and neo-adjuvant therapy and as palliative treatment. Palliation of bone pain can be a single treatment. Complications include ulceration, bleeding, delayed wound healing and lymphoedema.

45 D: Lower eight thoracic nerves

The rectus sheath contains the superior and inferior epigastric arteries and veins, rectus abdominis, pyramidalis and the lower six thoracic nerves.

46 D: The residual volume is 1900 ml

The normal values are tidal volume 500 ml, inspiratory reserve volume 3000 ml, expiratory reserve volume 2000 ml, vital capacity 5600 ml, and total lung capacity 6000 ml.

47 D: Total lung capacity is the sum of residual volume and tidal volume

Lung function tests are useful pre-operatively as they provide the anaesthetist with information about lung function and capacity. Lung volumes vary with sex/height but not weight. The tidal volume is the amount of air moved into/out of the lung during quiet respiration. The amount of air that can be inspired on top of this is the inspiratory reserve volume, and the amount of air that can be forcibly expired on top of the tidal volume is the expiratory reserve volume. Air left in the lung at the end of a maximal expiration is the residual volume. The residual volume together with the expiratory reserve volume is the functional residual capacity. This is important as it is the volume in which gas exchange takes place. Total lung capacity is the sum of the residual volume and the vital capacity, which is the volume expired after a maximum inspiration.

48 C: Cuboid

The medial longitudinal arch comprises the talus, navicular, calcaneum, cuneiforms and medial three metatarsals. The cuboid is lateral.

49 B: Level of the third costal cartilage

The plane of Louis lies at the lower border of T4, at the level of the second costal cartilage. It divides the mediastinum into superior and inferior parts. The trachea bifurcates at this level, the aorta arches and the azygos vein enters the SVC.

50 E: The fourth part lies at the level of L4

The fourth part of the duodenum lies at the level of L2.

51 A: Obturator externus

The sciatic nerve supplies both gemellae, quadratus femoris, semitendinosus, semimembranosus, both heads of biceps femoris, the hamstring half of adductor magnus and obturator internus. Obturator externus is supplied by the obturator nerve.

52 D: Musculocutaneous nerve

The branches of the posterior cord are the upper and lower subscapular nerves, thoracodorsal nerve, axillary nerve and radial nerve. The musculocutaneous nerve is a branch of the lateral cord.

53 C: They are associated with lipodermatosclerosis

Arterial ulcers are typically found at the 'pressure points' of the foot, ie tips of the toes, heel and over the malleoli. They are painful and have a 'punched out' appearance. Poor blood flow to the feet is associated with venous guttering and this can be seen in association with arterial ulcers. Conversely, venous ulcers are usually found around the gaiter area, have sloping edges and are associated with skin changes such as haemosiderin deposition and lipodermatosclerosis (skin induration due to fibrosis of subcutaneous fat).

54 D: Alcohol

There is no proved link between alcohol and bladder cancer; links have been shown to β-naphthylamine (in dyes and in cigarette smoke), schistosomiasis, benzidine, aromatic amines and trauma (eg from catheterisation or calculi).

55 D: Lack of response to painful stimulus

Apnoeic coma and a known cause of irreversible brain damage are pre-requisites for brainstem death testing. The patient must not be hypothermic, have uncorrected metabolic derangements (except Na^+ in diabetes insipidus), or be under the influence of sedative medications. Tests to be performed are: pupil responses, corneal reflexes, a caloric test, gag reflex, apnoea test and pain reflex. However, the pain reflex must be in the facial nerve distribution, as reflexes below the neck may be spinal.

56 D: Damage to the accessory nerve

Carotid endarterectomy is a procedure carried out to remove an atherosclerotic plaque from the carotid artery in patients who have suffered transient ischaemic attacks (TIAs) or (CVAs). The procedure is usually restricted to those who have 70% stenosis of the artery or above because it is at this point that the benefits outweigh the risks of the operation. It involves making an incision in the neck and locating the carotid artery, clamping it above and below the stenosis, creating a bypass for the blood to flow to the head during the operation and incising the artery to remove the plaque. The major risks involved include CVA (1–3%), MI (the most common cause of mortality), glossopharyngeal nerve injury and re-accumulation of the atheroma.

57 E: Increased temperature moves the curve to the right

Each gram of haemoglobin binds 1.34 ml of oxygen when fully saturated. The curve is moved to the left by alkaline pH, decreased temperature, decreased $Paco_2$, decreased 2,3 DPG, fetal haemoglobin and carboxyhaemoglobin. At a Pao_2 of 40 mmHg the saturation of Hb is 75%; at 26 mmHg the saturation is 50%.

58 E: Carbonic anhydrase catalyses the reaction of CO_2 and plasma

Around 30% is transported as carbaminohaemoglobin, 10% dissolved in the plasma and 60% transported as sodium bicarbonate. The carbaminohaemoglobin curve never saturates. Carbonic anhydrase catalyses the reaction of CO_2 and plasma.

59 E: Flexor carpi ulnaris

The contents of the carpal tunnel are:

- Median nerve
- Flexor digitorum superficialis
- Flexor digitorum profundus
- Flexor pollicis longus
- Flexor carpi radialis.

60 B: It passes from the lateral to the third ventricles via the foramen of Monro

CSF is produced by the choroid plexus and reabsorbed by the arachnoid villi. The rate of production is unrelated to the pressure in the ventricles, subarachnoid space, and systemic BP. It passes from the lateral to the third ventricles via the foramen of Monro, and from the third to the fourth ventricles via the aqueduct of Sylvius. It passes into the subarachnoid space via the foramina of Luschka and foramen of Magendie.

61 B: 21 ml

One per cent lidocaine contains 10 mg/ml. The maximum safe dose without adrenaline is 3 mg/kg. The maximum dose is therefore 210 ml, which is contained in 21 ml.

62 C: A decrease in serum magnesium

PTH secretion is decreased by decreased serum phosphate, increased free calcium ions, large decreased magnesium and increased 1,25(OH)$_2$ vitamin D. Its secretion is unrelated to serum potassium level. Mild decreases in serum magnesium may increase PTH secretion as will low calcium and high phosphate levels.

63 A: Vagus nerve

Structures passing through the foramen magnum are the medulla, meninges, tectorial membrane, anterior spinal artery, vertebral artery and spinal branches of the accessory nerve.

64 C: Is bounded laterally by the cystic duct

The boundaries of Calot's triangle are:

- Medially – the common hepatic duct
- Laterally – the cystic duct
- Superiorly – the visceral surface of the liver.

It contains:

- The cystic artery
- Cystic lymph nodes
- The right hepatic duct
- Occasionally the cystic vein.

65 E: Contains the hepatic artery lying on the left of the common bile duct in the anterior border

The epiploic foramen is the opening of the lesser sac on the right side of the abdomen.

The boundaries of the epiploic foramen are:

- Anteriorly – the free edge of the lesser omentum, containing the common bile duct on the right, hepatic artery on the left and the portal vein posteriorly
- Posteriorly – the inferior vena cava and right crus of the diaphragm
- Inferiorly – the first part of the duodenum
- Superiorly – the caudate lobe of the liver.

66 C: Percutaneous balloon angioplasty

Arterial stenoses that are short and localised in nature are amenable to treatment with percutaneous balloon angioplasty. Much better long-term results are achieved if the lesion is present in a proximal vessel such as the superficial femoral artery (SFA). The procedure is carried out by the Seldinger technique, where a flexible guidewire is passed across the stenosis and then a catheter with a plastic inflatable balloon is passed across it. The balloon is dilated when it reaches the stenosis, widening the vessel.

67 D: Oncofetal antibodies

Tumour markers can be enzymes, hormones, oncofetal antigens and ectopic hormones.

68 E: Lies halfway between the jugular notch and the pubic symphysis

The transpyloric plane of Addison lies midway between the jugular notch and the pubic symphysis at the level of the lower border of the L1 vertebra.

Structures lying at this level are the:

- Pyloris of the stomach
- Fundus of the gallbladder
- Duodenojejunal junction
- Neck of the pancreas
- Hila of the kidneys
- Ninth costal cartilages
- Superior mesenteric artery commencement
- Portal vein formation.

69 B: Left common iliac artery

Intermittent claudication is a pain in muscle caused by ischaemia, brought on by exercise and relieved by rest. The site of the pain often indicates the area of stenosis, for example calf pain suggests superficial femoral artery, thigh pain suggests external iliac artery and buttock pain suggests common iliac artery. Occlusion of the aorto-iliac region associated with buttock claudication and impotence is known as Leriche syndrome.

70 E: Neck of the pancreas

The stomach bed comprises the lesser sac of the peritoneum, left crus of the diaphragm, upper left kidney, left adrenal gland, body and tail of the pancreas, spleen, splenic artery, transverse mesocolon, aorta, coeliac trunk, coeliac ganglion and lymph nodes.

71 B: The transtubercular plane runs through the body of L5

The subcostal plane runs through the superior border of L3.

The transtubercular plane runs through the iliac tubercles, passing through the body of L5.

The transumbilical plane runs through the umbilicus at the level of the L3/4 intervertebral disc.

The sagittal planes are continuations of the midclavicular lines, running through the midinguinal points.

The transpyloric plane runs through the inferior border of L1.

72 D: The stylomastoid foramen

The facial nerve traverses the facial canal, the internal auditory meatus and the stylomastoid foramen. The superior orbital foramen contains the oculomotor, trochlear, trigeminal and abducent nerves. The trigeminal nerve passes through the foramen ovale and the foramen rotundum. The petrosquamous fissure has no contents.

73 C: They can cause emboli

Elective surgery is normally carried out for abdominal aortic aneurysm (AAA) only if the patient is relatively fit and has an aneurysm >5.5 cm in diameter, as the mortality for the operation is 5%. Endoluminal stenting is a relatively new alternative that can be used to treat infrarenal aneurysms. Overall mortality in ruptured aneurysms is 75% and unstable patients should proceed to urgent surgery. Ultrasound scan or CT scan can aid diagnosis, and regular ultrasound scans are a means of carrying out regular surveillance of aneurysms not large enough to require surgery. Thrombus formation within aneurysms can lead to distal emboli. AAAs are much more common in men.

74 C: Extensor carpi radialis

The contents of the extensor compartments are:

- I – Abductor pollicis longus and extensor pollicis brevis
- II – Extensor carpi radialis
- III – Extensor pollicis longus
- IV – Extensor digitorum and extensor indicis
- V – Extensor digiti minimi
- VI – Extensor carpi ulnaris.

75 B: *Clostridium tetani*

Clostridia are Gram-positive rods, as are *Listeria* and diphtheroids. Examples of Gram-negative rods include *Escherichia coli*, *Klebsiella*, *Yersinia*, *Haemophilus*, *Pseudomonas*, *Shigella*, *Legionella*, *Proteus* and *Salmonella*.

76 D: Is bounded inferiorly by teres major

The boundaries of the quadrilateral space are:

- Superiorly – subscapularis
- Inferiorly – teres major
- Medially – long head of triceps
- Laterally – medial shaft of humerus.

It contains:

- Axillary nerve
- Posterior circumflex humeral artery and vein.

77 D: Ulceration in primary lymphoedema is common

Lymphoedema is an abnormal collection of tissue fluid from defective lymphatics, and may be either primary or secondary in nature. Secondary causes include infection, malignancy and radiotherapy. Surgery is rarely used to treat it and management is usually conservative, with compression stockings, intermittent mechanical compression and treatment of cellulitis when it occurs. Ulceration is not commonly seen with primary lymphoedema.

78 A: Aldosterone is produced by the zona glomerulosa

The secretions of the adrenal glands by zone are:

- Zona glomerulosa – aldosterone
- Zona fasciculata – cortisol and testosterone
- Zona reticularis – oestradiol and progesterone
- Adrenal medulla – adrenaline, noradrenaline and dopamine.

79 A: The superior parathyroid glands are derived from the fourth pharyngeal pouch

The pharyngeal arches are composed of mesoderm, endoderm and ectoderm. The superior parathyroids are derived from the fourth pharyngeal pouch and the inferior parathyroids are derived from the third pharyngeal pouch. The mandible, maxilla and zygoma are derived from the first pharyngeal arch. The third pharyngeal arch is supplied by the glossopharyngeal nerve.

80 D: B-cell lymphoma

EBV is known to be carcinogenic for B-cell lymphoma, nasopharyngeal carcinoma and Hodgkin's lymphoma.

81 E: 5 mmol/l of potassium

Hartmann's contains 130 mmol of sodium, 111 mmol of chloride, no glucose and 2 mmol of calcium.

82 C: Bone cyst

Bone cysts are common benign fluid-containing lesions that usually occur in the metaphysis of long bones. Half of all bone cysts present as pathological fractures and most occur in children aged 4–10 years. Bone metastases usually present with pain, although occurrence of a pathological fracture may be the first presentation. Osteosarcoma has a bimodal distribution, with 75% of those affected being aged between 10 and 25 years. The remainder are elderly with a history of Paget's disease. It typically presents with a painful mass, most commonly affecting the lower femur and arising from the medullary cavity. Chondrosarcomas can present de novo or from malignant transformation of a benign cartilage tumour such an osteochondroma. They usually affect middle-aged or elderly people. Ewing's sarcoma usually affects young people aged between 5 and 15 years. It presents as a lytic lesion, which causes a periosteal reaction, giving it a characteristic 'onion skin' appearance.

83 C: The left adrenal lies posterior to the splenic artery

The left adrenal lies more medially than the right. The left adrenal lies posterior to the splenic artery and body of the pancreas, anterior to the left crus of the diaphragm, lateral to the coeliac ganglion and left gastric vessels, and medial to the left kidney. The right adrenal lies posterior to the right lobe of the liver and IVC, anterior to the right crus of the diaphragm, and lateral to the right inferior phrenic vessels.

The zona glomerulosa secretes aldosterone, the zona fasciculata cortisol and testosterone, and the zona reticularis oestradiol and progesterone.

84 D: 3500 ml of small-bowel secretions

Secretions per day: 1500 ml of saliva, 2000 ml of gastric secretions, 1000 ml of pancreatic juices, 1500 ml of bile, 3500 ml of small-bowel secretions and 500 ml of large-bowel secretions.

85 E: *Staphylococcus aureus*

Osteomyelitis is characterised by pain and swelling over the affected part and a fever. Bacteria can enter the bone via direct inoculation or haematogenous spread. People most susceptible are those with diabetes and immunosuppression. Radiological changes do not usually appear until 10 days after onset and consist of soft-tissue swelling and sclerotic bone changes with periosteal elevation. The most likely causative organism in this case is *S. aureus*. In young children, *Haemophilus influenzae* can also be a cause. *Salmonella* can cause osteomyelitis in sickle cell patients.

86 E: Hydrochloric acid is produced by the chief cells

Hydrochloric acid is produced by the parietal cells.

87 D: Factor VII

Factors XII, XI and IX are all part of the intrinsic pathway. Factor VII is common to both pathways. Factor III is part of the extrinsic pathway. Factor XIII is part of the final common pathway.

88 D: Wasting of the hypothenar muscles

Carpal tunnel syndrome is due to compression of the median nerve within the carpal tunnel, which is itself made up of the carpal bones and the transverse carpal ligament. It can be idiopathic or associated with pregnancy, rheumatoid arthritis, diabetes or hypothyroidism. It typically presents with pain and paraesthesia over the thumb and lateral two fingers, which is worse at night. There may be associated wasting of the thenar muscles. Tinel's test involves reproduction of symptoms on tapping over the carpal tunnel whereas Phalen's test involves reproduction of symptoms on flexing the wrist.

89 A: Folate reuptake

Answers B–E are the main functions of the terminal ileum. Folate reuptake is a function of the jejunum.

90 D: Stores can last for up to a year

Vitamin B_{12} is necessary for maturation of red cells; it is stored in the liver and also present in bile. Stores are large and can last 3–6 years. Intrinsic factor secreted by gastric parietal cells is necessary for its uptake.

91 C: Trypsinogen

Pancreatic polypeptide, somatostatin, glucagons and insulin are endocrine secretions of the pancreas. The exocrine secretions are trypsinogen, chymotrypsinogen, procarboxylase, procarboxypeptidases, phospholipase, amylase and lecithin.

92 D: Increased joint space

Characteristic radiological features of osteoarthritis are bone cysts, subchondral sclerosis, osteophytes, reduced joint space and joint effusion. In contrast, features of rheumatoid arthritis are periarticular soft-tissue swelling, loss of joint space, bony erosions, juxta-articular osteoporosis and pseudocysts.

93 E: Emphysema

Compliance is reduced by alveolar oedema, pulmonary hypertension, atelectasis and pulmonary fibrosis. It is increased by emphysema, acute asthma and increasing age.

94 C: Antidiuretic hormone (ADH)

The anterior pituitary secretes ACTH, FSH, LH, thyroid-stimulating hormone (TSH), GH and prolactin. The posterior pituitary releases ADH.

95 C: The popliteal artery is the deepest structure within the fossa

The popliteal fossa is a diamond-shaped area on the back of the knee. It is bounded superiorly by biceps femoris (laterally) and semimembranosus (medially) and the two heads of gastrocnemius (inferiorly). The roof is formed by deep fascia pierced by the short saphenous vein. It contains the branches of the sciatic nerve (tibial and common peroneal nerves), the popliteal vein and artery. The deepest structure is the artery. The common peroneal nerve lies laterally and winds around the head of the fibula, whereas the tibial nerve lies medially.

96 C: 70 mmol calcium

Daily requirements are: 1 mmol/kg potassium and chloride, 2 mmol/kg of sodium, 0.1 mmol/kg of calcium, and approximately 35 ml/kg of water.

97 D: The long thoracic nerve originates from trunks C5, C6 and C7

The brachial plexus is made up of five nerve roots (C5–T1), which then form trunks in the posterior triangle of the neck. C6 and C7 join to form the superior trunk, C7 continues as the middle trunk and C8 and T1 form the inferior trunk. The trunks divide into anterior and posterior divisions and then combine to form lateral posterior and medial cords. The cords divide to form the main nerves: musculocutaneous nerve (lateral cord), median nerve (lateral and medial cords), axillary nerve (posterior cord), radial nerve (posterior cord) and ulnar nerve (medial cord). There are several branches arising from the roots, trunks and cords, for example the long thoracic nerve, which supplies serratus anterior, arises from nerve roots C5–C7; the thoracodorsal nerve, which supplies the latissimus dorsi and the nerve to subscapularis both arise from the posterior cord.

98 A: Diarrhoea

Excess acid intake and excess bicarbonate loss, eg in diarrhoea, are causes of metabolic acidosis with a normal anion gap. The other conditions all cause an increased anion gap.

99 E: It is commonest in the fourth and fifth decades

Pleomorphic adenoma is the commonest salivary gland tumour. It is benign, although a small number undergo malignant transformation. It is commonest in the parotid gland, but can occur in any salivary gland. It is commoner in males, most often presenting in the fourth and fifth decades. Ten per cent of Warthin's tumours are bilateral.

100 B: Unconjugated bilirubin

Bile contains conjugated bilirubin with glucuronic acid, which make up the bile pigments. The other constituents are bile salts/acids, inorganic salts (eg sodium chloride and sodium bicarbonate), phospholipids (eg cholesterol and lecithins) and water, which makes up 97% of the bile.

101 B: Sciatic nerve

A posterior dislocation of the hip causes the leg to appear shortened and internally rotated. In 20% of fracture dislocations of the hip, the sciatic nerve is damaged. This results in paralysis of the hamstrings and all the flexors and extensors below the knee. Also, all of the skin below the knee loses its sensation apart from the areas supplied by the saphenous and posterior cutaneous nerve of the thigh (medial and upper posterior calf respectively).

102 A: Hodgkin's lymphoma

Reed–Sternberg cells are characteristic of Hodgkin's lymphoma.

103 C: Hepatitis E

Known risk factors for hepatocellular carcinoma include hepatitis B and C, aflatoxin, anabolic steroids, alcohol cirrhosis and primary liver disease.

104 D: Supraspinatus tendonitis

Supraspinatus tendonitis is usually caused by vigorous exercise in people aged over 40 years. They present with a 'painful arc' of shoulder movement when the arm passes through 60–120 degrees of abduction. In contrast, supraspinatus rupture makes active abduction impossible, although there is a full range of passive movement. Frozen shoulder occurs as a result of degenerative changes of the rotator cuff. Pain due to this causes the patient to hold the shoulder still and adhesions form, which limit movement even more until only scapular movement remains. Rupture of the long head of biceps usually occurs in a previously diseased tendon and causes pain, tenderness and bunching-up of the muscle in the lower arm.

105 E: Occurs in 1 in 31 000 live births

Infantile hypertrophic pyloric stenosis is present in 1 in 31 000 live births. It is more common in first-born males and usually presents between 3 and 6 weeks.

106 D: Carcinoembryonic antigen (CEA) for NSGCT

CEA is a non-specific marker for a variety of tumours and pathologies, but not for testicular tumours. Alpha-fetoprotein is a marker for NGSCT, but not for pure seminoma.

107 E: Femoral nerve injury is common

Fractured neck of femur is unfortunately a common injury in the elderly and mortality is in the region of 30% at 6 months. Patients usually present with a history of a fall and then inability to weight-bear on the affected side. On inspection the affected leg is shortened and externally rotated. The way in which fractured neck of femur is managed is dictated by the blood supply to the femoral head. A significant amount of the blood supply comes from the retinacular vessels, which pass proximally within the joint capsule. These vessels are therefore disrupted in intracapsular (subcapital) fractures. Undisplaced subcapital fractures have a good chance of maintaining the blood supply as there is minimal disruption of the capsule. They can generally be treated with insertion of cannulated screws. If they are displaced (ie Garden III and IV), there is a high risk of developing avascular necrosis of the femoral head and so hemiarthroplasty is the preferred management.

108 D: Hepatitis A

Epstein–Barr virus is linked to B-cell lymphoma, Hodgkin's lymphoma and nasopharyngeal carcinoma. Hepatitis B and C are linked to hepatocellular carcinoma, but no link has been shown to Hepatitis A. HIV is linked to leukaemia, lymphoma and Kaposi's sarcoma. HPV is linked to cervical cancer.

109 D: Systemic vascular resistance

A Swan–Ganz catheter can be used to directly measure mean arterial pressure, central venous pressure, pulmonary artery wedge pressure, cardiac output (using Fick's principle). Peripheral and systemic vascular resistance and ventricular stroke work are calculated, not directly measured.

110 C: Hartmann's procedure

The safest operation to carry out in these circumstances, where a patient is unstable and the operating field is highly contaminated, is a Hartmann's operation, where the affected segment of colon is excised and the proximal end is brought out as an end-colostomy. The rectal stump is closed and left inside or alternatively may be brought out as a mucous fistula. It is possible then to rejoin the two ends of bowel once the patient is in a more stable state and infection has settled to allow optimum conditions for forming an anastomosis.

111 E: Commonly includes hyperparathyroidism

MEN I is inherited in an autosomal dominant fashion; the gene is located on chromosome 11; the gene for MEN II is on chromosome 10. MEN IIA is known as Sipple syndrome. Phaeochromocytoma is a common feature of MEN IIB, not MEN I.

112 C: It can be caused by nitrous oxide

All inhalational anaesthetic agents except nitrous oxide can cause malignant hyperpyrexia; suxamethonium can also cause it. The treatment involves dantrolene. Malignant hyperpyrexia occurs in 1 in 150 000.

113 B: Pro-accelerin

Pro-accelerin is a plasma protein. All of the other factors (prothrombin, plasminogen, antithrombin and fibrinogen) are synthesised by the liver, as is factor VIII.

114 C: Malnutrition

Local factors delaying wound healing include infection, haematoma, foreign bodies, decreased blood supply and poor surgical technique. Malnutrition does affect wound healing, but is a systemic factor.

115 B: Renin is secreted by the granular cells of the juxtaglomerular apparatus

Renin is secreted by the granular cells of the juxtaglomerular apparatus. In the blood it converts angiotensin to angiotensin I. Angiotensin I is converted to angiotensin II by ACE in the lungs. Angiotensin II stimulates aldosterone and antidiuretic hormone. Antidiuretic hormone is produced by the hypothalamus and stored in the posterior pituitary, from which it is released.

116 C: Amino acids are actively reabsorbed

Sodium, glucose, bicarbonate and amino acids are actively reabsorbed in the proximal tubule. Phosphate and calcium are reabsorbed subject to control. Urea and water are passively reabsorbed. Hydrogen ions are secreted, dependent on pH.

117 D: Stimulated by high carbon dioxide levels

The chemoreceptors concerned with blood pressure maintenance are located at the carotid bifurcation and aortic bodies. The stretch receptors are located in the walls of the atria and pulmonary arteries. The chemoreceptors are stimulated by low oxygen levels, high carbon dioxide levels and acidic pH. The stretch receptors respond to stretching of the vessel walls.

118 B: Constriction of the pupils

The fight or flight response is controlled by the hypothalamus, which controls release of catecholamines from the adrenal medulla. It includes constriction of blood vessels, increased heart rate and increased contraction strength, sweating, decreased GI activity and dilatation of the pupils.

119 C: Phosphate

Sodium, magnesium, calcium and potassium are all cations. Chloride, phosphate, bicarbonate, lactate, sulphate and albumin are all anions.

120 E: Gastrinoma

Gastrinoma is a common feature of MEN I.

121 E: Rectus abdominis

The accessory muscles of expiration are the abdominal muscles, which can force the diaphragm upwards by contracting, including rectus abdominis, transversus abdominis, internal and external obliques. Sternocleidomastoid and the scalene muscles are the major accessory muscles of inspiration.

122 B: Palor

The characteristic features of acute inflammation are dolor (pain), rubor (erythema), tumour (swelling) and calor (heat).

123 E: Results in orderly vesicle formation

Answers A–D are characteristics of necrosis. Apoptosis is a physiological process of programmed cell death, which is irreversible once initiated, and energy-driven. The cells shrink and are packed into vesicles.

124 D: Adrenal

Tumours that commonly metastasise to bone are breast, bronchus, thyroid, prostate and kidney.

125 E: Is a remnant of the omphalomesenteric duct

Meckel's diverticulum is the commonest congenital developmental anomaly, more common in males. It is present in 2% of the population, 2-inches-long and 2 feet from the ileocaecal junction. It contains all layers of the intestinal wall. It can contain gastric or pancreatic mucosa. It is a remnant of the omphalomesenteric duct.

126 C: Ulcerative colitis

Granulomas are found in TB, leprosy, schistosomiasis, syphilis, sarcoidosis and Crohn's disease. The lack of granulomas in ulcerative colitis is one of the differences between the two types of inflammatory bowel disease.

127 D: A low nuclear-to-cytoplasmic ratio

Dysplasia is a premalignant change. It causes increased cell growth and mitosis. It causes abnormal differentiation with pleomorphism, hyperchromism and high nuclear-to-cytoplasmic ratio.

128 C: Papillary thyroid carcinoma

Psammoma bodies are a characteristic histological finding in papillary thyroid carcinoma.

129 C: Continuous sun exposure

Fair skin, albinism, xeroderma pigmentosum and family history are all risk factors for malignant melanoma. Intermittent sun exposure is a risk factor, with stronger links between continuous exposure and basal cell carcinoma and squamous cell carcinoma.

130 D: Merkel cell tumour

Pott's peculiar tumour is a trichilemmal cyst; a harmatoma is an overgrowth of one or more cell types that are normally present. A turban tumour is a type of cylindroma and seborrhoeic keratoses are benign overgrowths of the basal layer of the epidermis.

131 B: Vitamin B_3

Vitamin A is required for epithelial cell proliferation. Vitamin B_6 is required for collagen cross-links. Zinc is required for RNA and DNA synthesis. Copper is required for cross-linking of collagen.

132 A: EBV

Blood for transfusion is routinely screened for hepatitis B and C, HIV, CMV and syphilis.

133 D: Fibroblasts take 3 days to appear

Platelets appear immediately in a wound, followed by neutrophils within a day. Macrophages appear within 2 days, then fibroblasts and myofibroblasts in 2–4 days, then endothelial cells in 3–5 days.

134 E: Hamartoma is an overgrowth of cell not normally found in that tissue

Hypertrophy is an increase in cell size, and hyperplasia is an increase in cell number. Metaplasia is the conversion of one tissue type to another. Teratoma is a growth of cells originating from more than one germ-cell line. Hamartoma is an overgrowth of a cell normally found in that tissue.

135 A: Squamous carcinoma

Squamous cell carcinoma is the most common type, followed by small-cell, adenocarcinoma, large-cell and adenosquamous.

PRACTICE PAPER 2: QUESTIONS

PRACTICE PAPER 2: QUESTIONS

1 Structures derived from the first (mandibular) branchial arch include all of the following, EXCEPT:

- A Muscles of mastication
- B Stylohyoid ligament
- C Incus and malleus
- D Mylohyoid
- E Tensor tympani

2 Regarding branchial cysts, which of the following statements is FALSE?

- A They are lined by stratified squamous epithelium
- B Diagnosis is by clinical examination and needle aspiration
- C They occur at the junction of the lower third and upper two-thirds of sternocleidomastoid
- D They are present in 60% of males
- E A quarter of cysts become infected

3 Which one of the following statements regarding the development of the parathyroid glands is TRUE?

- A The superior parathyroids develop from the third pharyngeal pouch
- B The inferior parathyroids develop from the fourth pharyngeal pouch
- C Development of the superior parathyroids occurs in company with the thymus gland
- D Development of the inferior parathyroids occurs in company with the parafollicular C cells
- E The inferior parathyroids can be found in the superior mediastinum in association with the thymus gland

4 A 55-year-old man presents to you with back pain and paraesthesia along the medial border of the leg and foot. A disc prolapse is suspected with compression of which of the following spinal nerve roots?

- A L3
- B L4
- C L5
- D S1
- E S2

5 All of the following are complications of transurethral resection of prostate (TURP), EXCEPT:

- A Urethral stricture
- B Retrograde ejaculation
- C Hypernatraemia
- D Incontinence
- E Increased risk of myocardial infarction

6 Which of the following muscles of mastication inserts into the neck of the mandible and anterior surface of the disc of the temporomandibular joint?

- A Lateral pterygoid
- B Medial pterygoid
- C Masseter
- D Buccinator
- E Temporalis

7 Which one of these muscle and nerve pairings is correct?

- A Stylopharyngeus – glossopharyngeal nerve
- B Tensor veli palatini – pharyngeal plexus
- C Buccinator – cranial nerve Vc
- D Palatoglossus – hypoglossal nerve
- E Cricothyroid – recurrent laryngeal nerve

8 Concerning parasympathetic nerve supply, which one of the following pairings is correct?

- A Otic ganglion – submandibular gland
- B Pterygopalatine ganglion – lacrimal gland
- C Pterygopalatine ganglion – parotid gland
- D Auriculotemporal nerve – submandibular gland
- E Facial nerve – otic ganglion

9 A patient arrives in the Emergency Department with the following arterial blood gas results: Pao_2 8.0 kPa; $Paco_2$ 2.0 kPa; pH 7.54; bicarbonate 18 mmol/l. The most likely cause is:

- A Excessive vomiting
- B Pulmonary embolus (PE)
- C Diabetic ketoacidosis
- D CVA
- E Chest wall trauma

10 The operation of choice for treatment of a strangulated femoral hernia, which is likely to contain infarcted small bowel is:

- A McEvedy's abdominal approach
- B Lothiessen's high approach
- C Lockwood's crural or low approach
- D Bassini's low repair
- E Lower midline laparotomy

11 **A 21-year-old medical student presents to the Emergency Department with conjunctivitis. You prescribe him eye drops, but he mentions that he dislikes taking them as he gets a bitter taste at the back of his throat. You explain that the lacrimal drainage is connected to the nasopharynx, hence the bitter taste. He wishes to know exactly where the drainage occurs. Within the lateral wall of the nasal cavity the nasolacrimal duct opens at the:**

- A Superior meatus
- B Middle meatus
- C Inferior meatus
- D Spheno-ethmoidal recess
- E Nasopharynx

12 **An 18-year-old motorcycle accident victim is noted to have a fluctuating Glasgow Coma Scale (GCS) score and a dilated right pupil in the Emergency Department. You suspect an extradural haemorrhage and this is confirmed on computed tomography. Which one of the following branches of the maxillary artery is classically injured in an extradural haemorrhage?**

- A Deep auricular
- B Anterior tympanic
- C Middle meningeal
- D Deep temporal
- E Accessory meningeal

13 A patient of yours requires central venous access via the internal jugular vein. The internal jugular vein is formed by the union of the sigmoid sinus with which one of the following sinuses?

- A Superior petrosal sinus
- B Inferior petrosal sinus
- C Cavernous sinus
- D Straight sinus
- E Occipital sinus

14 All of the following statements about 5-fluorouracil (5-FU) are correct, EXCEPT:

- A It is indicated in the adjuvant treatment of rectal cancers
- B It interferes with DNA synthesis by reducing the availability of thymidylic acid
- C It is used in the treatment of solid cancers
- D It is an alkylating agent
- E It inhibits pyrimidine rather than purine synthesis

15 Which statement is true regarding the bladder?

- A Sympathetic fibres cause relaxation of the detrusor muscle and contraction of the internal sphincter
- B In the male, the external sphincter lies above the prostate
- C It receives its blood supply from branches of the external iliac arteries
- D It is entirely covered by peritoneum
- E The trigone is situated at the apex of the bladder

16 **Which one of the following structures passes through the foramen rotundum in the base of the skull?**

- A Mandibular division of the trigeminal
- B Maxillary division of the trigeminal
- C Lesser petrosal nerve
- D Middle meningeal artery
- E Facial nerve

17 **Structures entering through the jugular foramen in the base of the skull include all of the following, EXCEPT:**

- A Glossopharyngeal nerve (IX)
- B Vagus nerve (X)
- C Accessory nerve (XI)
- D Sigmoid sinus
- E Superior petrosal sinus

18 **Which of the following anti-cancer drugs would be classified as an alkylating agent?**

- A Doxorubicin
- B Methotrexate
- C Cytarabine
- D Vincristine
- E Cisplatin

19 **An obese 45-year-old waitress is referred to you by her GP with a diagnosis of meralgia paraesthetica. You would expect her symptoms to affect which one of the following areas?**

- A Lateral thigh region
- B Posterior thigh
- C Lateral thigh
- D Medial thigh
- E Groin area

20 **Cricoid pressure is often applied to assist anaesthetists during the intubation process. Anatomically, the cricoid cartilage can also be used to identify other vessels and landmarks in the neck. The surface marking of the cricoid cartilage in a normal male adult is represented by which of the following vertebral levels?**

- A C3
- B C4
- C C5
- D C6
- E C7

21 A patient has a tuning fork test with central vertex placement localising to the left ear; left ear bone conduction is better than air conduction on left mastoid tuning fork placement. The right ear demonstrates better air than bone conduction. Which one of the following statements is TRUE?

- A Weber's test is positive in the left ear
- B There is sensorineural hearing loss in the left ear
- C Rinne's test involves central tuning fork placement on the vertex of the skull
- D There is a conductive loss of greater than 20 dB in the left ear
- E Masking can be achieved with a Baroness sound box

22 A 3-year-old boy presents to the ENT Clinic with a 1-week history of unilateral purulent nasal discharge. His mother reports that he is otherwise well in himself and has no other symptoms. The initial management would be:

- A Swab discharge for microscopy, culture and sensitivity
- B Intravenous broad-spectrum antibiotics, eg Augmentin
- C Examination and attempted removal of foreign body
- D Plain facial X-rays
- E Orthopantomogram

23 The classic visual field defect caused by a pituitary adenoma will be a:

- A Homonymous hemianopia
- B Bitemporal hemianopia
- C Bitemporal inferior quadrantanopia
- D Binasal hemianopia
- E Unilateral visual loss

24 Which of the following veins accompanies the marginal branch of the right coronary artery?

- A Great cardiac vein
- B Middle cardiac vein
- C Small cardiac vein
- D Anterior cardiac vein
- E Oblique cardiac vein

25 A 17-year-old boy presents to the ENT Clinic for follow-up of his nasal fracture treatment. Incidentally, he mentions that he has had long-standing nasal stuffiness. A nasal speculum examination reveals bilateral polyps. Regarding nasal polyps, which one of the following statements is TRUE?

- A Co-existent asthma is rare
- B Polyps in childhood can indicate cystic fibrosis
- C Epistaxis is unlikely to be associated with neoplasia
- D Polyps are commonly treated with long courses of high-dose steroids
- E Surgery is not indicated

26 **A 5-year-old boy presents with a 2-hour history of sudden-onset distress while playing with Lego at nursery. He has very noisy inspiratory breathing from the neck, with raised respiratory and heart rates. The most likely site of obstruction would be at the level of the:**

- A Oropharynx
- B Nasopharynx
- C Larynx
- D Trachea
- E Main bronchi

27 **Which of the following features is NOT associated with a full-thickness burn?**

- A Black/white colour
- B Reduced blanching
- C No sensation
- D Usually require treatment with skin graft
- E Minimal healing

28 **A 52-year-old businessman is admitted to the Emergency Department with acute-onset chest pain, which radiates to the right arm and is associated with nausea and sweating. An ECG taken shows ischaemic changes within the heart and you suspect that he has angina. Transmission of activity within which of the following afferent nerves would explain the pain radiating down the arm from the chest?**

- A Phrenic nerve
- B Vagus nerve
- C Somatic nerves to the arm
- D Intercostal nerves
- E Splanchnic nerves

29 **A 42-year-old woman presents with a 6-month history of intermittent, sudden-onset, dizzy spells. She describes the world spinning suddenly, where she feels she is being thrown to the floor. She feels nauseous and lies as still as possible. It lasts for a few hours, and is associated with a ringing in her ears. She also notes that her hearing has slightly decreased between the attacks. Examination is unremarkable, but audiograms show low-frequency sensorineural hearing loss. Which one of the following is the most likely diagnosis?**

- A Benign positional vertigo
- B Acute labyrinthitis
- C Acoustic neuroma
- D Cardiovascular pathology
- E Ménière's disease

30 With regard to the synthesis and uptake of thyroid hormones, which one of the following statements is TRUE?

- A Like the catecholamines, the thyroid hormones are synthesised from the amino acid tyramine
- B Iodine is reduced to iodide and absorbed in the thyroid gland
- C The follicular cells take up iodide by simple diffusion
- D Thyroid-stimulating hormone (TSH) stimulates iodide trapping at all iodide-trapping sites within the body
- E Thiouracils inhibit T_4 production

31 Regarding TSH:

- A Low levels of circulating T_4 increase the TSH response to thyrotropin-releasing hormone (TRH)
- B TSH secretion is diurnal, peaking around midday
- C Plasma levels of TSH rise in hot environments
- D Glucocorticoids and oestrogens reduce the TSH secretory response to TRH
- E Secretion is stimulated by somatostatin and dopamine

32 A Richter's hernia refers to a hernia that:

- A Contains two loops of small bowel within it
- B Contains a perforated appendix
- C Contains part of the wall of the bowel
- D Protrudes through the linea semilunaris
- E Causes intestinal obstruction commonly

33 Innervation to the muscles of the back originate from:

- A Dorsal primary rami
- B Ventral primary rami
- C Grey rami communicantes
- D White rami communicantes
- E Lateral perforating branches of the ventral primary rami

34 Regarding multiple endocrine neoplasia (MEN) syndromes, which one of the following statements is correct?

- A Pituitary adenomas are mainly a feature of MEN II
- B Medullary carcinoma of the thyroid is a feature of MEN II
- C Phaeochromocytomas are best detected by urinary 5-HIAA measurement
- D MEN syndromes are always familial
- E Parathyroid adenomas tend to present with hypocalcaemia

35 The sensory nerve supply to the diaphragmatic pleura is derived from the:

- A Phrenic nerve
- B Vagus nerve
- C Intercostal nerve
- D Sympathetic chain
- E Pectoral nerves

36 **The intervertebral joint is an example of a:**

- A Primary cartilaginous joint
- B Seconday cartilaginous joint
- C Fibrous joint
- D Synovial condyloid joint
- E Synovial plane

37 **Which of the following blood results is most likely to indicate recent infection with hepatitis B?**

	HBsAg	HBeAg	Anti-HBsAg	Anti-HBcAg
A	–	–	+	+
B	–	+	–	+
C	+	–	+	–
D	+	+	–	+
E	+	+	+	+

38 **Which of the following nerves provides the afferent limb of the sneezing reflex?**

- A Ophthalmic division of the trigeminal nerve
- B Maxillary division of the trigeminal nerve
- C Mandibular division of the trigeminal nerve
- D Glossopharyngeal nerve
- E Vagus nerve

39 All of the following muscles are involved in abduction of the hip joint, EXCEPT:

- A Gluteus medius
- B Gluteus minimus
- C Sartorius
- D Quadratus femoris
- E Tensor fascia lata

40 Which of the following hereditary immune disorders is NOT correctly paired with the affected component of the immune system?

- A Chronic granulomatous disease (CGD) – macrophages
- B DiGeorge syndrome – T cells
- C Leucocyte adhesion deficiency (LAD) – neutrophils
- D Hereditary angioedema – complement pathway
- E X-linked hypogammaglobulinaemia – B cells

41 A 44-year-old-man presents to you with signs of a facial infection around the area of the pterygopalatine fossa following maxillary surgery. You initially suspect that the infection has tracked from the pterygoid venous plexus. All of the following structures are at risk of subsequent infection tracking down, EXCEPT:

- A Orbit
- B Oral cavity
- C Nasal cavity
- D Maxillary sinus
- E Middle cranial fossa

42 **All of the following nerves pass along the lateral wall of the cavernous sinus, EXCEPT:**

- A Oculomotor nerve
- B Trochlear nerve
- C Ophthalmic division of the trigeminal nerve
- D Maxillary division of the trigeminal nerve
- E Abducent nerve

43 **A 28-year-old woman gives birth to a healthy baby girl in the delivery suite. During her second stage of labour an episiotomy was necessary to allow delivery of her baby under local anaesthesia. Immediately after this procedure, the woman now complains that she is unable to maintain continence of faeces as she has no voluntary control of her anal sphincters. Which nerve in this clinical scenario has been anaesthetised?**

- A Pudendal nerve
- B Inferior gluteal nerve
- C Superior gluteal nerve
- D Ventral rami of S3 and S4
- E Inferior hypogastric nerve

44 A bleeding ulcer on the posterior aspect of the first part of the duodenum would classically erode through which of the following vessels?

- A Right gastric artery
- B Superior pancreaticoduodenal artery
- C Right gastroepiploic artery
- D Gastroduodenal artery
- E Hepatic artery

45 The lateral umbilical folds in the abdominal wall are formed by

- A Urachus
- B Obliterated umbilical arteries
- C Superior epigastric arteries
- D Inferior epigastric arteries
- E Falciform ligament

46 All of the following statements regarding Swan–Ganz pulmonary artery catheters are true, EXCEPT:

- A The insertion procedure may be complicated by arrhythmias
- B Pulmonary arterial pressures readings of 6–12 mmHg are normal
- C Left atrial pressure may be measured reasonably accurately
- D It can be used as part of the thermodilution mechanism to measure cardiac output accurately
- E It should always be inserted under strict aseptic technique

47 **Cerebrospinal fluid is connected to the subarachnoid space from the ventricles via the:**

- A Cisterna magna
- B Arachnoid villi
- C Choroid plexus
- D Foramen of Monro
- E Foramina of Magendie and Luschka

48 **A 42-year old alcoholic man is referred to you with ascites and liver cirrhosis. The mechanism of formation of ascites in this patient with cirrhosis is a combination of which of the following conditions?**

- A Hypoalbuminaemia and portal hypertension
- B Decreased hepatic lymph flow
- C Decreased hepatic lymph flow with decreased aldosterone secretion
- D Leaky capillaries in the portal circulation
- E Subacute inflammatory changes causing hepatic oedema and extravasation of fluid

49 A woman is brought to the Emergency Department after being rescued from a house fire. She has burns affecting her left arm and anterior surfaces of both legs. Using Wallace's rule of nines, the percentage of area burnt is:

- A 45%
- B 18%
- C 36%
- D 27%
- E 54%

50 A 35-year old businessman presents to you for an endoscopy following symptoms of epigastric pain which is worse at nights and on eating food. You suspect a gastric ulcer and proceed to perform endoscopy with a biopsy for *Helicobacter pylori*. On endoscopic biopsy, which of the following is the commonest location for finding *H. pylori* within the stomach?

- A Fundus
- B Lesser curve
- C Body
- D Pyloric antrum
- E Cardia

51 Damage to peripheral nerves results in specific areas of sensory loss. Which of the following nerve–sensory area pairings is INCORRECT?

- A Radial nerve – dorsal web space between thumb and index finger
- B Musculocutaneous nerve – lateral area of forearm
- C Median nerve – palmar aspect of index finger
- D Obturator nerve – lateral aspect of thigh
- E Deep peroneal nerve – dorsal aspect of first web space

52 All of the following structures would drain through the thoracic duct, EXCEPT:

- A Left arm and thorax
- B Left face and neck
- C Left side of abdomen
- D Right face and neck
- E Right side of abdomen

53 All of the following can be considered risk factors for compartment syndrome in trauma, EXCEPT:

- A Severe crush injury to muscles
- B Ischaemic reperfusion to limb muscles
- C Flexion–distraction spinal injuries
- D Presence of limb burns
- E Immobilisation of injuries in tight casts and dressings

54 Sick euthyroid syndrome consists of all of the following signs, EXCEPT:

- A Decreased number of binding proteins
- B Decreased affinity of binding proteins
- C Decreased TSH
- D Decreased peripheral conversion of T_3 to T_4
- E Normal thyroid functioning

55 All of the following principles are used in the management of chronic renal failure, EXCEPT:

- A High-dose loop diuretics in the management of hypertension
- B Fluid restriction to prevent the development of oedema
- C Sodium restriction to help limit fluid overload
- D High-protein diet to prevent muscle atrophy in catabolism
- E Calcium chloride to help bind gut phosphate in hyperphosphataemia

56 All of the following signs might be produced by a Pancoast's tumour at the apex of the right lung, EXCEPT:

- A Oedema and venous engorgement of the right upper limb
- B Hoarseness of the voice
- C Ipsilateral paradoxical diaphragmatic movement
- D Hyperhidrosis of the right side of the face
- E Enophthalmos and miosis in the right eye

57 All of the following statements regarding the chemical control of respiration are correct, EXCEPT:

- A The carotid bodies are sensitive to hypoxaemia
- B The carotid bodies are sensitive to hypercapnia
- C The central medullary chemoreceptors are sensitive to hypoxaemia
- D The central medullary chemoreceptors are sensitive to hypercapnia
- E The central medullary chemoreceptors are sensitive to changes in H^+

58 Which of the following structures can be injured in supracondylar fracture of the femur?

- A Sciatic nerve
- B Popliteal artery
- C Long saphenous vein
- D Short saphenous vein
- E Deep femoral artery

59 Which of the following is NOT a complication of mechanical ventilation?

- A Pneumothorax
- B Gastric dilatation
- C Acute respiratory distress syndrome (ARDS)
- D Atrophy of respiratory muscles
- E Reduced venous return

60 All of the following muscles are supplied by the posterior interosseous branch of the radial nerve, EXCEPT:

- A Extensor carpi radialis longus
- B Extensor digitorum
- C Extensor digiti minimi
- D Abductor pollicis longus
- E Extensor pollicis brevis

61 Which of the following statements regarding the triquetral bone is correct?

- A The degree of contact with the radioulnar articular disc is maximal in full adduction of the wrist joint
- B It lies just laterally to the lunate bone
- C It forms part of the radiocarpal joint in the wrist
- D The hamate lies just anterolaterally to the triquetral
- E During forced hyperextension of the wrist joint, anterior dislocation of the triquetral can cause carpal tunnel syndrome

62 A 23-year-old man undergoes open reduction and internal fixation of the right tibia after having sustained injuries from a road traffic accident. Shortly after his return to the ward, he begins to complain of paraesthesia in his toes as well as pain in his right leg, which is not relieved by analgesia. He has good distal pulses and sensation to his right foot. The first step in the management of this patient would be to:

- A Measure his compartment pressures in the right leg
- B Prescribe stronger analgesia as this is a common post-operative complaint
- C Call your seniors as he may have a trapped nerve from the surgery
- D Book theatres immediately for urgent fasciotomies as you are highly suspicious of compartment syndrome
- E Split the cast to relieve any pressure from post-operative swelling and reassess the situation in 10 minutes

63 Drainage of the right testicular vein normally occurs into the:

- A Portal vein
- B Inferior vena cava
- C Right renal vein
- D Right internal iliac vein
- E Right suprarenal vein

64 Which of these conditions does NOT predispose towards acute sinusitis?

- A Immunocompromise
- B Dental infection
- C Nasal polyposis
- D Kartagener syndrome
- E Waardenberg syndrome

65 Which of the following is NOT a feature of acute respiratory distress syndrome (ARDS)?

- A Severe hypoxaemia (Pao_2/Fio_2 <27)
- B Pulmonary infiltrates on chest X-ray
- C A known cause (eg pancreatitis)
- D Cardiac pulmonary oedema
- E Pulmonary artery wedge pressure (PAWP) <18 mmHg

66 A 43-year-old female patient has had a successful kidney transplant and is being discharged on the 5th post-operative day. One of the instructions she was given was not to eat grapefruit or drink grapefruit juice. This is because:

- A Grapefruit juice has large amounts of potassium
- B Grapefruit juice is sour and might interfere with the patient's digestion
- C Grapefruit juice can interfere with the metabolism of tacrolimus, one of the immunosuppressive agents being used
- D Grapefruit juice can interact with the action of the statin that has been prescribed for her hypercholesterolaemia
- E Grapefruit juice can cause diarrhoea and interfere with the patient's fluid balance

67 Which of the following is NOT a complication of tracheostomy?

- A Tracheal necrosis
- B Recurrent laryngeal nerve injury
- C Pneumothorax
- D Hypothyroidism
- E Tracheocutaneous fistula

68 A man presents to the Emergency Department with a very low urine output. Analysis of urine and serum samples gives the following results: urinary sodium 15 mmol/l; urine osmolality 520 mOsmol/kg; urine to serum osmolality ratio 1.5. The most likely cause is:

- A Bilateral pelvi-ureteric junction (PUJ) obstruction
- B Retention secondary to enlarged prostate
- C Excessive diarrhoea and vomiting
- D Interstitial nephritis
- E Glomerulonephritis

69 The most common site affected in oral cavity carcinoma is:

- A Hard palate
- B Lateral border of the tongue
- C Tonsils
- D Buccal mucosa
- E Soft palate

70 A 50-year-old woman is found to be febrile one day after her total gastrectomy for malignancy. The most likely cause of this is:

- A Urinary tract infection
- B Pulmonary embolus
- C Wound infection
- D Anastomotic leak
- E Atelectasis

71 **Which of the following is NOT a test used to determine brainstem death?**

- A Corneal reflex
- B Gag reflex
- C Caloric test
- D Pain reflex
- E Flexor response

72 **The following vessels all supply blood to the oesophagus, EXCEPT:**

- A Inferior thyroid artery
- B Inferior phrenic artery
- C Left gastric artery branches
- D Superior phrenic artery
- E Aortic and bronchial branches

73 **High anal fistulae:**

- A Are more common than low anal fistulae
- B Open into the rectum above the puborectalis muscle
- C Can be managed with a loose seton
- D Are typically associated with ulcerative colitis
- E May be laid open without hazard

74 Which of the following is NOT used in the definition of systemic inflammatory response syndrome (SIRS)?

- A Temperature >39 °C
- B Tachycardia >90 bpm
- C Temperature <36 °C
- D Bradycardia <45 bpm
- E Pa_{CO_2} <4.3 kPa

75 The developmental origin of the uterus and uterine tubes is the:

- A Pronephric ducts
- B Mesonephric ducts
- C Metanephric ducts
- D Paramesonephric ducts
- E Wolffian ducts

76 High-output stomas are associated with all of the following, EXCEPT:

- A Distal position
- B Electrolyte disturbances
- C Diarrhoea
- D Octreotide to reduce output
- E Loperamide to reduce output

77 A 57-year-old man was admitted to Neurointensive Care after a subarachnoid haemorrhage. He is not brainstem-dead, but the neurosurgeon is of the opinion that further treatment is futile. His long-standing partner of 15 years, a 55-year-old man, is in agreement that treatment should be withdrawn. Which of the following statements is TRUE?

- A The patient cannot be a kidney donor because he is gay
- B The patient cannot be a kidney donor because he is not brainstem-dead
- C The patient cannot be a donor because he is too old
- D The patient is a potential non-heart-beating donor of his liver and kidneys
- E Organ retrieval from such a patient is illegal

78 Concerning laparoscopic surgery, which of the following is NOT true?

- A Shoulder-tip pain is a common post-operative complaint
- B Bowel perforation should have consent
- C Verres needles should be inserted under direct vision
- D Conduction coupling is a recognised risk
- E Pneumoperitoneum can lead to pneumomediastinum

79 Smoking causes all of the following physiological effects, EXCEPT:

- A A shift of the oxygen dissociation curve to the left
- B Impaired wound healing and increased risk of wound breakdown
- C Impaired mucociliary function
- D No change in cardiovascular function when stopped 1 day before surgery
- E An increase in pulse rate and mean arterial pressure

80 Which of the following phases is correctly matched with its physiological action within the cardiac ventricular muscle action potential graph?

- A Phase 0 – resting membrane potential
- B Phase 1 – rapid depolarisation
- C Phase 2 – slow depolarisation plateau
- D Phase 3 – rapid repolarisation
- E Phase 4 – slow repolarisation

81 During observation of the venous pulse, you note that the *x* descent is:

- A Is prominent in atrial systole
- B Is synchronous with the carotid pulse wave
- C Reflects a rise in atrial pressure before the tricuspid valve opens
- D Is due to the tricuspid valve moving down during ventricular systole
- E Reflects opening of the tricuspid valve and a fall in right atrial pressure

82 **During the lateral (Hardinge's) approach to the hip, which one of the following nerves can be injured?**

- A Tibial
- B Sciatic
- C Inferior gluteal
- D Superior gluteal
- E Obturator

83 **A tumour marker used in surveillance after orchidectomy for non-seminomatous germ-cell tumours (NSGCT) of the testes is:**

- A Prostate-specific antigen (PSA)
- B Alpha-fetoprotein (AFP)
- C CA-125
- D Carcinoembryonic antigen (CEA)
- E CA-19-9

84 **In a healthy 70-kg male at rest, the normal coronary blood flow is:**

- A 100 ml/min
- B 250 ml/min
- C 500 ml/min
- D 750 ml/min
- E 1000 ml/min

85 The following are known to cause a metabolic acidosis, EXCEPT:

- A Myocardial infarction
- B Ischaemic bowel
- C Diabetic ketoacidosis
- D Sepsis
- E Persistent vomiting

86 Which of the following is true of ulcerative colitis?

- A It is commonly associated with anal fistulae
- B It is commonly associated with oral ulceration
- C It is worsened by smoking
- D It is associated with abdominal masses
- E It is associated with joint pain

87 Which of the following is NOT a feature of multiple endocrine neoplasia type II?

- A Medullary thyroid cancer
- B Phaeochromocytoma
- C Pituitary adenoma
- D Parathyroid tumours
- E Multiple mucosal neuromas

88 All of the following statements regarding malignant hyperpyrexia are true, EXCEPT:

- A Relatives of affected individuals should always be tested
- B Inheritance is in an autosomal recessive pattern
- C Incidence is 1 in 200 000
- D Treatment involves the use of dantrolene sodium and fluids
- E Conclusive diagnosis requires a muscle biopsy in addition to the clinical picture

89 The main host defences against bacterial exotoxins in a person with an intact immunological system are:

- A T-helper cells
- B T-cytotoxic cells
- C Activated macrophages that secrete proteases
- D IgM and IgG antibodies
- E Host-cell receptor modulation in response to toxins

90 The inguinal canal:

- A Is approximately 2.5-cm long
- B Has the fascia transversalis covering its whole posterior wall
- C Has an internal ring lying 5 cm above the middle of the inguinal ligament
- D Has the lacunar ligament in the medial part of its floor
- E Has the inferior epigastric artery lying medial to its deep ring

91 All of the following statements regarding interferons are correct, EXCEPT that they:

- A Are induced by dsRNA
- B Are typically specific to their host species cell of origin
- C Appear typically before antibodies in viral infections
- D Inhibit the growth of both DNA and RNA viruses
- E Enhance the metabolism of infected cells

92 Which of the following statements regarding the hepatitis B virus (HBV) is correct?

- A HBV belongs to the Picornaviridae group of viruses
- B Hepatitis B cannot be transmitted via breast milk
- C 25% of patients infected with hepatitis B become chronic carriers
- D Risk of transmission from needlestick injuries is greater for HBV than for HIV
- E HBV vaccines are live attenuated vaccines

93 The CHARGE syndrome is NOT associated with which of the following conditions?

- A Choanal atresia
- B Genital abnormalities
- C Facial nerve palsy
- D Retarded lung maturation
- E Coloboma

94 Indications for splenectomy include all of the following, EXCEPT:

- A Thrombotic thrombocytopenic purpura
- B Felty syndrome
- C Thrombocytopenia associated with drug abuse
- D Sickle cell disease without hypersplenism
- E Splenomegaly related to haemodialysis

95 The clinical presentation of neurogenic shock includes which one of the following combinations of signs?

- A Hypotension, bradycardia, warm skin
- B Hypotension, tachycardia, warm skin
- C Hypotension, bradycardia, cool skin
- D Hypotension, tachycardia, cool skin
- E Hypertension, bradycardia, cool skin

96 A woman with suspected breast cancer has fine-needle aspiration (FNA) of a breast lump. The report comes back as 'C3'. What does this mean?

- A Equivocal
- B Suspicious for cancer
- C Inadequate sample
- D Definitely malignant
- E Benign

97 Which of the following statements regarding suxamethonium is TRUE?

- A It is a non-depolarising muscle relaxant
- B It is not very useful in crash inductions
- C It is structurally similar to the acetylcholine molecule
- D Prolonged action can be due to the presence of too much plasma cholinesterase
- E It has a half-life of 10 minutes, making it short-acting

98 The following brachial plexus injuries would all give rise to the accompanying deficits, EXCEPT:

- A Radial nerve lesion – wrist drop
- B Ulnar nerve lesion – claw deformity
- C Axillary nerve injury – insensate shoulder patch
- D Median nerve palsy – weakened thumb movements + loss of sensation to lateral palm
- E Thoracodorsal nerve injury – winged scapula

99 Which of the following statements about the coronary circulation is FALSE?

- A Most of the perfusion of the left ventricle occurs during diastole
- B Direction of blood flow to the myocardium is from the outer surface of the heart inwards
- C Changes in blood flow in the coronary arteries occur by auto-regulation
- D The interventricular septum is supplied by the left coronary artery only
- E The right coronary artery arises from the right aortic sinus

100 Which of the following is the strongest of all the other risk factors in the development of gastric carcinoma?

- A *Helicobacter pylori*
- B Atrophic gastritis
- C Blood group A
- D Pernicious anaemia
- E Low socioeconomic class

101 A patient with a diagnosis of inflammatory bowel disease (IBD) may have the following extraintestinal manifestations, EXCEPT:

- A Episcleritis
- B Sclerosing cholangitis
- C Ankylosing spondylitis
- D Erythema nodosum
- E Sarcoidosis

102 Colonic diverticular disease:

- A Can present with a colo-vesical fistula
- B Does not present with colonic obstruction
- C Is an inherited condition
- D Is a premalignant condition
- E Is not a feature of ageing

103 Which of the following stoma complications makes closure technically easier?

- A Parastomal hernia
- B Prolapse
- C Stenosis
- D Retraction
- E Ischaemia

104 Which of the following statements regarding immunosuppressive drugs used in renal transplantation is CORRECT?

- A Azathioprine is more effective than mycophenolate in preventing acute rejection
- B Tacrolimus works by directly inhibiting nucleic acid synthesis
- C Mycophenolate works by inhibiting enzymes in the pathway for purine synthesis
- D Sirolimus has greater nephrotoxicity than ciclosporin
- E Basiliximab is not commonly used as an induction agent in renal transplants

105 Bowel obstruction can be caused by all of the following, EXCEPT:

- A Volvulus
- B Hiatus hernia
- C Adhesions from previous surgery
- D Intussusception
- E Polyp

106 The commonest infection to affect the asplenic patient following splenectomy is:

- A *Streptococcus pneumoniae*
- B *Neisseria meningitidis*
- C *Escherichia coli*
- D *Haemophilus influenzae*
- E *Staphylococcus aureus*

107 All of the following statements regarding the management of trauma in pregnant women are true, EXCEPT:

- A A qualified surgeon and obstetrician should always be consulted early in the evaluation of the pregnant patient
- B Small-bowel injury in commoner in upper abdominal penetrating wounds than lower penetrating injuries in late pregnancy
- C Pregnant women show earlier signs of hypovolaemia during haemorrhage
- D Unless contraindicated, pregnant women should be placed in the left-lateral position during assessment and management as early as possible
- E All Rh-negative pregnant patients should be considered for Rh immunoglobulin therapy in penetrating abdominal injuries

108 Which of the following is NOT part of the Glasgow Scale used to assess the severity of pancreatitis on initial assessment?

- A White cell count $>15\times10^9$/l
- B Pao_2 <60 mmHg
- C Age >55 years
- D Glucose <10 mmol/l
- E Lactate dehydrogenase (LDH) >600 units/l

109 Complications of intraosseous needle puncture in children include all of the following, EXCEPT:

- A Physeal plate injury
- B Skin pressure necrosis
- C Subperiosteal infiltration
- D Musculocutaneous fistula
- E Osteomyelitis

110 Which of the following volumes of blood loss would accurately fall into a class II haemorrhage?

- A 500 ml
- B 700 ml
- C 1000 ml
- D 1500 ml
- E 2000 ml

111 A man is found to have a PSA of 14 mg/ml on routine testing. He is entirely asymptomatic. Investigation with transrectal biopsy confirms prostate cancer. MRI scan shows a nodule on the left lobe, which extends into the seminal vesicles. The stage of prostate cancer based on this information is:

- A T4
- B T3a
- C T2a
- D T3b
- E T2b

112 The following statements about hernias are all true, EXCEPT:

- A Direct hernias are due to a deficiency at Hesselbach's triangle
- B A Littre's hernia contains a Meckel's diverticulum
- C A femoral hernia usually presents as a lump above and lateral to the pubic tubercle
- D Richter's hernia involves entrapment of the antimesenteric edge of the bowel
- E Spigelian hernias protrude from the lateral edge of the rectus abdominis muscle

113 Causes of spontaneous secondary pneumothorax include all of the following, EXCEPT:

- A Marfan syndrome
- B Lung cancer
- C Asthma
- D COPD
- E Lung abscesses

114 All of the following statements regarding dead-space ventilation are correct, EXCEPT:

- A Dead space refers to air that has to be ventilated, but does not take part in gas exchange
- B Anatomical dead space refers to air that does not reach the alveoli to take place in ventilation
- C Anatomical dead space can be measured using Fowler's method
- D Physiological dead space may be increased in positive-pressure ventilation
- E Anatomical dead space is reduced in the standing-up position

115 Which one of the following conditions would result in a positive base excess on a blood gas report?

- A Cushing syndrome
- B Starvation
- C Septicaemia
- D Pulmonary embolus
- E Myasthenia gravis

116 A 47-year-old male patient received a cadaver kidney transplant with immediate function 2 weeks ago. Within 3 days his serum creatinine had normalised to 110 μmol/l. He was discharged on the 5th post-operative day and has been followed up at the transplant follow-up clinic, attending thrice weekly. On attendance today his serum creatinine is 167 μmol/l and he is well in himself with no symptoms. You note on checking the blood results that the creatinine was 115 μmol/l 2 days ago. His tacrolimus (immunosuppression drug) level is normal. Ultrasound scan shows a normal transplant kidney. What is the most likely cause of his raised serum creatinine?

- A Acute rejection episode (and a transplant biopsy is urgently required to confirm the diagnosis)
- B Acute tubular necrosis
- C Volume depletion due to diarrhoea and vomiting
- D Ureteric obstruction
- E Transplanted renal artery stenosis

117 Fever can be caused by all of the following, EXCEPT:

- A Heatstroke
- B Hyperthyroidism
- C Posterior hypothalamic lesions
- D Dehydration
- E Exercise

118 Which of the following agents used in the treatment of urological conditions is NOT paired with its correct description?

- A Mitomycin C – intravesical chemotherapy agent
- B Finasteride – luteinising hormone-releasing hormone (LH-RH) agonist
- C Oxybutinin – anticholinergic agent
- D Tamsulosin – α-adrenergic blocker
- E Flutamide – anti-androgen agent

119 All of the following features are found in ARDS, EXCEPT:

- A Pulmonary oedema of non-cardiogenic origin
- B Hypoxaemia that is refractory to oxygen therapy
- C Reduced lung compliance
- D Pao_2/Fio_2 ratio <26.6 kPa (200 mmHg)
- E Pulmonary capillary wedge pressure >16 mmHg

120 The superficial radial nerve:

- A Runs between brachioradialis and extensor carpi radialis longus
- B Runs between the brachialis and brachioradialis
- C Is at a high risk of injury during the posterior approach to the forearm
- D Supplies most of the muscles in the posterior compartment of the forearm
- E Is difficult to see during surgery

121 In achondroplasia, clinical features include the following, EXCEPT:

- A Excessive lordosis
- B Trident hands
- C Small nasal bridge
- D Hypotonia during the first year of life
- E Short trunk

122 A man is found to have a hydrocele, which at operation is found to extend from the testis to the deep inguinal ring, but does not connect with the peritoneal cavity. Which of the following best describes this hydrocele?

- A Vaginal hydrocele
- B Congenital hydrocele
- C Infantile hydrocele
- D Hydrocele of cord
- E Malignant hydrocele

123 **A 23-year-old man is brought into the Emergency Department after having sustained three stab wounds to the abdomen with evisceration of small bowel. A laparotomy is performed where gross faecal contamination is found from large-bowel lacerations. The bowel injuries are resected and a defunctioning ileostomy is performed. On the 4th post-operative day, the patient develops a temperature of 39°C with peritonitis as well as buttock myonecrosis with foul-smelling discharge. In this clinical scenario, which of the following organisms is most likely to have caused this infection?**

- A *Helicobacter pylori*
- B *Bacteroides fragilis*
- C *Vibrio parahaemolyticus*
- D *Salmonella typhi*
- E *Shigella dysenteriae*

124 **The most common problem following total knee replacement involves:**

- A Infection
- B Incorrect prosthesis size
- C Chronic pain
- D Cosmesis
- E Patellar tracking

125 A 68-year-old man develops a massive acute myocardial infarction and dies in hospital while being resuscitated in the Emergency Department. An autopsy is performed and, while you are inspecting the heart, you note that it has undergone necrosis as expected. Which type of necrosis is found to be consistent with the pathology of this disease?

- A Coagulative necrosis
- B Liquefactive necrosis
- C Fat necrosis
- D Fibrinoid necrosis
- E Caseating necrosis

126 Which one of the following laboratory stains is used to identify amyloid staining in pathological tissue sections?

- A Prussian blue
- B Congo red
- C Haematoxylin and eosin
- D Oil red-O
- E Periodic acid–Schiff (PAS)

127 Diagnostic specificity is defined as:

- A Probability of a negative diagnostic test in the presence of disease
- B Probability of a positive diagnostic test in the presence of disease
- C Probability of a negative diagnostic test in the absence of disease
- D Probability of a positive diagnostic test in the absence of disease
- E Probability of being disease-free and test-negative within all people testing negative

128 Sertoli cells:

- A Are involved in the nurturing of sperm cells within the seminiferous tubules
- B Synthesise testosterone
- C Secrete testosterone in response to LH
- D Are known as interstitial cells of the testes
- E Are able to continue proliferating once fully differentiated

129 A 15-year-old boy presents with sudden-onset right testicular pain associated with nausea and vomiting. On examination, the right testis is found to be drawn up into the groin with a horizontal lie and is very tender. What is the most appropriate form of management?

- A Broad-spectrum antibiotics
- B Exploration of testis via inguinal incision
- C Bedrest and scrotal support
- D 'Watch and wait' policy
- E Exploration of testis via transverse incision over testis

130 In the induction of anaesthesia:

- A Thiopentone injection results in a delayed recovery because of its high lipid solubility
- B Propofol commonly causes nausea on recovery
- C Ketamine is a stimulant that works by dissociation
- D Ketamine is routinely used in adult anaesthesia
- E Ketamine can cause a bradycardia on injection

131 The first step in the management of an episode of massive haematemesis is:

- A Insertion of two large-bore intravenous cannulae
- B Urgent endoscopy
- C Urgent angiography
- D Clearing and securing the airway
- E Resuscitation with fluids and blood products

132 All of the following statements regarding polytetrafluoroethylene (polytef or PTFE) are correct, EXCEPT:

- A Pre-clotting is not required before use
- B It allows tissue ingrowth and neo-intima formation
- C It is a hydrophobic-non-elastic polymer
- D Platelet deposition can occur on its surface
- E It is used in the creation of arteriovenous (AV) fistulae

133 Which of the following features is found with a large pulmonary embolus?

- A Decreased pulmonary vascular resistance
- B Pulmonary hypertension
- C Increased left ventricular output
- D Decreased right ventricular afterload
- E Increased lung compliance

134 All of the following drugs can cause acute pancreatitis, EXCEPT:

- A Furosemide
- B Azathioprine
- C Didanosine
- D Tetracycline
- E Omeprazole

135 All of the following statements regarding prostate cancer are true, EXCEPT:

- A It is the second leading cause of male cancer deaths
- B The lifetime risk of microscopic prostate cancer in all men is 30%
- C The incidence is decreasing as a result of screening measures
- D The lifetime risk of developing overt disease is 10%
- E Consumption of carrots and cereals may have some protective effect

PRACTICE PAPER 2: ANSWERS AND TEACHING NOTES

PRACTICE PAPER 2: ANSWERS AND TEACHING NOTES

1 B: Stylohyoid ligament

Arch	Nerve	Bone	Muscles	Ligaments
First (mandibular)	V	Incus	Muscles of mastication	Sphenomandibular
		Malleus	Tensor tympani	Anterior ligament of malleus
			Tensor palati	
			Mylohyoid	
			Anterior belly of digastric	
Second (hyoid)	VII	Stapes	Stapedius	Stylohyoid
		Styloid process	Stylohyoid	
		Upper part of body of hyoid	Posterior belly of digastric	
		Lesser cornu of hyoid	Muscles of facial expression	
Third	IX	Greater cornu of hyoid	Stylopharyngeus	
		Lower part of body of hyoid		
Fourth – Sixth	X	Thyroid cartilage	Pharyngeal muscles	
		Arytenoid cartilage	Laryngeal muscles	
		Corniculate cartilage	Palatal muscles	
		Cuneiform cartilage		

2 C: They occur at the junction of the lower third and upper two-thirds of sternocleidomastoid

Branchial cysts are congenital epithelial cysts which arise on the lateral part of the neck from a failure of obliteration of the second branchial cleft in embryonic development. Branchial cysts are commonly found in young adults, 60% on the left and 60% in males. They are lined by stratified squamous epithelium and most arise deep to the anterior border of sternocleidomastoid at the junction of the upper third and the lower two-thirds of this muscle. Diagnosis is made by clinical assessment and needle aspiration. Depending on the size and the anatomical extension of the mass, local symptoms such as dysphagia, dysphonia, dyspnoea and stridor can occur. Needle aspiration might reveal cholesterol crystals. Approximately 25% of all cysts become infected.

3 E: The inferior parathyroids can be found in the superior mediastinum in association with the thymus gland

Embryology questions are common and simple derivatives of the arches and pouches should be known.

First arch (Meckel's cartilage): gives rise to malleus, incus, sphenomandibular ligament and the muscles of mastication; supplied by the mandibular division of the trigeminal nerve (Vc).

First pouch: gives rise to the Eustachian tube.

Second arch (Reichert's cartilage): gives rise to stapes, styloid process, lesser cornu and superior part of the hyoid bone, stylohyoid ligament and the muscles of facial expression; supplied by the facial nerve (VII).

Second pouch: contains the palatine tonsils.

Third arch: gives rise to the lower part and the greater cornu of the hyoid bone and stylopharyngeus; supplied by the glossopharyngeal nerve (IX).

Third pouch: gives rise to the inferior parathyroids (superior part) and thymus (inferior part). The inferior parathyroids might be dragged beyond the thyroid gland into the upper mediastinum to lie alongside the thymus gland.

Fourth and sixth arches: both give rise to thyroid cartilages and the muscles of the larynx; supplied by the vagus nerve (X).

Fourth pouch gives rise to the superior parathyroids and the sixth pouch the ultimobranchial body (parafollicular C cells).

4 B: L4

L4 dermatome supplies the sensation of the medial leg from the knee down to the medial aspect of the big toe. L3 primarily supplies the superior knee and medial thigh region. L5 supplies the lateral leg and S1 the lateral foot and heel.

5 C: Hypernatraemia

TURP is performed by passing a resectoscope through the urethra into the bladder and using a wire loop to pass electrical current to resect the prostate gland. It is a relatively safe procedure (mortality <0.25%) but is associated with certain complications. These include urinary incontinence (2–4%), erectile dysfunction (5%), urethral stricture (5%), retrograde ejaculation (65%) and increase risk of MI. In addition there is the risk of developing TUR syndrome, which is due to the absorption of irrigation fluid into the body. This presents with hypotension, bradycardia, nausea and vomiting and collapse. Blood tests show hyponatraemia.

6 A: Lateral pterygoid

Muscles of mastication include the lateral and medial pterygoids, the masseter muscle and the temporalis muscle. The buccinator muscle is a muscle of facial expression and not a mastication muscle. All of the muscles of mastication are supplied by the mandibular division of the trigeminal nerve. Buccinator is supplied by the facial nerve.

The lateral pterygoid arises as two heads from the lateral aspect of the lateral pterygoid plate and inserts into the neck of the mandible and the anterior surface of the disc of the temporomandibular joint. The medial pterygoid arises from the medial aspect of the lateral pterygoid plate and a small tubercle of the maxilla and its fibres insert inferolaterally into the roughened medial surface of the mandible near the angle.

The temporalis muscle arises from the temporal fossa and inserts into the coronoid process of the mandible. The masseter arises from the anterior two-thirds of the lower border of the zygomatic arch as well as the posterior third of the lower border and the whole of the deep surface of the arch. It then inserts into the outer surface of the ramus of the mandible from the mandibular notch above, down to the angle of the mandible. Both temporalis and masseter are palpable on the facial examination as superficial muscles.

7 A: Stylopharyngeus – glossopharyngeal nerve

There are a few simple rules for muscle innervation. All pharyngeal and palatal muscles are supplied by the pharyngeal plexus (IX, X and sympathetics), except stylopharyngeus, which is supplied by the glossopharyngeal nerve (IX) and tensor veli palatini, which is supplied by the nerve to the medial pterygoid (Vc). All tongue muscles are supplied by the hypoglossal nerve (XII), except palatoglossus, which is supplied by the pharyngeal plexus. Muscles of facial expression are supplied by the facial nerve (VII), except levator palpabrae superioris, which is supplied by the oculomotor nerve (III). Muscles of mastication are supplied by the mandibular division of the trigeminal nerve (Vc), except buccinator, which is supplied by the facial nerve. Laryngeal muscles are supplied by the recurrent laryngeal nerve (X), except cricothyroid, which is supplied by the superior laryngeal nerve (X).

8 B: Pterygopalatine ganglion – lacrimal gland

Parasympathetic supply arises from cranial nerves III, VII, IX and X. Oculomotor fibres (CN III, Edinger–Westphal nucleus) pass to the ciliary ganglion before supplying pupillary constriction and accommodation. Facial fibres (CN VII, superior salivary nucleus), via the nervus intermedius and greater petrosal nerve, pass to the pterygopalatine and submandibular ganglion, supplying the lacrimal, submandibular, sublingual and palatine glands. Glossopharyngeal fibres (CN IX, inferior salivary nucleus) run via the lesser petrosal to the otic ganglion and then in the auriculotemporal nerve to the parotid gland. Vagus fibres (CN X, dorsal motor nucleus of vagus) pass to the thorax and abdomen.

9 B: Pulmonary embolus

The example shows a patient with low PaO_2, low $PaCO_2$, high pH and low bicarbonate. When $PaCO_2$ is low, it shifts the following equilibrium to the left

$$CO_2 + H_2O <> H_2CO_3 <> H^+ + HCO_3^-$$

therefore reducing the concentration of H^+ and causing a respiratory alkalosis. From the given examples, PE is the most likely cause as this results in hyperventilation, which 'blows off' and therefore reduces blood levels of CO_2 but at the same time fails to achieve satisfactory oxygenation.

10 A: McEvedy's abdominal approach

The abdominal approach is best reserved where bowel resection is contemplated. An inguinal or high approach is used to repair co-existing inguinal hernias or where the diagnosis is in doubt. For small uncomplicated femoral hernias in the elective setting, the low or crural approach is preferable.

11 C: Inferior meatus

The nasolacrimal duct enters the nasal cavity under the anterior lip of the inferior concha in the inferior meatus and connects the conjunctival sac to the nasal cavity for drainage of tears. The frontal sinus, anterior and middle ethmoidal sinuses and the maxillary sinus open into the middle meatus under the middle concha at the hiatus semilunaris. The posterior ethmoidal sinus opens into the superior meatus and the sphenoidal sinus onto the spheno-ethmoidal recess. The opening of the pharyngotympanic tube, which is bounded by salpingopharyngeus, opens into the nasopharynx posterior to all the nasal turbinates.

12 C: Middle meningeal

The middle meningeal artery is classically injured in **extradural haemorrhage**. Such injuries usually result from a fracture of the squamous part of the temporal bone and require burr holes to drain the blood. Other types of haemorrhage include subdural and subarachnoid haemorrhages.

Subdural haematomas usually result from torn bridging veins or venous sinuses and are most commonly found in the elderly as a result of age-related cerebral atrophy and subsequent vulnerability of the bridging veins. Treatment involves drainage of the blood through burr holes, similar to the treatment of extradural haemorrhage.

Subarachnoid haemorrhage can result from trauma or can occur spontaneously from a ruptured berry aneurysm, resulting in blood within the ventricular system. Treatment includes coiling or clipping of aneurysms in addition to rest, supportive fluids, nimodipine therapy and analgesia. Occasionally, an external ventricular drain might be required to drain blood from within the ventricular system and prevent hydrocephalus.

13 B: Inferior petrosal sinus

The straight sinus usually runs into the left transverse sinus, which can also drain into the occipital and superior petrosal sinuses. The cavernous sinus receives drainage from the ophthalmic veins, sphenoparietal sinus, superficial middle cerebral vein and the basilar plexus. Subsequent drainage of the cavernous sinus is into the inferior petrosal sinus, although a large connection still exists to the superior petrosal sinus, running along the superior edge of the petrous temporal bone.

The superior sagittal sinus runs in the upper border of the falx cerebri and runs posteriorly to the internal occipital protuberance, where it usually deviates to the right to become continuous with the corresponding transverse sinus. The inferior sagittal sinus lies in the free lower margin of the falx cerebri. It joins the great cerebral vein to become the straight sinus, which usually becomes continuous with the left transverse sinus. The sigmoid sinus is continuous with the transverse sinus.

The petrosal sinuses drain the cavernous sinus. The superior petrosal sinus drains to the transverse sinus and the inferior petrosal sinus to the internal jugular vein.

The internal jugular vein is formed by the union of the inferior petrosal sinus and the sigmoid sinus on each side of the skull base, to emerge from the jugular foramen and run down caudally within the carotid sheath.

14 D: It is an alkylating agent

5-FU is commonly used in the treatment of colorectal cancers. It belongs to the group of antimetabolites and inhibits DNA synthesis accordingly by interfering with pyrimidine synthesis.

15 A: Sympathetic fibres cause relaxation of the detrusor muscle and contraction of the internal sphincter

The bladder is covered only on its upper aspect by peritoneum. Its muscular wall is formed by the detrusor muscle and it is lined by transitional epithelium. The triangular-shaped area at the bladder base, which lies between the two ureteric orifices, is the trigone. The detrusor muscle is supplied by parasympathetic fibres, which cause contraction, and sympathetic fibres, which cause relaxation. It has an internal sphincter formed by smooth muscle and an external sphincter, which lies below the prostate in the male. The blood supply comes from the superior and inferior vesical arteries, which are branches of the internal iliac artery.

16 B: Maxillary division of the trigeminal

17 E: Superior petrosal sinus

Foramen	Structures
Ovale	Mandibular division of trigeminal nerve Lesser petrosal nerve Accessory meningeal arteries
Spinosum	Middle meningeal vessels Meningeal branch of mandibular nerve
Rotundum	Maxillary division of trigeminal nerve
Stylomastoid	Facial nerve
Jugular	Internal jugular vein from sigmoid and inferior petrosal sinuses Cranial nerves IX, X and XI

The sigmoid and inferior petrosal sinuses enter the jugular foramen to combine and form the internal jugular vein, which exits the foramen and runs caudally within the carotid sheath. Cranial nerves IX, X and XI enter the foramen along with the sinuses and then course in their respective ways with only the vagus nerve continuing posterolaterally to the internal jugular vein within the carotid sheath.

18 E: Cisplatin

Cisplatin, along with busulfan, chlorambucil, chlormethine and cyclophosphamide are some of the drugs classed as alkylating agents. Doxorubicin is an antibiotic, vincristine is a vinca alkaloid, methotrexate is an antimetabolite, and cytarabine inhibits DNA polymerase.

19 C: Lateral thigh

Meralgia paraesthetica refers to compression of the lateral femoral cutaneous nerve as it passes through or just under the inguinal ligament, just medial to the anterior superior iliac spine. Compression of the nerve results in symptoms in the anteromedial thigh region.

20 D: C6

The cricoid cartilage is the most inferior of the laryngeal cartilages and lies at the level of the sixth cervical vertebral body. It is also here that the recurrent laryngeal nerve enters the larynx. The carotid artery pulse can also be felt here as it is compressed by the transverse processes of C6 vertebrae.

21 D: There is a conductive loss of greater than 20 dB in the left ear

Weber's test involves localising sound to one or other ear (signifies a 10-dB difference between the ears) or to the midline and involves central tuning fork placement, commonly on the vertex of the skull. Rinne's test is conducted by comparing air conduction with bone conduction on the mastoid bone, signifying a conduction loss of greater than 20 dB. A positive Rinne's test is one in which air conduction is better than bony conduction, signifying either a normal ear or sensorineural loss on that side. This patient has a Weber localising to the left, with a left negative and a right positive Rinne's test. This is consistent with a conductive loss on the left. Masking can be achieved with a Barany sound box (not Baroness).

22 C: Examination and attempted removal of foreign body

Children with a unilateral nasal discharge are most likely to have a nasal foreign body. These must be removed with some urgency because of the aspiration risk. Foreign bodies are often visible and amenable to removal by experienced instrumentation.

23 B: Bitemporal hemianopia

The central location of the pituitary gland within the sella turcica causes compression of the medial aspects of the optic chiasm. The resultant visual field defect is bitemporal hemianopia.

24 C: Small cardiac vein

The small cardiac vein accompanies the marginal artery along the inferior aspect of the heart and drains into the coronary sinus near its termination. The great cardiac vein accompanies the left anterior descending artery and the middle cardiac vein with the posterior interventricular artery.

25 B: Polyps in childhood can indicate cystic fibrosis

Inflammatory nasal conditions can lead to swelling of the nasal mucosa and formation of nasal polyps. Co-existent asthma is common. Childhood nasal polyps are rare and are associated with cystic fibrosis. Epistaxis and contact bleeding suggest the possibility of neoplasia. Polyps are initially treated medically with intranasal steroids, antihistamines or even short courses of high-dose steroids. Surgery can provide symptomatic improvement in cases of stubborn disease.

26 C: Larynx

This child has inspiratory stridor, most likely from a foreign object stuck at the level of the larynx. Inspiratory stridor characterises a laryngeal lesion. Tracheal lesions cause expiratory stridor, although high lesions can cause biphasic stridor. Wheezing is caused by chest pathology. Stertor is noisy breathing originating from the mouth and back of the nose.

27 B: Reduced blanching

Full-thickness burns are typically black/white in colour and insensate. They exhibit minimal healing and usually require skin grafting. They do not blanch when touched. In contrast, superficial burns are pink and painful and often associated with blistering;100% repair after 2 weeks but healing may be associated with pigment changes.

28 E: Splanchnic nerves

Pain arising from the heart travels within visceral afferent nerve fibres, which can run within the upper thoracic splanchnic nerves to reach the sympathetic chain, or within the middle and inferior cardiac cervical nerves to reach the sympathetic chain and then further onto T1–T2 levels.

29 E: Ménière's disease

This is a classic history of Ménière's disease, comprising paroxysmal vertigo with fluctuating hearing loss and tinnitus, attacks lasting minutes to hours. Benign positional vertigo is typified by vertigo associated with head movements lasting a few seconds to minutes. Acute vestibular failure (acute labyrinthitis) gives rise to vertigo that lasts for days, often preceded by an upper respiratory tract infection. Acoustic neuroma very rarely causes vertigo. Cardiovascular pathology can lead to pre-syncope, with light-headedness but not usually vertigo.

30 E: Thiouracils inhibit T_4 production

31 A: Low levels of circulating T_4 increase the TSH response to TRH

The synthesis depends on an adequate supply of dietary iodine (at least 75 µg daily is required to prevent goitre formation). Thyroid hormones, like catecholamines, are synthesised from the amino acid tyrosine. The synthesis of iodine requires the iodination of two tyrosine molecules and combination of two iodinated tyrosine residues. The iodine is reduced to iodide before absorption in the gastrointestinal tract. Follicular cells have an active iodide pump that acquires and concentrates iodide from the blood against an electrochemical gradient of more than 50 mV (inside negative). Iodide is rapidly oxidised by a peroxidase enzyme to iodine and incorporated into tyrosyl residues in thyroglobulin, which is located in the colloid. The multiple tyrosyl units on the thyroglobulin are iodinated at either one or two positions, forming mono-iodotyrosine (MIT) and di-iodotyrosine (DIT). When MIT couples with DIT it forms T_3, and two DIT molecules form T_4 of thyroxine. Thiouracils block the enzyme peroxidase and are very useful in treating states of thyroid hyperfunction. TSH has no effect on iodide traps in salivary glands, breast, placenta, cilary body or gastric mucosa.

The thyroid gland is controlled by hormone secretions from the hypothalamus–pituitary axis. The synthesis and secretion of TSH from the thyrotrophs is stimulated by TRH. TSH secretion is inhibited by other hormones including somatostatin and dopamine and also cytokines, particularly IL-1β, IL-6 and tumour necrosis factor (TNF). TSH is a complex glycoprotein hormone, and there are structural similarities between TSH, LH and FSH and a half-life of about 1 hour.

When circulating levels of T_4 are low, there is an increase in the number of TRH receptors and in TSH synthesis, resulting in an increased TSH response to TRH. The reverse is true in the presence of high circulating levels of thyroid hormones.

TSH is secreted in a pulsatile fashion with a diurnal variation, peaking around midnight. Cold weather will lead to an increase in the plasma concentrations of thyroid hormones, with a subsequent rise in basal metabolic rate. Glucocorticoids inhibit thyroid hormone secretions by reducing the TSH secretory response to TRH; oestrogens have the opposite effect.

32 A: Contains the two lops of small bowel within it

Richter's hernia contains only part of the bowel wall within it and so does not classically cause an obstruction. Amyand's hernia contains a perforated appendix within an inguinal hernia. A hernia through the linea semilunaris is called a Spigelian hernia. Maydl's hernia contains loops of small bowel, often forming a W-shaped configuration.

33 A: Dorsal primary rami

The dorsal primary rami supply the deep muscles of the back such as erector spinae. Rami communicantes are involved in autonomic communications and are classed as grey (unmyelinated) or white (myelinated). Ventral rami supply all other muscles anteriorly and make up the remaining nerve root plexuses.

34 B: Medullary carcinoma of the thyroid is a feature of MEN II

Multiple endocrine neoplasia syndromes are subdivided into types I and II. MEN I is characterised by pituitary adenomas, parathyroid adenomas and pancreatic endocrine tumours (eg insulinomas, gastrinomas, VIPomas). MEN II is characterised by medullary carcinoma of the thyroid, parathyroid adenomas and phaeochromocytomas. MEN IIB is a variant of this and is also associated with an appearance suggestive of Marfan syndrome. Phaeochomocytomas are usually tested for by measuring urinary VMA (vanillyl-mandelic acid). Raised urinary 5-HIAA is usually associated with carcinoid syndrome. Although MEN syndromes can show a genetic predisposition, most are due to sporadic mutations. Parathyroid adenomas can (but do not always) present with hypercalcaemia.

35 A: Phrenic nerve

The phrenic nerve is derived from the roots of C3, C4, and C5 and is the only motor supply to the diaphragm. It is also involved in the sensory supply of the diaphragmatic parietal pleura, the mediastinal parietal pleura, as well as the diaphragmatic peritoneum. The vagus (CN X, parasympathetic) supplies the visceral pleura and is only sensitive to stretch, in contrast to the parietal pleura, which is sensitive to pain. The intercostal nerves supply sensation to the costal pleura. There is no sympathetic nerve supply to the pleura, although within the lungs it is involved in bronchodilation. The pectoral nerves are derived from the brachial plexus and supply the pectoralis muscles.

36 B: Seconday cartilaginous joint

The intervertebral joints are an example of a **secondary cartilaginous joint**. This variety of joint occurs conveniently along the midline of the axial skeleton. Other examples include the manubriosternal and xiphisternal joints and the symphysis pubis. Structurally, they are similar to primary cartilaginous joints, except they also have a disc of fibrocartilage between the hyaline layers.

Fibrous joints are formed when two bones meet with fibrous tissue in-between. Examples include the teeth, skull sutures and interosseous membranes between the limb bones.

Synovial joints are joint cavities that are lined by a synovial membrane and contain synovial fluid for movement. They are seen in all joints which perform movements.

37 D

Hepatitis B is a hepadnavirus, which is a DNA virus. In the acute phase of infection, the virus releases its surface antigen (HBsAg) into the blood. This is also found to be present in persistent/chronic infections. The core antigen (HBcAg) causes production of HBc antibodies, which are the first antibodies to occur in the course of the infection. It is present in the blood in the brief period when HBsAg disappears and before Hbs antibodies appear, and thus it is an important diagnostic indicator of early infection. HBsAb confers immunity to the HBV virus. The 'e' antigen (HBeAg) is also found in the core of the virus and its presence in the blood indicates active viral production and infection. The antibody against HBeAG (HBeAb) is found at a much later stage of infection.

38 B: Maxillary division of the trigeminal nerve

The following nerves provide the afferent limb of the corresponding reflexes:

- Ophthalmic division of the trigeminal – blink reflex
- Maxillary division of the trigeminal – sneeze reflex
- Mandibular division of the trigeminal – jaw jerk
- Glossopharyngeal nerve – gag reflex
- Vagus nerve – cough reflex.

39 D: Quadratus femoris

Quadratus femoris is a lateral rotator of the hip joint as it connects the lateral border of the ischial tuberosity to the quadrate tubercle of the femur. All the others listed abduct the hip joint acting together.

40 A: Chronic granulomatous disease (CGD) – macrophages

CGD is an inherited deficiency in one subunit of NADPH oxidase used by phagocytes, thus causing patients to develop severe infections from bacteria such as *Staphylococcus aureus* and *Klebsiella*. DiGeorge syndrome is due to failure of development of the third and fourth pharyngeal pouches and therefore results in development of a hypoplastic thymus causing T-cell deficiency. LAD is a result of defects in the β chain of β2 integrins, which are important for leucocyte movement. This results in recurrent infections from extracellular bacteria owing to defective opsonisation, adhesion mobility and chemotaxis. Hereditary angioedema is due to a defect in the C1 inhibitor, and X-linked hypogammaglobulinaemia is due to a block in the maturation of the B cell, which results in recurrent pyogenic infections.

41 D: Maxillary sinus

The pterygopalatine fossa communicates with the mouth, nose, eyes and middle cranial fossa through many foramina directly. The maxillary sinus communicates via the nose through the middle meatus so any connection to the pterygopalatine fossa is indirect.

42 E: Abducent nerve

The abducent nerve runs into the medial wall of the cavernous sinus, running immediately lateral to the internal carotid artery before passing into the orbit through the superior orbital fissure. All the other nerves run in the lateral wall of the cavernous sinus.

43 A: Pudendal nerve

The pudendal nerve block can be useful in performing episiotomies. The pudendal nerve also supplies the external anal sphincters, thus rendering loss of faecal continence if it is anaesthetised. The inferior gluteal nerve supplies the gluteus maximus muscle and the superior gluteal nerve is motor supply to the gluteus medius and minimus as well as tensor fascia lata. The ventral rami of S3 and S4 are involved in supplying the levator ani muscle, which also contributes to the mechanism of continence, but in a more physiological mechanism via the puborectalis sling.

44 D: Gastroduodenal artery

The gastroduodenal artery classically passes behind the first part of the duodenum (D1). Posterior ulcers that perforate through the wall of the duodenum may erode into this artery, resulting in life-threatening haemorrhage.

45 D: Inferior epigastric arteries

Lateral umbilical folds – inferior epigastric arteries.

Medial umbilical folds – obliterated umbilical arteries.

Median umbilical fold – caudal remnant of ventral mesentery containing urachus.

46 E: It should always be inserted under strict septic technique

All CVP lines and Swan–Ganz catheters should be inserted under the strictest of aseptic technique, as infection is the commonest complication of these procedures.

47 E: Foramina of Magendie and Luschka

The foramina of Magendie (midline) and Luschka (lateral) in the roof of the fourth ventricle communicate directly into the subarachnoid space. The interventricular foramen of Munro connects the two lateral ventricles together. CSF is produced by the choroid plexus and absorbed by the arachnoid granulations (villi) to return to the venous system.

48 A: Hypoalbuminaemia and portal hypertension

Ascites formation in cirrhosis is due to disruption of Starling's forces within the abdominal circulation. The low protein (albumin) allows for a low oncotic pressure of fluid drawback into the portal circulation from the interstitial spaces and the venous hypertension also forces the outward hydrostatic pressure, equally contributing to ascitic formation. Spironolactone is useful in the treatment of ascites due to liver cirrhosis. This drug antagonises the effects of aldosterone, which is found in very high levels within the plasma due to its lack of metabolism in the cirrhotic liver.

49 D: 27%

Wallace's rule of nines is used to calculate the percentage body area involved. It works by attributing a percentage to a body part: Head = 9%; arm (each) = 9%; legs (each) 18% (9% each surface); trunk 36%; perineum 1%; palm 1.25%. Calculating the percentage burn helps to guide fluid resuscitation – intravenous fluids are essential when this exceeds 15%.

50 D: Pyloric antrum

Acid is secreted from the parietal cells within the stomach under neurohormonal influence. The highest concentration of these cells within the stomach is found in the gastric antrum. Evidence-based research also reveals that the pyloric antrum is the commonest location for *Helicobacter pylori* within the stomach and it is this location that is always biopsied in searching for *H. pylori*.

51 D: Obturator nerve – lateral aspect of thigh

The obturator nerve supplies the muscles in the medial compartment of the thigh and arises from the lumbar plexus (L1–4 ventral rami). It also supplies sensation to a patch of skin on the medial aspect of the thigh. Irritation of this nerve by pelvic pathology can result in pain in this distribution because the lateral pelvic peritoneum is supplied by the obturator nerve as it passes through the pelvis.

52 D: Right face and neck

The thoracic duct drains everything below the level of the diaphragm as well as all structures on the left-hand side of the body above the diaphragm.

53 C: Flexion–distraction spinal injuries

Flexion–distraction spinal injuries do not involve the limbs unless part of a multi-trauma case. Any injury or treatment to a limb in which muscles can become oedematous within a tight fascial compartment will lead to compartment syndrome. Isolated spinal injuries would not result in such a syndrome.

54 D: Decreased peripheral conversion of T_3 to T_4

Sick euthyroid syndrome consists of abnormalities in markers of thyroid function resulting from any acute illness without actually affecting thyroid function. The following changes can occur in a clinical euthyroid patient:

- Decreased binding proteins and affinity of binding proteins
- Decreased TSH
- Decreased peripheral conversion of T_4 to T_3.

55 D: High-protein diet to prevent muscle atrophy in catabolism

High-protein diets should be avoided in chronic renal failure as this increases the urea load on the kidney. Severe protein restriction is also not advised, especially in haemodialysis, as more protein is lost through filtration. A balanced protein intake is required at about 0.5 g/kg/day in chronic renal failure.

56 D: Hyperhidrosis of the right side of the face

Pancoast's tumour of the apex of the lung can produce an ipsilateral Horner syndrome, which results in the signs of miosis, enophthalmos, ptosis and anhidrosis of the side of the face.

57 C: The central medullary chemoreceptors are sensitive to hypoxaemia

The central medullary chemoreceptors are sensitive to changes in P_{CO_2} via changes in H^+ (pH). The peripheral chemoreceptors located in the carotid and aortic bodies are sensitive to hypercapnia, hypoxaemia, as well as acidaemia, and hyperkalaemia. The glomus cell (type I) is responsible for sensing these changes and appropriate feedback via cranial nerves IX and X.

58 B: Popliteal artery

Supracondylar fractures of the femur jeopardise the popliteal neurovascular bundle, in particular the popliteal artery. The sciatic nerve divides into its two terminal branches above the popliteal fossa, and the deep femoral artery has only a few geniculate branches participating around the knee. The long and short saphenous veins are subcutaneous veins lying medial to the knee or inferior to the popliteal fossa respectively.

59 C: Acute respiratory distress syndrome (ARDS)

Mechanical ventilation is used for unconscious patients and also to provide oxygen therapy where other methods have failed. It is unfortunately associated with several complications. As a result of the positive pressure required there is a risk of barotrauma (pneumothorax, pneumomediastinum, pneumoperitoneum and surgical emphysema) and venous return is reduced, which decreases cardiac filling. Ventilation can also cause gastric dilatation and ileus, and long-term use can lead to atrophy of the respiratory muscles. Infection and airway damage are other risks.

60 A: Extensor carpi radialis longus

The posterior interosseous nerve is the terminal motor branch of the radial nerve and supplies the extensor muscles from the common extensor origin distally. The brachioradialis and extensor carpi radialis longus muscles are directly supplied by the radial nerve and arise from the upper two-thirds and lower third of the lateral supracondylar ridge of the humerus respectively.

61 A: The degree of contact with the radioulnar articular disc is maximal in full adduction of the wrist joint

The triquetral bone participates in the ulnocarpal joint and articulates with the triangular articular disc proximally. The pisiform bone is related anteromedially and hamate bone distally. During forced hyperextension of the wrist joint, anterior dislocation of the lunate bone can cause a carpal tunnel syndrome.

62 E: Split the cast to relieve any pressure from post-operative swelling and reassess the situation in 10 minutes

This patient has undergone an internal fixation of the tibia following a fracture. He is at very high risk of a compartment syndrome in that leg. He could well have a compartment syndrome, but this might also be caused by a tight cast among the causes already listed, such as fractures and surgery. The first step in this case is to split the plaster cast and dressing and relieve any pressure as well as elevate the leg and prescribe analgesia. This should resolve most of his symptoms. However, if shortly afterwards he continues to have signs and symptoms then compartment syndrome should be suspected. Urgent senior review with fasciotomies in theatre is the next step. Compartment pressure monitoring is an adjunct to the clinical scenario here.

63 B: Inferior vena cava

Drainage of the right testicular vein normally occurs into the IVC and the left testicular vein into the left renal vein. Both testicular arteries arise from the abdominal aorta and so lymphatic drainage is to the para-aortic nodes.

64 E: Waardenberg's syndrome

Predisposing factors can be divided into local or general, the commonest causes being nasal. Any condition leading to blockage of the sinus ostia can lead to secretion retention and predisposition towards infection. Local causes can be due to upper respiratory tract infections, rhinitis, nasal polyps, tumours and foreign bodies, nasal anatomical variations, dental problems, swimming and diving and sinus fractures. General causes are debilitation, immunocompromise, mucociliary disorders (Kartagener syndrome, cystic fibrosis) and atmospheric pollutants (dust, fumes).

65 D: Cardiac pulmonary oedema

ARDS is a specific disease of the lungs characterised by hypoxaemia, alveolar inflammation and oedema and pulmonary fibrosis. Clinically the patient has a raised respiratory rate; cyanosis and arterial blood gases show hypercapnia. Lung compliance is greatly reduced, therefore increasing the work required. There are certain criteria that need to be met in order to make a diagnosis of ARDS. These are: severe hypoxaemia (Pao_2/Fio_2 of <27), pulmonary infiltrates on chest X-ray, pulmonary artery wedge pressure of <18 mmHg (therefore non-cardiogenic pulmonary oedema) and a recognised cause. There are a variety of causes, including pancreatitis, sepsis, disseminated intravascular coagulation (DIC), burns and aspiration.

66 C: Grapefruit juice can interfere with the metabolism of tacrolimus, one of the immunosuppressive agents being used

Drugs that interact with grapefruit and/or grapefruit juice undergo cytochrome p450 oxidative metabolism in the intestinal wall or liver. Grapefruit juice contains various furanocoumarins, which have been demonstrated to affect the cytochrome p450 system, especially at the isoenzyme CYP3A4. From the immunosuppressive agents, both ciclosporine and tacrolimus can show reduced metabolism with consumption of grapefruit juice, leading to toxic effects.

67 D: Hypothyroidism

Complications can be divided into immediate, intermediate and late:

- **Immediate:** anaesthetic, damage to local structures (cricoid cartilage, recurrent laryngeal nerve, oesophagus, brachiocephalic vein, thyroid – not enough to cause hypothyroidism, mostly bleeding), cardiac arrest and primary haemorrhage
- **Intermediate:** displacement of tube, surgical emphysema, pneumothorax, obstruction of tube, infection and tracheal necrosis
- **Late:** subglottic/tracheal stenosis, decannulation difficulty, tracheocutaneous fistula and scar (hypertrophic, keloid).

68 C: Excessive diarrhoea and vomiting

The cause of oliguria can be determined by looking at urine and serum samples. This helps to differentiate between renal and pre-renal causes. Pre-renal renal failure will have low urinary sodium (<20 mmol/l) and a serum osmolality ratio of >1.2, serum creatinine ratio of >40 and a high urine osmolality of >500 mOsmol/kg. Conversely; renal causes have high urinary sodium of >40 mmol/l, serum osmolality ratio of <1.2, serum creatinine ratio <20 and an osmolality of <350 mOsmol/kg.

69 B: Lateral border of the tongue

Some 90% of malignant oral cavity tumours are squamous cell carcinomas, accounting for <2% of malignancies in the UK. The commonest site is the lateral border of the tongue, presenting as an ulcer or an exophytic lesion. Aetiological factors include smoking and chewing tobacco, and high alcohol consumption. The tonsils and soft palate are actually within the oropharynx, not the oral cavity.

70 E: Atelectasis

The commonest cause of fever 1 day after upper gastrointestinal surgery is atelectasis from retained secretions in the small bronchi. Urinary tract infections are usually catheter-related and take a few days to develop rather than occurring in the immediate postoperative period. Pulmonary emboli develop from deep vein thromboses, which also take a few days to develop. Anastomotic leaks are classically seen from day 5 onwards, as are wound infections.

71 E: Flexor response

Brainstem death is defined as irreversible cessation of brainstem function and is diagnosed by carrying out specific tests. These tests cannot be carried out if the patient is hypothermic (<35 °C) has had depressant drugs or has metabolic derangements. The patient must be in an apnoeic coma requiring ventilation and have a known cause of brain damage. The tests are designed to test the cranial nerves and are: pupillary response, corneal reflex, pain reflex (facial nerve distribution), caloric test (instillation of ice-cold water into the ear, looking for nystagmus towards that side), gag reflex and apnoea test.

72 D: Superior phrenic artery

The blood supply to the oesophagus is classically divided into thirds. The upper third is supplied by branches of the inferior thyroid artery, the middle third from aortic oesophageal branches, and the lower third mainly from the left gastric artery, although contributions from the inferior phrenic are also received. The pericardiophrenic arterial branch of the internal thoracic acts as the superior diaphragmatic supply, but does not contribute branches to the oesophagus.

73 C: Can be managed with a loose seton

High anal fistulae can be difficult to manage as their treatment can involve dividing the anal sphincters. A loose seton helps establish drainage of sepsis, which is of great importance as the first step in managing any anal fistula. High fistulae are seen in Crohn's disease rather than ulcerative colitis.

74 D: Bradycardia <45 bpm

SIRS involves the systemic activation of the acute-phase response following an insult. It is defined by the presence of two or more of the following: tachycardia of >90 bpm, respiratory rate of >20 breaths per minute or $Paco_2$ of <4.3 kPa, temperature of >38 °C or <36 °C and white blood count of >12 or <4 $\times 10^9$/l.

75 D: Paramesonephric ducts

Pronephros – develops in the third week but never develops fully.

Mesonephric ducts – develop in males to form vas deferens and epididymis; also known as the Wolffian ducts.

Metanephric ducts – develop into the ureter, pelvis, calyces and collecting tubule.

Paramesonephric ducts – rise parallel to mesonephric ducts to form the uterus and uterine tubes

76 A: Distal position

Proximal stomas, such as jejunostomies for example, are associated with very high outputs because of the increased secretions from the gastroinstestinal tract and pancreaticobiliary enzymes. The more distal position allows these fluids, along with most of the oral intake, to be digested and absorbed to a greater degree, so there is less stoma output. Proximal stomas can be associated with dehydration, electrolyte abnormalities and renal failure.

77 D: The patient is a potential non-heart-beating donor of his liver and kidneys

A gay patient who has been in a long and stable relationship can be an organ donor; he is probably a lower risk group than, say, a young promiscuous heterosexual. Organ donation after cardiac death from withdrawal of treatment is permissible. The patient is not necessarily too old to be a donor. It depends on what other co-morbidities are present. If he is a diabetic and/or has long-standing hypertension and, at retrieval, the renal arteries show signs of heavy deposition of atheroma, then one is minded to turn down the kidneys for transplantation.

78 C: Verres needles should be inserted under direct vision

Verres needles are designed to be inserted blind to establish a pneumoperitoneum. Most surgeons do not recommend their use as it is a blind procedure and damage to viscera can occur, with a modest risk. When employing the open (Hasson's) approach, the dissection into the peritoneum is much safer as it is done under direct vision.

79 D: No change in cardiovascular function when stopped 1 day before surgery

Sudden cessation in smoking causes a rebound tachycardia and hypertension, which is temporary and mostly resultant from the irritability and depression of cravings. Cardiovascular and respiratory function will improve long term and aid in recovery from surgery, anaesthesia and wound healing on stopping smoking. Effects are related to the volume and frequency of smoking for individual patients.

80 D: Phase 3 – rapid repolarisation

Correct phases of the cardiac action potential of ventricular muscles cell are:

- Phase 0 – initial rapid depolarisation
- Phase 1 – rapid repolarisation
- Phase 2 – slow repolarisation plateau
- Phase 3 – rapid repolarisation
- Phase 4 – resting membrane potential.

81 D: Is due to the tricuspid valve moving down during ventricular systole

- a wave – prominent in atrial systole
- c wave – synchronous with the carotid pulse wave
- v wave – reflects a rise in atrial pressure before the tricuspid valve opens
- x descent – due to the tricuspid valve moving down during ventricular systole
- y descent – reflects opening of tricuspid valve and a fall in right atrial pressure

82 D: Superior gluteal

In the lateral approach, the skin and the fascia lata are incised to expose the gluteus medius and the vastus lateralis muscles. The gluteus medius is incised from the greater trochanter, leaving a cuff of tissue. This incision is extended to split the gluteus medius proximally, and distally the vastus is split along its anterior part down to the femoral shaft. The gluteus minimus is detached from its insertion and the hip is exposed after incising the joint capsule. The superior gluteal nerve can be damaged (and the gluteus medius denervated) if the gluteus medius is split >5 cm proximal to the greater trochanter.

83 B: Alpha-fetoprotein (AFP)

Tumour markers are substances found in the blood that are associated with certain cancers. They are used in diagnosis, surveillance and staging. Non-seminomatous germ cell tumours of the testis are associated with a raised AFP and raised βhCG). PSA is a tumour marker for prostate cancer but is also elevated in benign prostatic hypertrophy (BPH) and prostatitis. CA-125 is mainly elevated in mucinous ovarian carcinoma but is also seen in breast and pancreatic cancer. CEA is a marker for colorectal cancer, as well as ovarian and breast cancer. CA-19-9 is sometimes elevated in pancreatic cancer and advanced colorectal cancer.

84 B: 250 ml/min

The normal coronary blood flow to the heart is 250 ml/min in the average 70-kg healthy young male adult at rest. This can rise to 1000 ml/min on exercise.

85 E: Persistent vomiting

Any cause of shock can result in metabolic acidosis as the inadequate perfusion results in an anaerobic metabolic response in addition to the production of lactate. Persistent vomiting typically results in a large loss of gastric acid and so a metabolic alkalosis.

86 E: It is associated with joint pain

Extraintestinal manifestations of ulcerative colitis include ankylosing spondylitis, arthritis, uveitis, pyoderma gangrenosum, erythema nodosum and sclerosing cholangitis. Smoking, unusually, appears to be protective against the development of ulcerative colitis.

87 C: Pituitary adenoma

MEN is a familial autosomal dominant disorder. There are two types, MEN I (pituitary adenomas, pancreatic islet tumours, hyperplasia of the parathyroids and tumours of the adrenal cortex) and MEN II, which is further subdivided into MEN IIa (medullary thyroid carcinoma, phaeochromocytoma, parathyroid adenoma/hyperplasia) and MEN IIb (parathyroid tumours, medullary thyroid carcinoma, phaeochromocytoma, multiple mucosal neuromas and marfanoid habitus). MEN syndromes can be picked up by genetic screening techniques.

88 B: Inheritance is in an autosomal recessive pattern

Malignant hyperpyrexia is an autosomal dominant condition with an incidence of 1 in 200 000. It produces a hypermetabolic state of skeletal muscle on exposure to general anaesthetics or muscle relaxants, which produces hyperthermia as a side effect. Muscle rigidity and rhabdomyolysis can occur, with resulting hyperkalaemia and multi-organ failure. Treatment is supportive, with intravenous fluids, dantrolene sodium, cooling, forced diuresis and intensive care as necessary.

89 D: IgM and IgG antibodies

Exotoxins are secreted by both Gram-positive and Gram-negative bacteria, whereas endotoxins are found within cell walls of Gram-negative bacteria only. The main defence against these secreted toxins are antibodies such as IgG and IgM. A clinical example of this is the tetanus toxin and the tetanus immunoglobulin injected to help counter its effects.

90 E: Has the inferior epigastric artery lying medial to its deep ring

The deep ring of the inguinal canal is a defect in the transversalis fascia and is situated 2 cm above the midpoint of the inguinal ligament. It has the inferior epigastric artery on its medial aspect and it is this structure that is used to define Hasselbach's triangle. Indirect inguinal hernias pass through the deep ring and are lateral to this vessel. Direct hernias, in contrast, pass through the posterior wall, medial to the inferior epigastric artery.

91 E: Enhance the metabolism of infected cells

Interferons are a heterogeneous group of endogenous glycoproteins which inhibit the growth of viruses, bacteria, protozoa and cancer cells by blocking the translation of proteins. They are the most important part of the non-specific defence response to viral infections. Interferons classically appear within hours of initiation of viral replication, in contrast to antibodies, which take some days to appear. They are species-specific, so therapy with animal interferons is ineffective in humans.

92 D: Risk of transmission from needlestick injuries is greater for HBV than for HIV

Hepatitis B is a dsDNA virus which belongs to the Hepadnaviridae group. Transmission occurs via three main routes: blood inoculation, sexual transmission, or vertically through childbirth or breastfeeding. The risk of HIV transmission following needlestick injury is 0.3% and for HBV this is around 3%. The HBV vaccine is a recombinant DNA vaccine.

93 D: Retarded lung maturation

The CHARGE association is a sporadic condition associated with multiple congenital anomalies: C, coloboma (failure of eyeball closure) and cranial nerve palsies (facial nerve); H, heart disease; A, atresia choanae; R, retarded growth; G, genital abnormalities; E, ear abnormalities and deafness. Patients may also have laryngotracheal abnormalities.

94 D: Sickle cell disease without hypersplenism

Numerous reasons exist for splenectomy in the non-trauma setting. The incidence of elective splenectomy in the UK has declined as this was used in the staging of lymphomas previously. Any cause of hypersplenism or thrombocytopenia resulting from hypersplenism can justify a splenectomy, as very large spleens can be symptomatic as well as have a very high incidence of rupture from trauma. Spleens, occasionally can cause pressure symptoms if large enough.

95 A: Hypotension, bradycardia, warm skin

Neurogenic shock is shock caused by the sudden loss of the sympathetic nervous system signals to the smooth muscle in vessel walls. This results in the triad of bradycardia, hypotension and peripheral vasodilatation, resulting from loss of sympathetic tone. This should be distinguished from septic shock, which results classically in a tachycardia and hypotension.

96 A: Equivocal

Cytology reports grade samples according to the cellular appearances by a 5-point system. C1 = inadequate sample, C2 = benign, C3 = equivocal, C4 = suspicious for malignancy and C5 = malignant. Fine-needle aspiration cytology (FNAC) forms part of the triple assessment for suspected breast cancer, along with clinical examination and imaging (mammogram or ultrasound).

97 C: It is structurally similar to the acetylcholine molecule

Suxamethonium is a short-acting, depolarising muscle relaxant useful in anaesthesia for performing intubation in the induction phase. It is structurally similar to the ACh molecule (double-ACh structure) and has a very short half-life of a few minutes, and complete metabolism by plasma cholinesterase in 5–10 minutes.

98 E: Thoracodorsal nerve injury – winged scapula

The thoracodorsal nerve supplies the latissimus dorsi muscle, which is one of the major adductors of the shoulder joint as well as an extensor and medial rotator. A winged scapula would result from an injury to the long thoracic nerve of Bell, which arises from the roots of C5, 6 and 7 of the brachial plexus. Both of these nerves are commonly encountered in axillary dissection procedures and can be injured here as well.

99 D: The interventricular septum is supplied by the left coronary artery only

Blood flows in an 'outward to inward' direction towards the myocardium. During systole, contraction of the ventricles causes compression of the coronary vessels, reducing or even reversing blood flow. This means that it is in diastole when the most blood reaches the myocardium of the left ventricle. Changes in myocardial activity and demand result in release of mediators, which autoregulate the coronary flow according to need. The right coronary artery, which arises from the right aortic sinus, mainly supplies the right ventricle. The left coronary artery, which arises from the left aortic sinus, supplies the left ventricle. Blood supply to the atria is variable. The interventricular septum is supplied by both arteries.

100 B: Atrophic gastritis

Atrophic gastritis and hypogammaglobulinaemia are both associated with a 30-fold increase in risk of developing gastric carcinoma. The other conditions listed have proved risks but not as great.

101 E: Sarcoidosis

Inflammatory bowel disease is associated with several extraintestinal manifestations. These include erythema nodosum, pyoderma gangrenosum, uveitis, iritis, episcleritis, seronegative arthritis, sclerosing cholangitis and cirrhosis. Rarely, systemic amyloidosis can occur, but sarcoidosis is not a known association.

102 A: Can present with a colo-vesical fistula

Diverticular disease occurs in the colon more frequently in the developed countries and increases with increasing age. It is not inherited and has no known risk of causing colorectal cancers. There are theories suggesting that their development may be due to high intraluminal pressures arising from diets that lack fibre and cause the colon to strain in propelling the stools along. Diverticular disease may present as diverticulitis, although it may also present as obstruction, perforation, or even as a fistula into surrounding organs such as bladder, uterus, vagina and even skin.

103 A: Parastomal hernia

Parastomal hernias spread and stretch the tissue planes, making stoma closure technically easier than a normal stoma. On reversal of the stoma, the hernia repair can be undertaken at the same operation.

104 C: Mycophenolate works by inhibiting enzymes in the pathway for purine synthesis

Mycophenolate inhibits enzymes in the pathway of purine synthesis and is more effective and selective than azathioprine in preventing acute rejection episodes in transplanted organs. It blocks proliferation of T and B cells, thereby inhibiting formation of antibodies and generation of cytotoxic T cells.

105 B: Hiatus hernia

Hiatus hernia is a protrusion of a viscus, usually stomach or upper oesophagus, through the oesophageal hiatus. These hernias are usually classed as being of the sliding or rolling variety and may even result in strangulation or perforation, although obstruction does not typically occur from these hernias.

106 A: *Streptococcus pneumoniae*

The asplenic patient is at risk of infections from encapsulated organisms such as streptococci, *Neisseria meningitidis*, *Haemophilus influenzae*. The commonest infection to affect the asplenic patient out of this group is *Streptococcus pneumoniae*. Regular immunisations as well as penicillin prophylaxis is mandatory for these patients.

107 C: Pregnant women show earlier signs of hypovolaemia during haemorrhage

The management of a pregnant woman in the trauma setting is no different from that of a normal patient. In this case the mother rather than the fetus takes priority and an obstetrician needs to be involved from early on. A special consideration that needs to be addressed is that, in mid- to late pregnancy, a large uterus can compress the IVC when lying in the supine position, and so a left-lateral position whenever possible will provide a better volume return to the heart, as there is lack of caval compression. Pregnant women exhibit slightly altered physiology, which needs to be considered as well; they may not show signs of haemorrhage as they have a larger vascular volume.

108 D: Glucose <10 mmol/l

The Glasgow scale is one of the scoring systems used to determine the severity of an attack of pancreatitis. The criteria used are: age >55, WBC >15 × 10^9/l, blood glucose >10 mmol/l, serum urea >16 mmol/l, PaO_2 <8 kPa, serum calcium <2.0 mmol/l, albumin <32 g/l, LDH >600 units/l, AST/ALT >100 U/l. The other scoring system in use is Ranson's criteria.

109 D: Musculocutaneous fistula

Intraosseous needle insertion is not without its recognised complications. Musculocutaneous fistulae are not recognised complications as they do not exist. A fistula is an abnormal communication between two epithelial surfaces and an abscess or infection can drain from the muscle into the skin. However, this would by definition not be called a musculocutaneous fistula.

110 C: 1000 ml

	Vol of blood loss	% blood loss
Class I	<750 ml	up to 15%
Class II	750–1500 ml	15–30%
Class III	1500–2000 ml	30–40%
Class IV	>2000 ml	>40%

111 D: T3b

Prostate cancer is staged using the tumour-node-metastasis or TMN system. Staging often determines the management plan. T1 disease is present when the tumour is not palpable or visible and is picked up on examination of the chips obtained at TURP. T2 disease is when the tumour is confined to the prostate and can be further subdivided into 2a (one lobe) and 2b (two lobes). T3 disease is when there is extension through the capsule, with T3a being extracapsular disease and T3b being invasion into the seminal vesicles. T4 is when the tumour is fixed or is invading into adjacent structures. In this example, the patient has T3b disease, which would be treated with hormone therapy and radiotherapy.

112 C: A femoral hernia usually presents as a lump above and lateral to the pubic tubercle

Femoral hernias occur through the femoral canal, which is under the inguinal ligament, just medial to the femoral vein. These hernias present as a lump in the groin situated below and lateral to the pubic tubercle, often as an emergency, and more commonly in elderly women. Inguinal hernias present as a lump in the groin just above and medial to the pubic tubercle.

113 A: Marfan syndrome

Spontaneous secondary pneumothoraces occur secondary to lung pathology such as cancer, infection or airways disease. Marfan syndrome results in a primary (ie cause unknown) pneumothorax.

114 E: Anatomical dead space is reduced in the standing-up position

Dead space is the volume of air that has to be ventilated, but does not actually take part in gas exchange. Anatomical dead space is the volume that does not mix with air in the alveoli, and physiological dead space is the volume of air that may reach the alveoli, but does not take part in gas exchange, eg due to lack of perfusion. Anatomical dead space will be increased in the standing position, with larger lung volumes and bronchodilatation. Physiological dead space is increased in hypotension, hypoventilation, pulmonary embolus, emphysema and positive-pressure ventilation.

115 A: Cushing syndrome

Cushing syndrome classically causes a hypokalaemia and metabolic alkalosis resulting in a high bicarbonate serum level and positive base excess. Starvation and septicaemia will both result in metabolic acidosis. Respiratory acidosis in myasthenia gravis due to hypoventilation and respiratory alkalosis occurs in pulmonary embolus due to hyperventilation and tachypnoea.

116 A: Acute rejection episode (and a transplant biopsy is urgently required to confirm the diagnosis)

Volume depletion is not likely as the patient did not complain of diarrhoea or vomiting. The ultrasound scan would have excluded ureteric stenosis (hydronephrosis) and transplanted renal artery stenosis. Residual acute tubular necrosis does not usually lead to a jump in the serum creatinine level. The serum creatinine levels tend to plateau at a level above the normal range in such a case. Acute rejection should be suspected in this case and can be proved on an urgent biopsy.

117 C: Posterior hypothalamic lesions

Causes of fever include, but are not limited to: illness, exercise, heatstroke, hyperthyroidism, malignant hyperpyrexia, failure of the heat-loss mechanism (dehydration), and by anterior hypothalamic lesions (neoplasia, ischaemia, surgery).

118 B: Finasteride – luteinising hormone-releasing hormone (LH-RH) agonist

Mitomycin C is an agent instilled intravesically for the treatment of superficial transitional cell carcinoma of the bladder, to prevent a recurrence. Finasteride is a 5α-reductase inhibitor. By blocking the action of 5α-reductase, it reduces the formation of dihydrotestosterone, therefore reducing the stimulatory effect this has on prostate gland growth. Oxybutynin is an anticholinergic agent used in the management of detrusor instability. Tamsulosin is an α-adrenergic blocker used in the management of BPH. It causes smooth-muscle relaxation of prostate and bladder neck, therefore improving urine flow rates. Flutamine is used in the management of prostate cancer. It is an anti-androgen and works by preventing testosterone from causing growth of the tumour.

119 E: Pulmonary capillary wedge pressure >16 mmHg

ARDS is an acute syndrome characterised by respiratory failure with the formation of non-cardiogenic pulmonary oedema, leading to reduced lung compliance and hypoxaemia refractory to oxygen therapy. The pulmonary wedge pressure is <16 mmHg. Diffuse pulmonary infiltrates are seen and the Pao_2/Fio2 ratio is <26.6 kPa (200 mmHg).

120 A: Runs between brachioradialis and extensor carpi radialis longus

The radial nerve enters the forearm anterior to the lateral epicondyle, runs between brachialis and brachioradialis and divides into the superficial radial and posterior interosseous nerve (PIN). The PIN splits the supinator (site of damage during retraction of the muscle) and supplies all of the extensor muscles except brachioradialis, extensor carpi radialis brevis and extensor carpi radialis longus. The superficial radial nerve passes to the dorsal radial surface of the hand in the distal third of the forearm by passing between brachioradialis and extensor carpi radialis longus. It can be visualised during the anterior approach to the forearm.

121 E: Short trunk

Clinical features of achondroplasia include small nasal bridge, button nose, trident hands (inability to approximate extended middle and ring fingers), lumbar stenosis, excessive lordosis, hypotonia during the first year of life, radial head subluxation, frontal bossing and a normal trunk but short limbs (rhizomelic).

122 C: Infantile hydrocele

A hydrocele is an abnormal collection of fluid in the tunica vaginalis surrounding the testis or spermatic cord. They occur in males of any age but are most common at extreme ends of the age spectrum. They can present from birth because during descent of the testis from the abdomen to the scrotum, a sac of peritoneum is pulled along, which envelops the testis and epididymis, creating a tubular communication between the abdomen and the tunica vaginalis of the scrotum. Usually the part surrounding the spermatic cord obliterates, therefore closing off this communication. If it does not, a congenital hydrocele is formed, where fluid accumulates within the patent processus vaginalis and around the testis. If the processus vaginalis obliterates at the level of the deep inguinal ring, the resulting hydrocele is an infantile hydrocele. If fluid is present in the tunica vaginalis surrounding the testis but not the spermatic cord, this is a vaginal hydrocele. A hydrocele of the cord is formed when the distal portion of the processus vaginalis closes, the midportion remains patent and fluid-filled and the proximal portion may be open or closed. In older men, an increase in the production of serous fluid by the tunica vaginalis (eg due to infection, trauma or tumour) can result in a hydrocele. In 10% of cases a testicular tumour is associated with a hydrocele.

123 B: *Bacteroides fragilis*

Bacteroides organisms are anaerobic, non-spore-forming, Gram-negative rods normally found within the human colon. They can cause endogenous infections and lead to peritonitis, sepsis and abscess formation. The polysaccharide capsule of the *Bacteroides* organisms is responsible for the high virulence factor. *Shigella*, *Salmonella*, and *Vibrio* are all enteric pathogens that cause gastroenteritis. *Helicobacter pylori* is a well-known cause of gastritis and is limited to the upper gastrointestinal tract.

124 E: Patellar tracking

The technical goals of a knee replacement are (1) restoration of mechanical alignment; (2) preservation of joint line; (3) balanced ligaments; and (4) maintenance of the Q angle (the angle formed by the intersection of the extensor mechanism axis above the patella with the axis of the patella tendon). To avoid lateral subluxation of the patella the femoral component is positioned laterally and rotated externally; internal rotation of the tibial component is avoided; the patellar component is medialised, and the joint position is maintained.

125 A: Coagulative necrosis

Coagulative necrosis commonly occurs in fibrous or muscular tissue where the outline of the cell is retained, but not the cell nucleus. The brain classically undergoes liquefactive necrosis, which results from complete hydrolysis of the cell. Caseating necrosis is seen in cases of TB and may represent a combination of coagulative and liquefactive necrosis. Fat necrosis usually occurs in abdominal wall, pancreatic or breast tissue that has sustained trauma and has been damaged by lipases. Fibrinoid necrosis may be seen in damaged vessel walls where plasma proteins accumulate.

126 B: Congo red

Congo red stains are used to identify and stain tissues containing amyloid. When polarised light is used, the amyloid is identified by its apple-green birefringence.

127 C: Probability of a negative diagnostic test in the absence of disease

Specificity refers to how well a test picks up disease-free individuals. It is expressed as a proportion of those disease-free individuals testing negative (true negatives) out of all disease-free individuals (true negatives plus false positives).

128 A: Are involved in the nurturing of sperm cells within the seminiferous tubules

Sertoli cells are regarded as 'mother cells', providing nutrition and wellbeing to the sperm cells within the seminiferous tubules. Once differentiated, they stop proliferating. Leydig cells or interstitial cells synthesise and secrete testosterone in response to hormonal stimulation by LH and FSH.

129 E: Exploration of testis via transverse incision over testis

These symptoms are most likely to be due to a testicular torsion. This has to be considered a surgical emergency as the longer this is left, the higher the chance of testicular infarction. The purpose of surgery is to correct the torsion in the affected testis and to anchor the other testis to prevent future torsion. This can be achieved via a transverse incision over the testis or via a small midline incision in the scrotal raphe. If the testis is found to be clearly necrotic, it should be removed.

130 C: Ketamine is a stimulant that works by dissociation

Ketamine is a stimulant that works by dissociation. It commonly causes a tachycardia and rise in blood pressure on injection. Its use is commonly within paediatric anaesthesia. The commonest side effects are nightmares and hallucinations.

131 D: Clearing and securing the airway

Airway, breathing and circulation in that order are always the mainstay of any resuscitation measures. Massive haematemesis requires resuscitation first; then proceed or transfer to definitive treatment.

132 D: Platelet deposition can occur on its surface

The smooth inert surface of PTFE as well as the negatively charged surface inhibits platelet deposition. Bleeding can sometimes be a problem through pores made by suture needles.

133 B: Pulmonary hypertension

Physiological changes resulting from a large pulmonary embolus include:

- Increased pulmonary vascular resistance
- Pulmonary hypertension
- Decreased left ventricular output
- Increased right ventricular afterload
- Decreased lung compliance
- Impaired gas exchange.

134 E: Omeprazole

H2 antagonists such as cimetidine and ranitidine can lead to pancreatitis but not proton-pump inhibitors.

135 C: The incidence is decreasing as a result of screening measures

The incidence of prostate cancer is rising as the general elderly population increases. The average age of death in men is rising and so prostate cancer will be more prevalent.

PRACTICE PAPER 3: QUESTIONS

PRACTICE PAPER 3: QUESTIONS

1 All of the following muscles are usually supplied by the obturator nerve, EXCEPT:

- A Pectineus
- B Adductor longus
- C Gracilis
- D Obturator externus
- E Adductor brevis

2 Select the correct statement regarding action potentials:

- A The size and shape of the action potential becomes smaller as it spreads across the membrane
- B The size and shape of action potentials are the same from one excitable tissue to another
- C The accumulation of positive charges due to Na^+ influx promotes further depolarisation of the cell membrane
- D Repolarisation after an action potential is due to inactivation of the postassium channels
- E Tetrodotoxin (TTX) is a specific blocker of the potassium channel

3 Select the correct statement regarding cerebrospinal fluid (CSF):

- A It is produced by specialised endothelial cells covering the choroid plexuses
- B It has similar composition to plasma EXCEPT for glucose
- C It is produced at 1.5 ml/min, allowing it to be turned over four times a day
- D About half of the volume is distributed in the ventricles at any one time
- E It plays a critical role in important brain functions and in providing nutritive support

4 All of the following special precautions should be taken when operating on a patient with known HIV status, EXCEPT:

- A Use of disposable gowns and drapes
- B Double gloving and use of indicator systems
- C Minimising the presence of unnecessary theatre staff
- D Operating in a theatre with negative-pressure air ventilation
- E Use of the kidney dish to pass all instruments

5 The correct 'shelf-life' of platelet concentrates is:

- A 4 °C, maximum 35 days
- B Room temperature, maximum 5 days
- C –30 °C, maximum 12 months
- D –65 °C, maximum 3 years
- E Room temperature, maximum 24 hours

6 Which one of the following statements regarding skeletal muscle is CORRECT?

- A Increasing tension in a muscle depends on modulation of the firing frequency of motor neurones
- B It can be innervated by parasympathetic nerves
- C An action potential in a skeletal muscle only lasts 1–2 ms
- D Fatigue results from depletion of muscle ATP levels
- E Fast muscle fibres contain myosin with high ATPase activity

7 A 23-year-old patient with myasthenia gravis is admitted under your care for a thymectomy. On further reading you discover that this autoimmune disorder affects the neuromuscular junction. Which one of the following statements concerning neuromuscular junctions is CORRECT?

- A It is also known as a 'gap junction'
- B Noradrenaline (norepinephrine) is the primary neurotransmitter in the neuromuscular junctions in the somatic nervous system
- C Choline is synthesised in adequate amounts in the ends of motor neurones
- D In myasthenia gravis the number of acetylcholine (Ach) molecules released is dramatically reduced
- E It is an example of a chemical synapse

8 **A 12-year-old boy presents to the Emergency Department with spontaneous hip pain and inability to walk. You suspect that the patient might have slipped upper femoral epiphysis (SUFE). Which of the following statements regarding SUFE is CORRECT?**

- A The incidence of SUFE is approximately 2%
- B SUFE is commoner in girls than in boys
- C The incidence of bilateral SUFE in children with symptomatic disease is around 10%
- D The clinical presentation can be with pain located in the foot
- E It can be managed non-operatively

9 **You are looking after a 73-year-old woman in ITU who requires total parenteral nutrition (TPN) via a central venous catheter in her right internal jugular vein. All of the following are recognised complications of central venous pressure (CVP) line insertion, EXCEPT:**

- A Tension pneumothorax
- B Air embolus
- C Cardiac arrythmias
- D Pleural effusions
- E Thrombophlebitis

10 **Down syndrome (trisomy 21) is associated with an increased risk of all of the following surgical conditions, EXCEPT:**

- A Endocardial cushion defect
- B Cryptorchidism
- C Duodenal atresia
- D Diaphragmatic hernia
- E Hirschsprung's disease

11 **Which of the following is the most common cause of osteomyelitis in adults?**

- A Sickle cell disease
- B Following a compound fracture
- C Haematogenous spread
- D Immunosuppression
- E Following orthopaedic surgery

12 A 39-year-old woman presents to the Orthopaedic Clinic complaining of severe pain and tingling in both hands at night-time, especially in her thumb, index and middle fingers, and occasionally her ring finger. You confirm that she has carpal tunnel syndrome on nerve conduction tests. The following are all recognised causes of carpal tunnel syndrome, EXCEPT:

- A Acromegaly
- B Rheumatoid arthritis
- C Pregnancy
- D Addison's disease
- E Repetitive strain injury

13 Select the correct statement regarding compartment syndrome:

- A It presents early with a pulseless limb
- B Ischaemia occurs initially because compartment pressures exceed capillary pressures
- C Operative management is only mandatory after failed conservative treatment
- D Compartment pressures must be measured prior to any surgical procedure
- E Fasciotomy is a recognised cause

14 All of the following are true statements regarding diverticular disease, EXCEPT:

- A It is found more commonly in the developed world
- B Surgical treatment is usually unnecessary in acute uncomplicated disease
- C Diverticulae are most commonly found in the descending colon
- D Perforation and fistula formation can result from an attack of acute diverticulitis
- E Resolution of the diverticulae can occur with a high-fibre diets and adequate hydration

15 A patient has blood sent away for clotting studies and the results show a raised prothrombin time, but activated partial thromboplastin time, thrombin time and platelet count are normal. What is the most likely reason?

- A Heparin treatment
- B Liver disease
- C Disseminated intravascular coagulation
- D Warfarin treatment
- E Vitamin K treatment

16 Risk factors for squamous cell carcinoma include the following, EXCEPT:

- A UV radiation
- B Burn scars
- C Surgery
- D Vitiligo
- E Actinic keratoses and Bowen's disease

17 Clinical features of a basal cell carcinoma include the following, EXCEPT:

- A Pink, pearly nodules
- B Surface telangiectasia
- C Ulceration
- D Nodular
- E Associated adenopathy

18 Types of radiation-induced cell damage include all of the following, EXCEPT:

- A DNA strand breakage
- B Free radical peroxidation in cell membrane lipids
- C DNA base alterations
- D Catalytic dismutation of the superoxide anion
- E DNA cross-linking

19 All of the following statements regarding the anion gap are true, EXCEPT:

- A Normal range is between 10 and 19 mmol/l
- B It reflects the concentrations of normally unmeasured anions in the serum
- C It will be abnormal in conditions where bicarbonate is lost, such as diarrhoea and fistulae
- D It is calculated by taking the difference between the main cations and anions in the serum (Na^+, K^+, HCO_3^-, Cl^-)
- E It would be increased in the serum of a runner immediately after a marathon

20 All of the following features are associated with necrotising enterocolitis, EXCEPT:

- A Pneumatosis coli
- B Bleeding per rectum
- C Metabolic acidosis
- D Haematemesis
- E Disseminated intravascular coagulation

21 Which of the following is NOT a possible long-term complication of gastrectomy?

- A Bolus obstruction
- B Dumping
- C Weight gain
- D Vitamin B_{12} deficiency
- E Low serum calcium

22 All of the following statements regarding fracture healing are true, EXCEPT:

- A The internal callus lies within the medullary cavity
- B The external callus is related to the periosteum and acts as a splint
- C Lamellar bone is subsequently replaced by woven bone
- D Maximum bony girth is normally attained within 3 weeks of the injury
- E Remodelling takes place according to the direction of mechanical stress

23 Which of the following chemical mediators of acute inflammation is correctly paired with its source?

- A Lysosomes – mast cells
- B Histamine – red cells
- C Prostaglandins – platelets
- D Nitric oxide – neutrophils
- E Leukotrienes – eosinophils

24 All of the following products of complement activation are correctly associated with their functions, EXCEPT:

- A C3a – cytolytic activity
- B C3b – opsonisation
- C C4b – histamine release from mast cells
- D C5a – opsonisation
- E C8 – chemotaxis

25 A complete division of the right oculomotor nerve (N III) would result in all of the following signs, EXCEPT:

- A Ptosis
- B Diplopia
- C Convergent squint
- D Dilated pupil on the right side
- E Loss of a consensual pupillary reflex when the left eye is examined

26 A 66-year-old man comes into the Emergency Department with severe tearing chest pain, which radiates to the back. His past medical history includes hypertension and diet-controlled diabetes. Examination reveals an early diastolic murmur and blood pressure differences in both arms of >15 mmHg. The gold-standard investigation of choice in confirming your diagnosis would be:

- A CT chest with contrast
- B MRI chest
- C Echocardiogram
- D Electrocardiogram
- E Angiogram of the arch vessels

27 Which of the following statements regarding HIV is CORRECT?

- A It is a double-stranded RNA retrovirus
- B HIV infection results in a fall of CD8+ T cells
- C HIV can be transmitted in normal saliva
- D There is an increased risk of malignancies other than Kaposi's sarcoma
- E Newborn haemophiliacs will have an increased lifetime risk of contracting the virus

28 A 40-year-old woman presents with right upper quadrant pain and nausea. Ultrasound scan reveals that she has cholecystitis and your consultant asks you to place the patient on a course of ciprofloxacin therapy. Which one of the following statements correctly represents the mechanism of action of ciprofloxacin?

- A It binds to the 30s subunit of ribosomes
- B It inhibits transpeptidase and cell wall synthesis
- C It binds to the 50s subunit of ribosomes
- D It inhibits DNA gyrase
- E It competitively inhibits dihydrofolate reductase

29 A 46-year-old man is noted to have a platelet count of 28×10^9/l as part of his full blood count results taken at a pre-admission clinic. You decide to postpone elective surgery and investigate this further to find the cause of his condition. Causes of thrombocytopenia include all of the following, EXCEPT:

- A Multiple myeloma
- B Alcohol abuse
- C Heparin administration
- D Uraemia
- E Hypersplenism

30 Which of the following statements is true regarding the aetiology of colorectal carcinoma?

- A Crohn's disease poses a similar risk in the development of colorectal carcinoma as does ulcerative colitis
- B Malignancy developing from ureterosigmoidostomy classically occurs at some distance from the anastomosis site
- C Colon cancer is more prevalent in non-urban areas compared with urban areas
- D Hereditary non-polyposis colon cancer (HNPCC) causes over 60% of tumours proximal to the splenic flexure
- E Gardner syndrome results from a mutation on chromosome 6

31 All of the following statements about carcinoma of the gallbladder are correct, EXCEPT:

- A The neoplasm usually starts in the cystic duct and neck of the gallbladder
- B It is found more commonly in women than in men
- C It is associated with the presence of gallstones in >85% of cases
- D Prognosis is generally poor with <1-year survival with local invasion
- E Chemotherapy and radiotherapy do not alter disease progression

32 A 15-year-old boy complains of easy bruising while playing sport and bleeding gums while brushing his teeth. He is seen by the GP, who orders a blood test for coagulation studies. His APTT is normal, but the PT is abnormal. The explanation for this result is a deficit in:

- A Platelet function
- B Vessel wall
- C Common pathway
- D Factor VII deficiency
- E Intrinsic pathway

33 Failure of normal organ differentiation is defined as:

- A Agenesis
- B Atresia
- C Hypoplasia
- D Dysgenesis
- E Heterotopia

34 All of the following factors stimulate the progression of the cell cycle, EXCEPT:

- A P53
- B PDGF (platelet-derived growth factor)
- C EGF (epidermal growth factor)
- D IGF-1 (insulin-like growth factor 1)
- E IGF-2 (insulin-like growth factor 2)

35 Which of the following statements about the differences between jejunum and ileum are TRUE?

- A The ileum has a thicker wall than the jejunum
- B The jejunum has fewer arterial arcades
- C The ileum has a wider lumen
- D The jejunum has fewer villi on its inner surface
- E The ileum has more valvulae conniventes

36 All of the following statements about Herceptin are correct, EXCEPT:

- A It is a form of immunotherapy as opposed to chemotherapy
- B Patients receiving Herceptin need regular cardiac function monitoring
- C It can be used in combination with paclitaxel as a first-line agent for metastatic breast cancer with HER2 overexpression
- D Up to 40% of patients may get an infusion reaction in the first 24 hours
- E Polycythaemia and leukaemia may occur

37 The sensitivity of a test is defined by which one of the following:

- A True positives / (true positives + false positives)
- B True positives / (true positives + false negatives)
- C True negatives / (true negatives + false positives)
- D True negatives / (true negatives + false negatives)
- E True positives / (true negatives + false positives)

38 Risk factors for oesophageal carcinoma include all of the following, EXCEPT:

- A Vitamin A deficiency
- B Opium ingestion
- C High intake of tannic acid
- D Pharyngeal pouch
- E Lye strictures

39 Which of the following statements regarding malignant bone tumours is CORRECT?

- A Primary malignant bone tumours account for 3% of all deaths from malignant disease in the UK
- B Ewing's sarcoma is more common in prevalence than chondrosarcoma
- C Pain is an unusual presenting feature of bone tumours
- D The commonest presenting sites of osteosarcoma are the proximal femur and proximal humerus
- E Radiographic features of an osteosarcoma reveal a sclerotic intramedullary lesion of the metaphysis

40 Which of the following is NOT a feature of ulcerative colitis?

- A Crypt abscesses
- B Granulomas
- C Perianal infection
- D Pseudopolyps
- E Backwash ileitis

41 Which of the following vessels used in coronary artery bypass grafting has been shown through evidence-based practice to have the best outcome for long-term graft patency rates?

- A Internal thoracic artery
- B Radial artery
- C Long saphenous vein
- D Short saphenous vein
- E Cephalic vein

42 Which of the following diseases is the commonest indication for a bilateral lung transplant?

- A Chronic obstructive pulmonary disease
- B Primary pulmonary hypertension
- C Fibrotic lung disease
- D Cystic fibrosis
- E Severe asbestosis

43 Which of the following statements regarding dumping syndrome is correct?

- A Can be avoided by performing a gastroenterostomy
- B Results from hyperosmolar fluid reaching the small bowel
- C Reduced by eating high-carbohydrate meals frequently
- D Can cause constipatory symptoms
- E Can be avoided by pylorus-preserving surgery

44 All of the following staements about a hiatus hernia are correct, EXCEPT:

- A They are more common in males
- B Rolling types are more common than sliding
- C Sliding types are more common in the elderly
- D Dysphagia is accounted for by extrinsic compression
- E Gastric volvulus is rare

45 Which of the following cases should be considered to have the highest priority on the emergency theatre list?

- A Laparoscopic appendicectomy for suspected appendicitis
- B Pyloroplasty for congenital pyloric stenosis
- C Incarcerated inguinal hernia in a young man
- D Strangulated femoral hernia in an elderly woman
- E Hemiarthroplasty for fractured neck of femur

46 A 69-year-old man presents with mechanical bowel obstruction confirmed by barium enema. Which of the following is NOT a possible cause?

- A Diverticular disease
- B Angiodysplasia
- C Crohn's disease
- D Gallstones
- E Carcinoma of the colon

47 Which of the following statements regarding the management of colorectal carcinoma is true?

- A 5-FU is commonly used in the adjuvant treatment of Duke's B colon cancer
- B Post-operative adjuvant radiotherapy for locally extensive but resectable colon cancer is preferred over pre-operative radiation
- C Patients presenting with large-bowel obstruction from an ascending colon tumour are best treated with a primary resection with a defunctioning colostomy to aid healing of the anastomosis
- D Surveillance colonoscopy should be performed annually for the first 10 years to assess the presence of local recurrence and metachronous tumours
- E Hand-sewn anastomoses in bowel resections for cancer have been shown to be structurally and functionally superior to stapled anastomoses

48 Which of the following hepatobiliary conditions would typically result in an unconjugated hyperbilirubinaemia?

- A Crigler–Najjar syndrome
- B Primary biliary cirrhosis
- C Mirizzi syndrome
- D Congenital biliary atresia
- E Hepatitis B infection

49 The following are all recognised complications of acute pancreatitis, EXCEPT:

- A Toxic psychosis
- B Gastric ulceration
- C Chronic renal failure
- D Pancreatic abscess
- E Hypocalcaemia

50 Which of the following is NOT a cause of constipation?

- A Volvulus
- B Fissure in ano
- C Digoxin
- D Aspirin
- E Cerebral vascular accident (CVA)

51 A 24-year-old woman, who is 2 months post-partum and is breastfeeding, attends your clinic with symptomatic hyperthyroidism. Which of the following treatments would you initiate in this patient to treat her hyperthyroidism?

- A Radioactive iodine
- B Carbimazole
- C Proplythiouracil
- D Atenolol therapy
- E Iodine therapy with recommended cessation of breastfeeding

52 A 35-year-old woman presents to the Endocrine Clinic with complaints of lethargy and easy skin bruising. She appears to have cushingoid features and you decide to investigate this in the Outpatient Department with some simple blood tests. All of the following are features of Cushing's disease found on blood testing, EXCEPT:

- A Hypernatraemia
- B Hypokalaemia
- C Hyperglycaemia
- D Lowered plasma adrenocorticotropic hormone (ACTH)
- E Raised plasma cortisol levels

53 A 34-year-old woman undergoes a right mastectomy and axillary clearance for a 4-cm carcinoma of the right breast with fixed unilateral axillary nodes. A staging CT scan confirms that there are no metastases present. Which of the following TNM stages does this patient's clinical picture represent?

- A T1 N0 M0
- B T1 N1 M0
- C T2 N0 M0
- D T2 N1 M0
- E T2 N2 M0

54 The commonest site for peripheral vascular aneurysms after the aorta is:

- A Iliac artery
- B Femoral artery
- C Popliteal artery
- D Splenic artery
- E Radial artery

55 Which of the following statements is TRUE?

- A Veins are better than arteries as conduits for bypass procedures
- B Superficial veins may be stripped in the presence of deep venous insufficiency
- C The radial artery is safe to be harvested if Allen's test reveals a time of 15 seconds
- D Veins may need valves to be stripped with a valvulotome before use in bypass procedures
- E Off-pump coronary artery bypass graft (CABG) procedures increase the risk of TIA or CVA

56 Which of the following is NOT a cause of splenomegaly?

- A Syphilis
- B Polycythaemia
- C Congestive cardiac failure
- D Familial adenomatous polyposis
- E Amyloidosis

57 Which of the following ulcers are correctly associated?

- A Cushing's ulcer – burns
- B Venous ulcer – haemochromatosis
- C Curling's ulcer – head injury
- D Neuropathic ulcer – glucosuria
- E Marjolin's ulcer – chronic scarring

58 Which one of the following statements regarding acoustic neuroma is CORRECT?

- A Acoustic neuromas make up 1% of all intracranial tumours
- B The majority are bilateral
- C Vertigo is a common symptom
- D Acoustic neuromas arise from Schwann cells
- E Most patients have normal hearing

59 Which of the following statements about pharyngeal pouch is TRUE?

- A Also known as Zenker's diverticulum
- B Arises from the anterior pharyngeal wall, known as Killian's dehiscence
- C Hoarseness is a common symptom
- D Barium swallow should not be performed because of the risk of perforation
- E Commonly, a pouch contains an invasive squamous cell carcinoma (SCC) in its wall

60 **A 42-year-old woman attends your clinic to discuss her management options after recieving her results of a triple assessment scan. She is found to have ductal carcinoma in situ (DCIS) on Trucut biopsy of a 5-cm mass in her right breast. Which of the following treatment options would you advise for this woman?**

- A Right mastectomy
- B Right mastectomy with axillary clearance
- C Right mastectomy with sentinel node biopsy
- D Right wide local excision
- E Right wide local excision with axillary clearance

61 **A 1st-year medical student attends a dental appointment for a filling of a right lower 7th molar tooth under local anaesthetic. After injection of the anaesthetic, she notices that the right half of her chin has gone numb, although she still retains normal movements of the jaw. Which of the following nerves has been infiltrated by local anaesthetic in this clinical scenario?**

- A Lingual nerve
- B Buccal nerve
- C Mental nerve
- D Mandibular nerve
- E Inferior alveolar nerve

62 **Which of the following statements about salivary gland tumours is FALSE?**

- A 80% of parotid gland tumours are benign
- B 15% of salivary gland neoplasms are submandibular
- C Excision of the submandibular gland can result in Frey syndrome
- D Malignant parotid tumours can cause facial nerve palsy
- E Adenolymphoma of the parotid (Warthin's tumour) is benign

63 **All of the following sinuses drain into the middle meatus below the middle concha of the maxilla, EXCEPT the:**

- A Posterior ethmoidal sinus
- B Middle ethmoidal sinus
- C Anterior ethmoidal sinus
- D Frontal sinus
- E Maxillary sinus

64 **A 4-year-old child is brought into the Emergency Department by his mother after having fallen from a slide at a height of 2 metres. His vital signs are: heart rate 135/min, BP 90/70mmHg, respiratory rate 28/min, and temperature 36.5 °C. Which one of the following signs would you consider abnormal in this child?**

- A Heart rate
- B Blood pressure
- C Respiratory rate
- D Temperature
- E None of the above

65 In acute arterial occlusion, the tissue that is most sensitive to arterial hypoxaemia is:

- A Skin
- B Subcutaneous tissue
- C Nerve
- D Muscle
- E Bone

66 Which of the following is the commonest cause of vocal cord palsy in an adult?

- A Idiopathic
- B Malignant disease
- C Trauma
- D CVA
- E Iatrogenic

67 A 73-year-old woman presents with a lump in her neck. Biopsy and imaging indicate that this is an early anaplastic thyroid tumour. What is the most appropriate management?

- A Radiotherapy
- B Chemotherapy
- C Resection and radiotherapy
- D Total thyroidectomy only
- E Radiotherapy and chemotherapy

68 A 34-year-old man wants to donate a kidney to his sister. His BMI is 31 Kg/m^2. His glomerular filtration rate (GFR) is 110 ml/min. The patient and his sister have the same blood group but they have no HLA antigens in common. On arteriography, he has a single renal artery and single renal vein on the left and single renal artery and single vein on the right. Based on the above findings, which of the following statements is TRUE?

- A The patient and his sister do not have the same biological parents
- B The patient is too overweight to be a living kidney donor
- C The patient's kidney function is not adequate for him to be a donor
- D The kidney of choice for donation and transplant is the left kidney
- E The kidney of choice for donation and transplant is the right kidney

69 Presence of all of the following factors will predispose to the development of an anal fistula, EXCEPT:

- A Infection
- B Foreign bodies
- C Radiation
- D Neoplastic disease
- E Inadequate vascularisation

70 A 25-year-old right-handed woman is brought into the Emergency Department after a traumatic amputation of her right middle finger less than 1 hour ago. The finger has been preserved on ice and a decision is taken to re-implant the finger under general anaesthetic. The correct order in which the structures will be re-anastomosed (excluding the finger tendons) is which of the following?

- A Artery, vein, bone, nerve, skin
- B Artery, bone, vein, nerve, skin
- C Bone, artery, vein, nerve, skin
- D Bone, vein, artery, nerve, skin
- E Vein, artery, bone, nerve, skin

71 The following endocrine conditions are paired with the correct hormone abnormality, EXCEPT:

- A Cushing syndrome – excess glucocorticoid
- B Phaeochromocytoma – excess catecholamines
- C Conn syndrome – excess ACTH
- D Addison's disease – reduced cortisol secretion
- E Congenital adrenal hyperplasia – 21-hydroxylase deficiency

72 All of the following arteries are named direct branches of the axillary artery, EXCEPT:

- A Superior thoracic artery
- B Lateral thoracic artery
- C Suprascapular artery
- D Subscapular artery
- E Acromiothoracic artery

73 A 46-year-old woman presents with a small mass to the left of the hyoid bone and anterior to the sternocleidomastoid muscle. It is smooth and compressible and mobile in the horizontal but not the vertical plane. There is also a bruit. The probable diagnosis is:

- A Sternocleidomastoid tumour
- B Dermoid cyst
- C Carotid body tumour
- D Laryngocele
- E Cystic hygroma

74 Which of the following structures are skeletal derivatives of the third branchial arch?

- A Stapes
- B Styloid process
- C Incus and malleus
- D Lesser cornu of the hyoid bone
- E Greater cornu of the hyoid bone

75 Which of the following pathological changes is correctly associated with the named disease?

- A Familial adenomatous polyp (FAP) – metaplasia
- B Peutz–Jehger – hamartoma
- C Barratt's oesophagus – dysplasia
- D Paget's disease of the nipple – metaplasia
- E Gardner syndrome – hamartoma

76 Which of the following is NOT a possible complication of thyroidectomy?

- A Laryngeal oedema
- B Hypercalcaemia
- C Hypothyroidism
- D Haematoma
- E Superior laryngeal nerve palsy

77 A 45-year-old patient presents to the Emergency Department 1 hour after falling from his mountain bike. He is complaining of left hip pain and X-rays reveal an undisplaced intracapsular fracture of his left femoral neck. The best method of treatment for this patient is:

- A Dynamic hip screw
- B Hemiarthroplasty
- C Partially threaded cancellous screws
- D Intramedullary reconstruction nail
- E Total hip replacement

78 The conjoint tendon of the biceps and coracobrachialis is retracted medially during an anterior approach to the shoulder. Post-operatively the patient has weakness of elbow flexion and reduced sensation over the lateral forearm. Which nerve has been injured?

- A Radial
- B Median
- C Ulnar
- D Musculocutaneous
- E Axillary

79 In the spine, the intervertebral disc which is most commonly implicated in causing nerve root symptoms is the disc between:

- A L5/S1
- B L4/5
- C L3/4
- D L1/2
- E T12/L1

80 Following pneumonectomy for carcinoma of the lung, which of the following statements is TRUE?

- A A chest drain is always required
- B Mortality rates are higher for left-sided pneumonectomy compared with right-sided pneumonectomy
- C Bronchopleural fistulae occur in <5% of cases
- D A double-lumen endotracheal tube is contraindicated
- E Mediastinal shift is a major problem, requiring further surgery

81 Which of the following systemic conditions is NOT associated with pruritus ani?

- A Cell-mediated lympholysis
- B Systemic lupus erythematosus (SLE)
- C Obstructive jaundice
- D Diabetes
- E Lymphoma

82 A 50-year-old woman has a Colles' fracture manipulated in theatre, followed by application of a full below-elbow cast. One hour after being on the ward with her arm elevated, she starts to complain of paraesthesia in the index and middle fingers, along with wrist pain. The correct initial treatment should be:

- A Observe for another hour to see if the symptoms settle
- B Split the cast and lower the arm
- C Take her back to theatre for a remanipulation
- D Split the cast and keep the arm elevated
- E Perform an urgent carpal tunnel decompression

83 **A 23-year-old man is brought into the Emergency Department after having been involved in a motorbike accident at high speed. He is unconscious and has a cervical collar on as a C-spine injury cannot be excluded without X-rays. A decision to intubate him using the nasotracheal route is taken. Contraindications to blind nasotracheal intubation in this patient would include all of the following, EXCEPT:**

- A Apnoea
- B Cervical spine injury
- C Skull base fracture
- D Frontal bone fracture
- E Facial fractures

84 **A 55-year-old woman treated for 6 months with carbimazole for thyrotoxicosis is no longer getting any control of her symptoms. What is the most appropriate form of management?**

- A Subtotal thyroidectomy
- B Total thyroidectomy
- C Radio-iodine treatment
- D Propylthiouracil
- E Propranolol

85 Complications of a surgical cricothyroidotomy include all of the following, EXCEPT:

- A Subglottic stenosis
- B Mediastinal emphysema
- C Vocal cord paralysis
- D Oesophageal laceration
- E Carotid artery puncture

86 Which one of the following associations between daily gastrointestinal secretion volume (in a normal 70-kg young adult) and fluid type are CORRECT?

- A Saliva – 0.5 litres
- B Gastric juice – 2 litres
- C Bile – 0.2 litres
- D Pancreatic juice – 3 litres
- E Intestinal secretions – 5 litres

87 All of the following conditions would result in decreased lung compliance, EXCEPT:

- A Alpha$_1$-antitrypsin deficiency
- B Pulmonary oedema
- C Supine position
- D Mechanical ventilation
- E Increased age

88 **A 24-year-old male is brought into the Emergency Department having sustained multiple stab wound injuries to the chest and abdomen. His HR is 130/min, BP 90/50 mmHg, RR 34/min, with a narrow pulse pressure and reduced urine output. Given this clinical scenario, how much blood volume loss do you expect in this patient?**

- A 600 ml
- B 950 ml
- C 1300 ml
- D 1650 ml
- E 2000 ml

89 **How much crystalloid fluid volume resuscitation does this patient require immediately as cross-matched blood is being awaited?**

- A 1900 ml
- B 2600 ml
- C 3300 ml
- D 3900 ml
- E 4950 ml

90 **A 60-year-old male smoker who is under your care undergoes a laryngectomy for cancer of the larynx. In assessing the sterility of this operation, you would best classify this procedure as a:**

- A Clean procedure
- B Clean-contaminated procedure
- C Contaminated procedure
- D Contaminated-dirty procedure
- E Dirty procedure

91 The following statements about the anatomy of the orbit are all FALSE, EXCEPT:

- A All the muscles that move the eye originate from a fibrous ring except lateral rectus
- B The ethmoid bone forms the lateral wall
- C The wings of the sphenoid form the posterior wall
- D The lateral rectus is supplied by cranial nerve III
- E The frontal bone forms the medial wall

92 An advantage of using povidone-iodine disinfectant over chlorhexidine solution while a surgical scrub is being performed is that iodine:

- A Causes less skin sensitivity and irritation than does chlorhexidine
- B Has a longer duration of action than chlorhexidine
- C Is more effective than chlorhexidine against spores and fungi
- D Has greater bactericidal activity than chlorhexidine for Gram-positive bacteria
- E Is resistant to deactivation in the presence of organic material such as blood, pus and faeces

93 **A 42-year-old opera singer presents with a laryngeal carcinoma of the vocal cord. Staging investigations show this to be limited to the vocal cord with no evidence of spread. What is the most appropriate form of management?**

- A Chemotherapy alone
- B Radiotherapy alone
- C Radiotherapy and chemotherapy
- D Partial laryngectomy
- E Endoscopic resection

94 **While performing a small-bowel resection for strictures following Crohn's disease, you notice that, on inspection, there are marked differences between jejunal and ileal anatomy. Such differences include all of the following, EXCEPT:**

- A Wider lumen in the jejunum
- B Fewer lymphatics in the jejunal mesentery compared with ileal
- C More prominent and multiple arcades of vessels in the ileum
- D Thicker wall of the ileum
- E Thicker and more fat-laden mesentery increasing towards the ileum

95 Which of the following statements regarding monopolar diathermy is TRUE?

- A It uses a very-high-frequency direct current to cut and coagulate
- B Cutting of tissues is accomplished by pulsed output of currents at short intervals
- C Currents as high as 500 mA can be passed through the body at frequencies of 5 mHz
- D When monopolar diathermy forceps are used, the current is passed between the two limbs of the forceps at the tip
- E It can be used in surgery on the penis or digits

96 The following statements about the anatomy of the thyroid gland are all true, EXCEPT:

- A The superior thyroid artery supplies the upper pole
- B The inferior thyroid artery is a branch of the external carotid artery
- C The isthmus of the gland overlies the second and third tracheal cartilages
- D The inferior thyroid vein drains into the brachiocephalic veins
- E There may be a pyramidal lobe

97 Which of the following statements about immediate care of a patient with burns is CORRECT?

- A Third-degree burns are usually painless
- B Intravenous lines may be placed in burnt skin provided no other site is accessible and good venous access is obtained
- C Priority is given to the airway and breathing before attending to stopping the burning process
- D Fluid resuscitation is calculated by a formula involving the body weight, percentage area burned, and the degree of burns
- E The most important complication found in the hospital phase of recovery from a large (>40%) burn is renal failure

98 All of the following signs are found in re-feeding syndrome, EXCEPT:

- A Hypophosphataemia
- B Hypocalcaemia
- C Hypokalaemia
- D Hypoglycaemia
- E Hypomagnesaemia

99–101 For the following questions regarding blood gas interpretations, please select the best answer from the one of the following. Each clinical scenario has one best answer. Each answer may be used once, more than once or not at all.

- A Uncompensated metabolic acidosis
- B Uncompensated respiratory acidosis
- C Compensated metabolic acidosis
- D Compensated respiratory acidosis
- E Mixed metabolic acidosis with metabolic alkalosis

99 A 23-year-old female patient has just been admitted following an aspirin overdose. She does not state how many tablets she has ingested; but, she is complaining of tinnitus. She has vomited six times before presenting and appears to be tachypnoeic on arrival to the Emergency Department. Her blood gas reveals the following: pH 7.4; HCO_3^- 22 mmol/l; base excess –2 mmol/l; Pco_2 5 kPa.

100 You are asked to review a patient who is 2 days post-laparotomy for a perforated duodenal ulcer. On blood gases, the following results are noted: pH 7.35; HCO_3^- 35 mmol/l; base excess +9 mmol/l; Pco_2 7 kPa.

101 A 33-year-old insulin-dependent diabetic patient attends the Day Surgery Unit for an inguinal hernia repair on the afternoon list. In the anaesthetic room, she collapses and is immediately resuscitated by the anaesthetist present. A blood gas taken shows pH 7.2; HCO_3^- 12 mmol/l; base excess –14 mmol/l; Pco_2 5.3 kPa.

102 A 14-year-old girl is admitted as an inpatient under your care with suspected acute appendicitis. She is competent to understand the diagnosis and management decision along with complications of undergoing an appendicectomy. She consents to the procedure. However, her parents do not want her to undergo the treatment as your diagnosis is not guaranteed, and fear that their daughter may undergo unnecessary surgery. Assuming that this case has been discussed with all relevant hospital personnel and team members, which of the following options should you carry on with?

- A Proceed against the parents' wishes to an appendicectomy
- B Agree with the parents' wishes and withhold from operating
- C Obtain a court order to carry out treatment in the patient's best interests
- D Adopt a 'wait and see' policy in this particular case
- E Treat the patient with antibiotics in the first instance

103 A 16-year-old boy is hit over the head with a bat while playing cricket. He loses consciousness for 10 minutes but then recovers and wants to carry on playing. His parents take him to the hospital, which is an hour's drive away. On arrival he is drowsy with a Glasgow Coma Scale (GCS) score of 12. The most likely diagnosis is:

- A Basal skull fracture
- B Subdural haemorrhage
- C Extradural haematoma
- D Subarachnoid haemorrhage
- E Diffuse axonal injury

104 Which of the following statements regarding FAP is TRUE?

- A It accounts for up to 10% of colorectal carcinomas
- B It may be treated with a prophylactic right hemicolectomy
- C It usually takes 30–40 years to present as a colorectal carcinoma
- D The gene is located on the long arm of chromosome 5
- E It is inherited as an autosomal recessive condition

105 Which of the following pairings is correct regarding complement function?

- A C5a – cytolytic activity
- B C3a – neutrophil chemotaxis
- C C3b – release of histamine from mast cells
- D C8 – neutrophil chemotaxis
- E C7 – cytolytic activity

106 All of the following familial cancer syndromes are correctly associated with the resultant neoplasm, EXCEPT:

- A Li–Fraumeni – cerebral astrocytoma
- B Retinoblastoma (*Rb1*) – osteosarcoma
- C von Hippel–Lindau (*VHL*) – renal carcinoma
- D *BRCA1* and *2* – ovarian carcinoma
- E MEN I – phaeochromocytoma

107 Following splenectomy, which of the following organisms can cause overwhelming sepsis?

- A *Pseudomonas* species
- B Fungal infections
- C *Neisseria meningitidis*
- D *Salmonella*
- E *Staphylococcus aureus*

108 Which of the following statements regarding the spleen is correct?

- A Red pulp consists of central arteries ensheathed by lymphoid nodules and lymphocytes
- B Red pulp forms most of the splenic volume
- C Most of the antibody synthesis in the spleen occurs in the red pulp
- D White pulp contains sinusoids, which trap defective red cells
- E White pulp contains B lymphocytes located in the immediate vicinity of the central artery

109 Which of the following phases in a cell cycle is the most resistant to chemotherapeutic agents and requires higher doses in order to obtain a response?

- A G0
- B G1
- C S
- D G2
- E M

110 Capacitance coupling in laparoscopic surgery can be avoided by:

- A Careful use of prep solution
- B Having the surgery performed by the most experienced surgeon available
- C Use of an insulated instrument with a metal cannula
- D Use of all-metal instruments and cannula
- E Use of lower power settings on the diathermy machine

111 A 55-year-old man on the surgical high dependency unit is being treated with dobutamine for congestive heart failure. The mechanism of action of dobutamine is:

- A α-adrenergic agonist
- B β-adrenergic agonist
- C β-cholinergic agonist
- D α- and β-cholinergic agonist
- E α- and β-adrenergic agonist

112 All of the following vitamins are synthesised in the gut by colonic bacteria, EXCEPT:

- A Vitamin K
- B Vitamin B_{12}
- C Vitamin B_2 (riboflavin)
- D Vitamin B_1 (thiamine)
- E Vitamin B_3 (niacin)

113 Regarding pulmonary blood flow, which of the following statements is CORRECT?

- A Both hypoxia and hypercapnia result in constriction of smaller alveolar vessels
- B Hypercapnia results in dilatation of smaller alveolar vessels
- C Pulmonary arterioles play an important role in the regulation of pulmonary blood flow
- D Perfusion of blood with alveolar ventilation is better matched towards the base of the lung rather than at the apex
- E Perfusion of blood with alveolar ventilation is better matched towards the apex of the lung rather than at the base

114 Which of the following statements regarding ANP (atrial natriuretic peptide) is correct?

- A It stimulates ADH secretion
- B It increases the GFR by simultaneous dilation of renal afferent arterioles and constriction of efferent arterioles
- C It is secreted in response to hyponatraemia
- D Secretion increases as central venous pressure decreases
- E It acts on selected parts of the nephron to increase water and salt resorption

115 A 43-year-old postman presents to your clinic with troublesome PR bleeding and a feeling of a prolapse. Examination reveals third-degree haemorrhoids. Ideal management of this patient would include which one of the following treatment options?

- A Injection sclerotherapy
- B Banding of piles
- C Prolapse and haemorrhoidopexy (PPH)
- D Open haemorrhoidectomy with a Delorme's procedure for prolapse
- E Fibre diet alone and observe in the outpatient setting

116 A 65-year-old male ex-smoker undergoes a single left main-stem LIMA (left internal mammary artery) CABG operation by a median sternotomy approach. During the recovery period, 1 week post-operatively, it is noted that he still has a persistent hoarse voice after extubation 5 days earlier. The nerve most likely to be damaged during surgery is:

- A Right recurrent laryngeal nerve
- B Superior laryngeal nerve
- C Left recurrent laryngeal nerve
- D Left phrenic nerve
- E Right phrenic nerve

117 All of the following mechanisms are involved in the secretion of gastric acid, EXCEPT:

- A Release of ACh from the vagus nerve in response to gastric distension
- B Release of gastrin from the G cells in response to acetylcholine stimulation
- C Release of gastrin from the G cells in response to histamine stimulation
- D Release of histamine from the enterochromaffin cells to act on the parietal cells
- E Neural stimulation arising from the hypothalamus in anticipation of food ingestion

118 All of the following muscles are lateral rotators of the hip joint, EXCEPT:

- A Gluteus maximus
- B Pectineus
- C Gemellus superior
- D Obturator externus
- E Quadratus femoris

119 A 54-year-old woman inpatient is referred to your surgical team with a diagnosis of small-bowel obstruction. Which one of the following clinical signs would you look for in trying to identify the commonest cause of this condition?

- A Previous abdominal surgery scar
- B Lump in the groin above and medial to the pubic tubercle
- C Lump in the groin below and lateral to the pubic tubercle
- D Cachexia and nodule at the umbilicus
- E Circumoral pigmentation and a family history of previous obstruction

120 All of the following causes of peptic ulceration may be cured by a course of proton-pump inhibitor (PPI) therapy, EXCEPT:

- A Non-steroidal anti-inflammatory drug (NSAID)-induced ulceration
- B *Helicobacter pylori* ulceration in addition to triple therapy
- C Cushing's ulceration
- D Curling's ulceration
- E Zollinger–Ellison syndrome

121 The main effect of ADH (antidiuretic hormone) on the kidney is to:

- A Reduce urine volume production by decreasing the GFR
- B Concentrate the urine by increasing Na^+ excretion
- C Increase water retention by upregulating Na^+/K^+ receptors in the distal nephron
- D Increase water retention by increasing distal nephron permeability to water
- E Increase water retention by increasing Na^+ resorption by acting on the Na/K-ATPase pump in the distal nephron

122 An example of a depolarising muscle relaxant used in anaesthesia is:

- A Vecuronium
- B Gallamine
- C Propofol
- D Suxamethonium
- E Neostigmine

123 All of the following statements regarding renal artery stenosis are true, EXCEPT:

- A It can cause acute renal failure in patients who are taking ACE inhibitor therapy
- B It is a cause of secondary hypertension
- C It is most commonly caused by atherosclerosis in younger patients
- D Treatment can include stenting of the involved vessels
- E It can lead to hypokalaemia

124 A 14-year-old boy is referred from the Emergency Department to you with sudden onset right-sided testicular pain of 6 hours' duration. On examination, you find the right testicle is hard, swollen, and lying transversely, with severe tenderness on light palpation. The next step in management is:

- A Urgent ultrasound scan of the testis
- B Analgesia, antibiotics and outpatient follow-up
- C Urgent theatre for testicular exploration
- D Admission for observation and analgesia
- E Elective arrangement for bilateral orchidopexy

125 The following are all management options in the definitive treatment of urethral strictures, EXCEPT:

- A Optical urethrotomy
- B Open urethroplasty
- C Urethral dilators
- D Urethral catheterisation
- E Urethral stenting

126 All of the following are correct boundaries of the foramen of Winslow, EXCEPT:

- A Free edge of the lesser omentum
- B Inferior vena cava posteriorly
- C First part of the duodenum
- D Quadrate lobe of the liver
- E Porta hepatis

127 The following layers of tissue are encountered during a Pfannenstiel incision, EXCEPT:

- A Subcutaneous tissue layers of Camper and Scarpa
- B Anterior rectus sheath
- C Linea alba
- D Posterior rectus sheath
- E Peritoneum

128 A 55-year-old woman is referred to you by the GP with an adenocarcinoma of the distal transverse colon recently found on colonoscopy and biopsy. Following the multidisciplinary team meeting, a decision to undertake an extended right hemicolectomy is agreed. You know that all of the following structures may be at risk of damage from direct or indirect effects when extended right hemicolectomy is performed, EXCEPT:

- A Right ureter
- B Right gonadal vessels
- C Fourth part of the duodenum
- D Right ovary or testis
- E Spleen

129 **A 67-year-old man who is an inpatient on your ward undergoes a thyroidectomy and right radical neck dissection. On the first post-operative day he complains that he is unable to initiate shoulder abduction. Which one of the following nerves is most likely to be injured?**

- A Axillary nerve
- B Suprascapular nerve
- C Dorsal scapular nerve
- D Lateral pectoral nerve
- E Thoracodorsal nerve

130 **A 24-year-old motorcyclist has a collision with a car and is thrown 2 metres, landing on his head. When assessed at the scene he is mumbling incoherently, moving in response to command and opening his eyes only in response to painful stimuli. His GCS score is:**

- A 9
- B 10
- C 6
- D 12
- E 8

131 A 23-year-old man sustains a stab wound to his cubital fossa during a fight. You suspect that there may be damage to the median nerve. All of the following muscles would lose their motor innervation, EXCEPT:

- A Palmaris longus
- B Abductor pollicis brevis
- C Pronator teres
- D Adductor pollicis
- E Opponens pollicis

132 The following are true statements about the trachea, EXCEPT:

- A The trachea commences at the cricoid cartilage at C6
- B The trachea ends at the bifurcation (carina) at the level of the second rib
- C The tracheal bifurcation varies with respiration between T4 and T6
- D The trachea is laterally related to the thyroid lobes and carotid arteries
- E The trachea is lined by stratified squamous, non-keratinising epithelium

133 A 16-year-old boy is brought into the Emergency Department after having injured his right knee during a rugby game. After careful history-taking, the injury he describes indicates that his knee was forcibly abducted and externally rotated while in a flexed position. This scenario would classically result in a tear of:

- A Anterior cruciate ligament
- B Posterior cruciate ligament
- C Medial meniscus
- D Lateral meniscus
- E Lateral collateral ligament

134 Which of the following statements is true regarding HbF (fetal haemoglobin)?

- A HbF contains two α and two β chains in its structure
- B The oxygen dissociation curve for HbF is shifted to the left because of the decreased affinity for O_2
- C HbF responds to an increase in 2,3-DPG by a right shift towards the adult Hb curve
- D HbF production is increased with the administration of erythropoietin (Epo)
- E Decreased levels are found in patients from African and Arabian populations

135 Structures passing through the greater sciatic foramen include all of the following, EXCEPT:

- A Piriformis muscle
- B Posterior cutaneous nerve of the thigh
- C Nerve to obturator internus
- D Tendon of obturator internus
- E Internal pudendal artery

PRACTICE PAPER 3: ANSWERS AND TEACHING NOTES

PRACTICE PAPER 3: ANSWERS AND TEACHING NOTES

1 A: Pectineus

The **obturator nerve** is derived from the anterior primary rami of L2, L3 and L4 of the lumbar plexus. It is principally the nerve supply to the adductors and the skin overlying these muscles on the medial side of thigh. The nerve travels medially in relation to the psoas major muscle and passes through the obturator foramen. It divides into anterior and posterior divisions around the adductor brevis muscle. The corresponding branches supply the following muscles:

- **Anterior branch:**
  - Adductor brevis
  - Adductor longus
  - Gracilis
- **Posterior branch:**
  - Adductor magnus (also partly supplied by the tibial nerve – hamstring portion)
  - Obturator externus.

The pectineus muscle occasionally receives a nerve twig from the obturator nerve, although it is classically supplied by the femoral nerve.

2 C: The accumulation of positive charges due to Na^+ influx promotes further depolarisation of the cell membrane

An action potential is a sequence of changes in the membrane potential that occurs when a nerve or muscle membrane impulse spreads over its surface. Any factor that increases the permeability of the cell to Na^+ can elicit an action potential. Action potentials take different forms in terms of size and shape in different tissues (eg motor 2 ms, skeletal 5 ms and cardiac ventricle 200 ms). However, the action potential is propagated without decrement down the entire length of nerve or muscle fibres.

The action potential is based on successive increases in conductance of Na^+, then K^+; there would be no net movement of ions across the membrane if this were to occur simultaneously. Action potentials are most often initiated by the opening of the ligand-gated ion channels that increase the permeability of the membrane to Na^+, allowing these ions to enter the cells and thus cause E_m (membrane potential) to move closer to E_{Na}. In a resting cell the membrane potential is very close to the equilibrium potential of potassium. During an action potential, opening of the voltage-gated sodium channels leads to further depolarisation. This process becomes explosively self-regenerating when E_m reaches about −45 mV to −50 mV. At the peak of depolarisation, around +35 mV, sodium channels deactivate and the permeability to Na^+ rapidly diminshes. At the same time, voltage-gated potassium channels open so that E_m moves back towards E_K. During an action potential it is only the voltage-gated sodium channels that inactivate and not the potassium channels. TTX is a selective sodium-channel blocker that binds to the extracellular side.

3 E: It plays a critical role in important brain functions and in providing nutritive support

CSF is produced largely by the choroid plexuses, which are capillary loops covered by specialised ependymal cells located in the ventricular system. It is produced at a rate of 0.35–0.5 ml/min, distributed approximately as 20 ml in the ventricles, 45 ml in the cranial subarachnoid space and the rest in the spinal subarachnoid space and central canal. CSF has lower concentrations of K^+, glucose and protein but greater concentrations of Na^+ and Cl^- than blood. CSF is important in regulation of brain function in many ways, for example: CSF pH and P_{CO_2} on respiration; CSF sodium chloride on AVP (vasopressin); CSF carriage of neuromodulators, eg opioids. It plays a minor role in supplying glucose to inaccessible areas.

4 D: Operating in a theatre with negative-pressure air ventilation

Standard HIV precautions exist to minimise any chance of inoculation from blood contact. Double gloving, disposable gowns, and kidney-dish passing of sharp instruments are just some of the few precautions listed. There are no suggestions for specific theatre ventilation in HIV as this is not transmitted via airborne routes.

5 B: Room temperature, maximum 5 days

Platelet transfusions are used for various reasons, for example to correct thrombocytopenia prior to an operation. They should be ABO-compatible. They have a shelf-life of 5 days at room temperature. In contrast, red blood cell concentrates have a shelf-life of 35 days at 4 °C, fresh frozen plasma (FFP) can be stored for a maximum of 12 months at –30 °C and granulocytes can be kept for 24 hours at room temperature.

6 E: Fast muscle fibres contain myosin with high ATPase activity

A graded increase in tension is produced by recruiting more motor units as well as by increasing the firing rate of the motor neurones of each motor unit. Skeletal muscle is innervated by the somatic nervous system and not by the autonomic nervous system. An action potentials lasts 2–4 ms and travels at a rate of 5 m/s. The reason for muscle fatigue is unknown, but the following contribute to it: H^+ ion, lactate, Po_4^{3-} ion rise, and failure of the Ca^{2+}-ATPase of the sarcoplasmic reticulum. The contraction to peak tension is much quicker in fast muscle fibres than in a slow ones, where there is low ATPase activity.

7 E: It is an example of a chemical synapse

The chemical synapses between the axons of motor neurones and skeletal muscle are called 'neuromuscular junctions'. Gap junctions are the contact points between neurones which act as electrical synapses. The axon terminals are unmyelinated and contain many 40-nm-diameter synaptic vesicles containing ACh, the neurotransmitter employed at this synapse. The choline subunit cannot be synthesised by the motor neurone; it is obtained by active uptake from the extracellular fluid by Na^+-coupled secondary active transporter in the nerve terminal.

Myasthenia gravis occurs as a result of the production of autoantibodies against the nicotinic receptor. This results in the production of a smaller action potential and subsequent weakened muscle contraction. There is a normal discharge of 100–220 vesicles even in myasthenia gravis. (Each vesicle or quantum contains 100 000 molecules of Ach.)

8 C: The incidence of bilateral SUFE in children with symptomatic disease is around 10%

SUFE facts:

- Incidence is 2 per 100 000 of the population
- Commoner in boys than girls (3:2)
- Commonly occurs in the 10–15-years age group
- Associated with hypogonadism, pituitary dysfunction and hypothyroidism
- Reported incidence of bilateral disease in cases which are symptomatic is 10%
- Usual presenting symptom is pain in the groin, thigh or knee, and a limp
- X-rays should include an AP X-ray as well as a frog-lateral to avoid missing a SUFE
- Cannulated screws are used to fix the femoral head very soon after diagnosis to prevent progression
- In severe cases where avascular necrosis has occurred, salvage procedures such as osteotomy, joint replacement or arthrodesis may be required.

9 E: Thrombophlebitis

Thrombophlebitis does not usually occur in such large-bore veins. It is recognised in peripheral veins with the use of hyperosmolar solutions, which is why a central vein is used instead.

10 D: Diaphragmatic hernia

Although case reports show that diaphragmatic hernias can occur in children with Down syndrome, there is no increased risk above that of the normal population. Endocardial cushion defects, duodenal atresia, Hirschsprung's disease and cryptorchidism are all known associations with Down syndrome.

11 B: Following a compound fracture

The commonest cause of osteomyelitis in adults is following a compound fracture of the bone, where organisms contaminate the wound. Haematogenous spread is another common cause of spreading infection from a septic focus elsewhere in the body. Sickle cell, TB, immunosuppression and post-surgical causes are recognised but are much less common.

12 D: Addison's disease

Typically, carpal tunnel syndrome affects women aged 40–60 years who perform chronically repetitive tasks that involve the hand. The median nerve can become compressed within the carpal tunnel in such cases. Patients often present with nocturnal symptoms of frequent burning, tingling, itching or numbness in the palm of the hand and fingers. This especially affects the thumb, index and middle fingers. There is loss of coordination and strength in the thumb because the median nerve innervates abductor pollicis brevis, flexor pollicis brevis and opponens pollicis. Adduction of the thumb is not affected as it is controlled by abductor pollicis, which in turn is innervated by the ulnar nerve. Sensation over the lateral aspect of the palm is controlled by the median nerve, although the branch innervating the palm (palmar cutaneous branch) passes superficially to the carpal tunnel. Sensation over the medial aspect of the dorsum of the hand is mediated by the ulnar nerve, as is the medial aspect of the palm.

Some causes of carpal tunnel syndrome include:

- Idiopathic
- Repetitive strain injury
- Pregnancy
- Rheumatoid arthritis

- Acromegaly
- Diabetes
- Cushing's disease
- Hypothyroidism
- Lipomata and ganglia of the wrist
- Post-traumatic wrist injuries.

13 B: Ischaemia occurs initially because compartment pressures exceed capillary pressures

Compartment syndrome occurs within a limb compartment or other closed space (such as the abdomen) when pressure builds up and compromises the blood supply to the tissues within that compartment. It can occur following trauma (including surgical trauma), revascularisation or any other situation leading to tissue oedema.

In the limbs, muscle oedema within a tight fascial compartment raises the pressure within that compartment. In the first instance, the venules are compressed due to the higher external pressures and this shifts the Starling's forces towards further tissue oedema. As the pressure from the worsening oedema rises, the capillary become compressed and ischaemia begins. This occurs at about 40 mmHg, which is much less than the arterial pressure (so a pulse might be palpable during the earlier stages). As the pressure rises the ischaemia worsens and the cycle must be broken to prevent permanent muscular and tissue necrosis.

The diagnosis is clinical and treatment is by performing fasciotomies on the affected compartment. Compartment pressure monitoring is helpful but not mandatory, and most people would advise surgery on a purely clinical diagnosis. A high index of suspicion is necessary to clinch the diagnosis.

14 E: Resolution of the diverticulae can occur with a high-fibre diet and adequate hydration

Diverticular disease is more prevalent in the developed world and theories suggest this may be due to dietary factors. Prevention and not resolution of diverticular disease may occur with the use of a high-fibre diet, which theoretically puts less strain on the colon. Once diverticular disease is established, only surgery can completely eradicate it; however, attacks of diverticulitis are usually managed conservatively unless these symptoms are troubling enough with frequent attacks, or complications from the initial disease have occurred (fistula or abscess formation).

15 D: Warfarin treatment

Prothrombin time (PT) assesses the extrinsic factor VII as well as the common pathway factors. Activated partial thromboplastin time (APTT) assesses both intrinsic and common pathway factors, and thrombin time (TT) detects a deficiency of fibrinogen or inhibition of thrombin. In the question, the PT alone is elevated. This is most likely to be due to warfarin administration, which blocks the synthesis of vitamin K-dependent factors (II, VII, IX). Heparin treatment causes a raised APTT and TT by binding and activating antithrombin III, therefore reducing fibrin formation. Liver disease results in a reduction in the synthesis of all the coagulation factors except factor VIII and also impairs absorption of vitamin K. There is therefore raised APTT and PT and also reduced platelets. Disseminated intravascular coagulation (DIC) is a pathological response to many disorders, for example malignancy and infections. It involves haemolysis of red blood cells, fibrinolysis and consumption of haemostatic factors. It therefore results in elevated PT, APTT, TT and reduced levels of platelets.

16 D: Vitiligo

Squamous cell carcinoma is a malignant epidermal tumour whose cells show maturation towards keratin formation. Squamous cell carcinoma has a number of risk factors, but vitiligo is not one of them. Clinically this is a firm skin tumour normally found on the dorsum of the hand, the scalp or the face. It can have everted edges and a keratotic crust and well-differentiated tumours will have a keratin horn.

17 E: Associated adenopathy

Basal cell carcinoma is a malignant tumour composed of cells derived form the basal layer of skin. It is the commonest malignant tumour of the skin in white races, with increased prevalence in locations of high sun exposure. Other risk factors include UV and ionising radiation and immunosuppression. Locally invasive and rarely metastasises to lymphatics.

18 D: Catalytic dismutation of the superoxide anion

Radiation-induced cell damage can generate the formation of several types of free radicals, which can be damaging to the cell membranes and DNA. DNA damage can include:

- Strand breakages
- Base alterations
- Cross-linking.

The free radicals can also cause peroxidation of the unsaturated lipids in the cell membrane to cause damage to the cell. Free radical scavengers such as the superoxide dismutases (SODs) catalyse the dismutation of the superoxide anion, which is an important byproduct of oxidative metabolism. The resulting hydrogen peroxide and molecular oxygen products of the reaction are further detoxified to water by catalases and peroxidases.

19 C: It will be abnormal in conditions where bicarbonate is lost, such as diarrhoea and fistulae

The anion gap would be increased in conditions where unmeasured anions exist in the blood in metabolic acidosis. Examples include lactic acidosis, ketones from diabetic ketoacidosis, and drugs that are taken in overdose. Diarrhoea and loss of bicarbonate do not result in an increased anion gap.

20 D: Haematemesis

Necrotising enterocolitis (NEC) is the most common gastrointestinal surgical emergency occurring in neonates. With mortality rates approaching 50% in infants who weigh <1500 g, NEC represents a significant clinical problem.

Initial symptoms can include the following:

- Feeding intolerance and delayed gastric emptying
- Abdominal distension and/or tenderness
- Haematochezia.

Systemic signs can include the following:

- Apnoea
- Lethargy
- Decreased peripheral perfusion and shock (in advanced stages)
- Cardiovascular collapse
- Bleeding diathesis (DIC)
- Pneumatosis coli and metabolic acidosis result; however, haematemesis is not classically found in this condition.

21 C: Weight gain

Gastrectomy is an effective treatment for gastric carcinoma but is associated with possible long-term complications. Dumping syndrome is caused by food and liquid passing too quickly into the small intestine causing abdominal cramps, diarrhoea, dizziness, sweating, nausea and vomiting. It is thought to be due to accelerated gastric emptying of hyperosmolar contents into the small bowel. This leads to fluid shifts from the intravascular compartment into the bowel lumen. It is often relieved by dietary changes. Another possible problem is vitamin B_{12} deficiency: the stomach is where intrinsic factor is secreted by the parietal cells and stomach acid also helps to release vitamin B_{12} from ingested food. Bolus obstruction can occur from the relative reduction in volume of the small intestine compared with the stomach. Hypocalcaemia can also occur post-gastrectomy and is due to increased transit time and therefore reduced time over which absorption can occur. Because of this malabsorption, weight loss is commonly seen post-gastrectomy.

22 C: Lamellar bone is subsequently replaced by woven bone

Bone healing occurs in well-defined stages after the initial trauma. The first stage is the formation of a haematoma from ruptured vessels and periosteum from the ends of the fracture. Following this, macrophages invade the haematoma, together with fibroblasts and polymorphs, to allow new vessel formation, fibrosis and the formation of an organised clot by the end of the first week. Osteoblasts then proceed to grow into the haematoma and form trabeculae of woven bone. This new bone is called 'callus' and can also contain some islands of cartilage, which are chondroblast-induced. Woven bone is subsequently replaced by lamellar bone and remodelling occurs over time. Normal restoration can take up to a year, although, functionally, most bone is clinically healed within 8 weeks.

23 C: Prostaglandins – platelets

Chemical mediator	**Source (cell type)**
Lysosomes	Neutrophils
Histamine	Mast cells, basophils, eosinophils, platelets
Prostaglandins	Platelets, endothelium, macrophages, others
Nitric oxide	Endothelium, macrophages, free radicals
Leukotrienes	Neutrophils, mast cells, macrophages, others
Cytokines	Many cells

24 B: C3b – opsonisation

The complement system is a cascade of enzymatic proteins which become activated during the acute inflammatory response. The components of the cascade have specific roles in the process of inflammation. Some examples include:

- C5a – neutrophil chemotaxis, histamine release from mast cells, increase in vascular permeability
- C3a – similar activity as above but less potent
- C5, C6, C7 – neutrophil chemotaxis
- C5, C6, C7, C8, C9 – MAC (membrane attack complex) = cytolytic activity
- C2a, C3b, C4b – bacterial opsonisation and phagocyte facilitation.

25 C: Convergent squint

All of the following signs are seen as well as a divergent squint. This occurs because of the unopposed action of the lateral rectus and superior oblique muscles.

26 E: Angiogram of the arch vessels

The gold standard in investigations for aortic dissection in a stable patient is an arch aortogram to assess accurately the extent and nature of the dissection. This is also essential in planning a surgical approach to treatment.

27 D: There is an increased risk of malignancies other than Kaposi's sarcoma

The HIV or human immunodeficiency virus is a single-stranded RNA retrovirus that produces DNA, which is incorporated into host cells using the reverse transcriptase enzyme. HIV infection results in a fall in CD4+ T-helper cells and subsequent widespread immunological dysfunction. Opportunistic infections and a wide variety of neoplastic disorders can occur in HIV infection.

Transmission of HIV occurs via:

- Sexual transmission
- Vertical transmission (childbirth or breastfeeding)
- Intravenous drug abuse
- Blood transfusion.

Individuals at risk of HIV include:

- Promiscuous individuals and prostitutes (and their partners)
- Homosexual or bisexual males
- Intravenous drug abusers
- Children of affected mothers
- Haemophiliacs treated before October 1995, when routine testing of blood became available.

28 D: It inhibits DNA gyrase

Ciprofloxacin works by blocking DNA synthesis in bacteria by inhibiting DNA gyrase. It is part of the quinolone group of antibiotics.

Aminogylcosides such as gentamicin, as well as the tetracycline group of antibiotics, work by binding to the 30s subunit of ribosomes and preventing bacterial protein synthesis. In a similar way, chloramphenicol and macrolides such as erythromycin work by binding to the 50s subunit of bacterial ribosomes and so prevent protein synthesis as well.

Penicillins and cephalosporins both inhibit transpeptidase and so inhibit bacterial cell wall synthesis. Resistant bacteria that possess the penicillinase enzyme can break down penicillin and render it inactive.

Competitive inhibition of dihydrofolate reductase occurs when trimethoprim is administered. This inhibits the production of tetrahydrofolic acid, which subsequently inhibits bacterial nucleic acid (precursor) synthesis.

29 D: Uraemia

Uraemia can cause bleeding even with a normal platelet count because of loss of or abnormal platelet function.

Other causes of abnormal platelet function include:

- Drugs (eg aspirin, NSAIDs)
- Septicaemia
- von Willebrand's disease
- Bernard–Soulier syndrome
- Glanzmann's thromboaesthenia.

Causes of thrombocytopenia include:

- Decreased production
- Hereditary thrombocytopenia
- Aplastic anaemia
- Drugs (cytotoxic agents)
- Alcohol abuse
- Viral infections (cytomegalovirus or CMV)
- Myelodysplasia, myelofibrosis and bone marrow infiltration.

Causes of increased destruction/decreased survival of platelets:

- Thombocytopenic purpura (idiopathic/thrombotic)
- Drugs (heparin, antibiotics)
- Post-transfusion
- Infections
- Disseminated intravascular coagulation (DIC)
- Hypersplenism.

30 D: HNPCC causes over 60% of tumours proximal to the splenic flexure

Gardner syndrome and familial adenomatous polyposis (FAP) share the same *APC* gene that mutates on the long arm of chromosome 5. Risk factors for colon cancer include genetic causes, diet, irradiation, surgical procedures and inflammatory bowel disease. Cancers occurring post-ureterosigmoidostomy classically occur at or near the ureterocolic anastomosis. Interestingly, around two-thirds of cancers are proximal to the splenic flexure in HNPCC.

31 A: The neoplasm usually starts in the cystic duct and neck of the gallbladder

Gallbladder tumours occur in the fundus in 60% of patients, in the body in 30% of patients, and in the neck in 10% of patients. They are rarely found in the UK and are associated with gallstones and porcelain gallbladders.

32 D: Factor VII deficiency

The coagulation pathway ends by the conversion of fibrinogen to fibrin by thrombin. There are two systems which interact to form the coagulation cascade: the intrinsic and extrinsic pathways. The intrinsic pathway involves normal blood components whereas the extrinsic pathway is activated by the release of thromboplastin from damaged cells.

Abnormalities of coagulation can best be understood by examining the cascade and available blood tests hand-in-hand. The prothrombin time (PT) tests the integrity of the extrinsic pathway and the common pathway. It will be increased in deficiencies of factors I, II, V, VII and X. The PT is normally 12–16 seconds. The activated partial thromboplastin time (APTT) tests the integrity of the intrinsic system. It will be abnormal in deficiencies of all clotting factors EXCEPT for factor VII. The APTT is normally 24–31 seconds.

Test results	**Conclusion**
PT and APTT normal	Platelet or vessel defect
PT and APTT abnormal	Common pathway deficit
PT abnormal and APTT normal	Factor VII deficiency
PT normal and APTT abnormal	Intrinsic system deficit

33 D: Dysgenesis

Agenesis is defined as the failure of development of an organ or structure. Examples include renal agenesis, thymic agenesis in DiGeorge syndrome, and anencephaly.

Atresia is the failure of development of a lumen in a normally tubular structure. Examples include oesophageal atresia, duodenal atresia and biliary atresia.

Hypoplasia is the failure of an organ to attain its normal size, for example developmental dysplasia of the hip.

Dysgenesis (dysplasia) is the failure of normal organ differentiation or persistence of primitive embryological structures. Examples of this include renal dysgenesis and patent urachus.

Heterotopia or **ectopia** is the development of mature tissue at an abnormal site. The presence of gastric mucosa in Meckel's diverticulum is an example.

34 A: p53

The *TP53* and *Rb* (retinoblastoma) genes are tumour suppressor genes which send inhibitory signals to the cell cycle at the G1–S transition phase.

Stimulatory growth factors that promote progression of the cell cycle include PDGF, EGF, and IGF-1 and IGF-2. These growth factors act on cells in the G0 phase, which leads to DNA synthesis followed by mitosis.

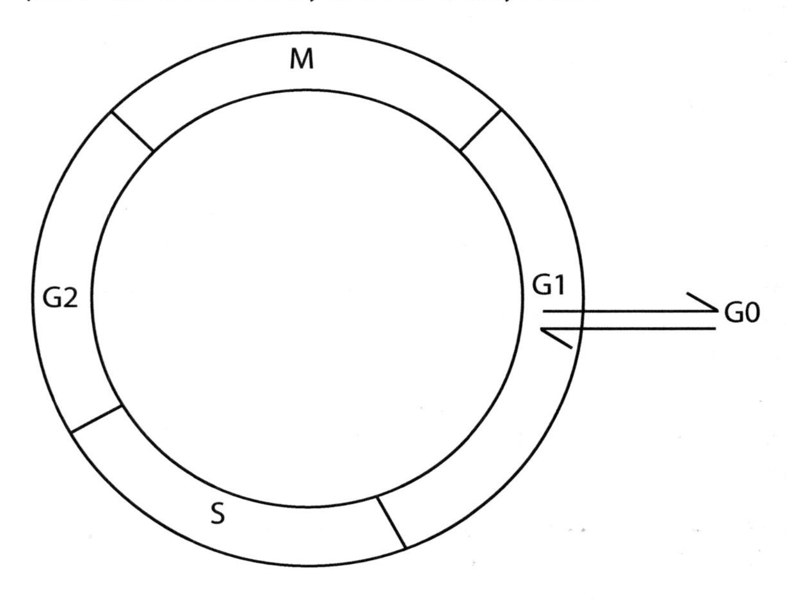

M = mitosis; G1 = gap 1; S = synthesis (DNA); G2 = gap 2; G0 = quiescent phase (resting).

35 B: The jejunum has fewer arterial arcades

The jejunum forms the upper 2/5ths of the small bowel and the ileum forms the lower 3/5ths. There are certain anatomical differences between the two. Compared with the ileum, the jejunum has a thicker wall, more valvulae conniventes, a greater number of villi and a wider lumen. There is also a difference in the arrangement of the blood vessels in the small bowel mesentery. The ileal vessels form complex branching arcades before reaching the bowel, whereas the jejunal vessels have a much simpler arrangement.

36 E: Polycythaemia and leukaemia may occur

Herceptin is the first humanised antibody (immunotherapy) approved for the treatment of HER2-positive metastatic breast cancer. Herceptin is designed to target and block the function of HER2 protein overexpression. Herceptin administration can result in the development of certain heart problems, including congestive heart failure. Severe allergic reactions, infusion reactions, and lung problems have been observed. Anaemia and leucopenia have also been reported when it is used in combination with chemotherapy.

37 B: True positives / (true positives + false negatives)

Sensitivity = true positives / (true positives + false negatives)

Defined as the probability of a positive diagnosis in all patients with the disease.

Specificity = true negatives / (true negatives + false positives)

Defined as the probability of a negative diagnosis in all patients without the disease.

Positive predictive value = true positives / (true positives + false positives)

The ability of a test to correctly report patients with the disease in all patients who test positive.

Negative predictive value = true negatives / (true negatives + false negatives)

The ability of a test to correctly report patients without the disease in all patients who test negative.

38 D: Pharyngeal pouch

Oesophageal carcinoma accounts for around 2% of all malignant disease in the UK. Other risk factors include:

- Barratt's oesophagus
- Lye strictures
- Smoking

- Alcohol consumption
- Oesophageal webs
- Achalasia
- Peptic strictures
- Plummer–Vinson syndrome
- Dietary deficiencies of zinc, riboflavin, vitamin A
- High intake of tannic acid
- Thermal injury
- Fungal contamination of food
- Opiate ingestion.

39 E: Radiographic features of an osteosarcoma reveal a sclerotic intramedullary lesion of the metaphysis

Primary malignant bone tumours account for 1% of all deaths from malignant disease in the UK. The order of frequency of bone tumours from commonest to least common is osteosarcoma, chondrosarcoma, and then Ewing's sarcoma. Pain and swelling are the commonest presenting features. Radiographic features of an osteosarcoma reveal a sclerotic intramedullary lesion of the metaphysis which expands and destroys the cortex. Unfortunately, by the time of presentation, over 90% of patients already have cortical destruction.

40 B: Granulomas

Ulcerative colitis is a disease of the mucosa lining the rectum that spreads proximally in a continuous manner to involve a variable proportion of the colon. In a few cases the terminal ileum is involved and this is known as backwash ileitis. Even less commonly, the perianal region may be involved, although this is much more common in Crohn's disease. Unlike Crohn's disease, which is transmural, the inflammation in ulcerative colitis is restricted to the mucosa, causing oedema, ulceration and pseudopolyps. Granulomas are a typical feature of Crohn's disease but not of ulcerative colitis.

41 A: Internal thoracic artery

The internal thoracic or internal mammary artery has been demonstrated to have the best patency rates in the surgical treatment of coronary main-vessel disease. The other vessels listed can be used, but the long-term patency rates are not as good.

42 D: Cystic fibrosis

The only absolute indication for a bilateral lung transplant is cystic fibrosis. Other indications such as severe COPD, fibrosis and pulmonary hypertension are relative indications and patients with these conditions might also be considered for single lung transplantation in certain cases.

43 B: Results from hyperosmolar fluid reaching the small bowel

Dumping syndrome occurs after gastrectomy surgery due to the rapid emptying of hyperosmolar contents into the small bowel and resultant rapid fluid shift into the lumen of the bowel. Patients complain of dizziness, faintness, nausea, and vomiting within 15 minutes of eating a meal. Patients are advised to take small meals frequently with a low carbohydrate and high fibre component. A late dumping syndrome may result in a reactive hypoglycaemia from a delayed insulin secretory response.

44 C: Sliding types are more common in the elderly

Hiatus hernias are protrusions of viscus through the oesophageal hiatus. They are more common in the elderly and are usually (80%) of the sliding variety. Dysphagia is only reported in about 20% of patients and the most common symptom is upper abdominal discomfort.

45 D: Strangulated femoral hernia in an elderly woman

A laparoscopic appendicectomy for suspected appendicitis should be done within 12 hours of diagnosis, although ideally as soon as possible. Patients can be maintained on intravenous antibiotics in the meantime. The laparoscopic approach should have no difference in priority from the open approach. Pyloroplasty for congenital pyloric stenosis should also be surgically operated within a day; however, neonates usually require a period of resuscitation pre-operatively due to the loss of fluid and electrolytes from all the vomiting. An incarcerated inguinal hernia in a young man that is not strangulated or obstructed can wait until the next elective list, provided it is not symptomatic. A strangulated femoral hernia in an elderly woman might contain ischaemic bowel and requires urgent operation. A long period of resuscitation is not recommended as the cause of any sepsis may worsen in delaying surgery. Hemiarthroplasty for fractured neck of the femur can wait at least a day before being booked onto the trauma list for surgery.

46 B: Angiodysplasia

Diverticular disease can cause bowel obstruction, either as a result of repeated episodes of inflammation, which causes fibrosis and strictures, or due to a diverticular mass, which obstructs the lumen. Similarly an adenocarcinoma of the bowel, particularly if it is annular in nature, can also cause obstruction. Crohn's disease causes transmural inflammation and this also results in stricturing. Gallstones may erode into the duodenum causing a gallstone ileus. Angioplasia is a vascular malformation that can result in PR bleeding, most commonly in the elderly. It does not cause obstruction.

47 A: 5-FU is commonly used in the adjuvant treatment of Duke's B colon cancer

5-FU is commonly used in the adjuvant chemotherapy in managing colorectal cancers. Colorectal cancers should be treated with excision where possible, although in some cases a limited course of pre-operative chemoradiotherapy may be required. The management of ascending colon tumour in the acute obstructed setting would include a right hemicolectomy plus a defunctioning loop ileostomy and not a colostomy. Surveillance colonoscopy should be performed for the first 5–10 years every 2 years and not annually, although local guidelines may differ slightly. Numerous studies have shown that there is no difference between hand-sewn and stapled bowel anastomoses.

48 A: Crigler–Najjar syndrome

Unconjugated hyperbilirubinaemia results from prehepatic haemolysis or hepatic disorders of bilirubin conjugation such as Gilbert syndrome and Crigler–Najjar syndrome. The remainder of causes listed result in jaundice from an elevated level of conjugated bilirubin.

49 C: Chronic renal failure

Acute pancreatitis can cause acute renal failure, ARDS, and DIC in very severe cases. However, chronic (long-term) renal failure is not a recognised complication.

50 C: Digoxin

Constipation can occur for many different reasons. Volvulus is a twisting of a loop of bowel around its mesenteric axis, resulting in partial or complete obstruction and therefore constipation. It also causes abdominal pain and nausea and vomiting. Painful anal conditions, such as anal fissure, can also result in constipation as the patient is reluctant to pass stool. CVA, Parkinson's disease and Hirschsprung's disease all cause adynamic bowel and therefore constipation. Drugs such as opiate analgesics, aspirin and anticonvulsants are also known causes. Digoxin is known to cause diarrhoea.

51 C: Proplythiouracil

Propylthiouracil is the treatment of choice in the management of hyperthyroidism in pregnant and lactating women. Carbimazole and iodine therapy may be considered after cessation of breastfeeding, but you should not encourage the mother to stop breastfeeding. Atenolol is also contraindicated in breastfeeding women.

52 D: Hyperglycaemia

Cushing's disease is due to a pituitary adenoma, which secretes ACTH. The resulting clinical picture is no different from Cushing syndrome. However, the plasma ACTH is raised in contrast to an adrenal adenoma or exogenous source where the plasma ACTH is lowered due to the negative feedback of cortisol on the pituitary.

53 E: T2 N2 M0

Tis – in-situ carcinoma
T1 – <2 cm
T2 – 2–5 cm
T3 – >5 cm
T4 – involvement of chest wall or skin

N0 – no regional nodes
N1 – palpable unilateral axillary nodes
N2 – fixed unilateral axillary nodes
N3 – unilateral internal mammary nodes

M0 – no distant metastases
M1 – distant metastases

54 C: Popliteal artery

The commonest site of vascular aneurysms is the abdominal aorta. Following this, the commonest site of peripheral vascular aneurysms is the popliteal artery, followed by the femoral artery. Although rare, the commonest site of abdominal vascular aneurysms is the splenic artery.

55 D: Veins may need valves to be stripped with a valvulotome before use in bypass procedures

Arteries have been shown to have better outcomes than veins in bypass procedures. Before superficial veins are harvested for use, a deep vein thrombosis must be excluded. An Allen's time of 15 seconds indicates that the radial artery might be the only main blood supply to the hand, in which case removing it may render the hand ischaemic. Before veins are used, they may need to be stripped of any valves inside and reversed to act as a conduit; otherwise, an immediate blockage of flow might occur.

56 D: Familial adenomatous polyposis

Early splenomegaly is usually asymptomatic but, as the spleen increases in size, it may cause abdominal discomfort and early satiety from gastric compression. Causes include infection (eg CMV, malaria/TB/syphilis), autoimmune disease (eg rheumatoid arthritis and SLE), haematological disorders (eg leukaemia, lymphoma, polycythaemia and haemolytic anaemia) and amyloidosis.

57 E: Marjolin's ulcer – chronic scarring

Cushing's ulcer – stress ulceration from head injuries.

Venous ulcer – lipodermatosclerosis and haemosiderin deposits.

Curling's ulcer – stress ulcer from burns.

Neuropathic ulcer – diabetes.

Marjolin's ulcer – squamous cell carcinoma occurring in a chronic ulcer or scar tissue.

58 D: Acoustic neuromas arise from Schwann cells

Acoustic neuromas arise from Schwann cells and make up 8% of all intracranial tumours. The majority are unilateral (95%). Patients usually present with gradual progressive unilateral deafness (90%) associated with tinnitus (70%). Vertigo is unusual. The investigation of choice is a gadolinium-enhanced MRI scan.

59 A: Also known as Zenker's diverticulum

Pharyngeal pouches arise from Killian's dehiscence, which is a posterior pharyngeal weakness between thyropharyngeus and cricopharyngeus. It is also known as Zenker's diverticulum. Patients may present with a lump in the throat, dysphagia and regurgitation of food. Only very rarely does a pouch contain an invasive SCC. Barium swallow is the initial definitive investigation.

60 C: Right mastectomy with sentinel node biopsy

A right mastectomy is recommended for any solid tumour >4 cm; however, this may also be dependent on general breast size and breast-conserving surgery may be considered. Although the biopsy reveals a DCIS, there may be areas of carcinoma in the solid tumour that were missed and so complete excision along with a sentinel node sampling is recommended.

61 E: Inferior alveolar nerve

The branches of the posterior division of the mandibular nerve supply the tongue and oral cavity. The lingual nerve is sensory to the anterior two-thirds of the tongue and also contains within it the chorda tympani branch, which allows for detection of taste. The inferior alveolar nerve branch passes through the inferior alveolar foramen of the mandible and supplies sensation to the lower teeth. This nerve ends as the mental nerve as it emerges from the mental foramen to supply sensation to the skin overlying the chin and lower lip.

62 C: Excision of the submandibular gland can result in Frey syndrome

The parotid gland is known as the 80% gland because: 80% of salivary tumours are found in the parotid. Of these, 80% are benign in nature and 80% of these are pleomorphic adenomas. Another benign tumour of the parotid is an adenolymphoma. Adenocarcinoma of the parotid makes up 3% of all parotid tumours. It may infiltrate the facial nerve, which runs through the parotid, causing a facial palsy. Management is by parotidectomy, with the aim of preserving the facial nerve if it is not involved. Damage to the innervation of the parotid gland during surgery can result in Frey's syndrome. This is due to inappropriate regeneration of parasympathetic nerve fibres, which stimulate the sweat glands of overlying skin resulting in gustatory sweating. 15% of salivary gland neoplasms are located in the submandibular gland.

63 A: Posterior ethmoidal sinus

The posterior ethmoidal sinus drains into the superior recess underlying the superior concha. The remaining named sinuses drain below the middle concha.

64 E: None of the above

Age (years)	HR (bpm)	BP (mmHg)	RR (breaths/min)
0–1	<160	>60	<60
1–3	<150	>70	<40
3–5	<140	>75	<35
6–12	<120	>80	<30
>12	<100	>90	<30

65 C: Nerve

Nervous tissue is the most sensitive tissue in the human body to hypoxaemia and can undergo irreversible ischaemic changes within minutes of being deprived of oxygen.

66 B: Malignant disease

Unilateral vocal cord palsy produces hoarseness. The commonest cause is malignant disease (30%), especially of the bronchus, followed by iatrogenic causes (25%), ie thyroid surgery or any surgery along the course of the recurrent laryngeal nerve. Trauma, idiopathic and other causes, eg central and myopathies, are unlikely (15% each).

67 C: Resection and radiotherapy

Anaplastic thyroid tumours are most commonly found in elderly women and present as a rapidly expanding neck mass. Fifty per cent present with distant metastases and the prognosis is poor. Radiotherapy can be used for palliation of local disease whereas chemotherapy has a role in treating distant metastases. In early anaplastic cancer the outlook is better and this can be treated by surgery followed by radiotherapy.

68 D: The kidney of choice for donation and transplant is the left kidney

The left kidney is the kidney of choice as it has the longer renal vein (the cava being to the right of the aorta). A BMI of 31 kg/m^2 is not an absolute contraindication to donation; and a GFR of 110 ml/min is within the normal range for his age. It is possible for siblings not to have HLA antigens in common. The proof for consanguinity is to check the parents' HLA type or the HLA type of other siblings.

69 E: Inadequate vascularisation

Anal fistulae can may form from any infection or systemic irritation occurring around the anus. Examples include neoplasia, inflammatory bowel disease, foreign bodies and radiation damage. Inadequate vascularisation does not predispose to the development of a fistula, although it may prevent its healing.

70 D: Bone, vein, artery, nerve, skin

Bony fixation needs to be done first as this will act as the strut for the finger re-implantation. After this the venous return is established as this can often be the most difficult part of the operation and if the veins are damaged beyond repair or avulsed, then there would be no point in establishing arterial continuity. The artery is then re-anastomosed on one side as this is often adequate and then the nerves and tendons can be repaired. The skin is closed last.

71 C: Conn syndrome – excess ACTH

Cushing syndrome is a disease caused by an excess of cortisol production or by excessive use of cortisol or other similar steroid (glucocorticoid) hormones. It can be diagnosed either by measuring 24-hour urinary free cortisol or by an overnight dexamethasone suppression test, which fails to suppress morning cortisol levels in affected patients. Cushing's disease is the name given to a type of Cushing syndrome caused by too much ACTH production in the pituitary. Phaeochromocytomas are tumours of the adrenal medulla arising from chromaffin cells and secreting excess catecholamines. Vanilly-mandelic acid (VMA) is a breakdown product of catecholamines and therefore urinary levels become elevated and are used as a diagnostic test. Conn syndrome is caused by an aldosterone-secreting adrenocortical adenoma and causes raised plasma aldosterone. Addison's disease is often associated with other autoimmune disorders and is characterised by low serum cortisol. It can be investigated for by using the short Synacthen test, which doesn't cause a rise in plasma cortisol in affected patients whereas it does in unaffected people. Congenital adrenal hyperplasia occurs as a result of 21-hydroxylase deficiency.

72 C: Suprascapular artery

The suprascapular artery is a branch of the thyrocervical trunk of the subclavian artery. All of the others listed are direct branches of the axillary artery in addition to the anterior and posterior circumflex humeral arteries from the third part.

73 C: Carotid body tumour

Carotid body tumours present as masses adjacent to the hyoid bone and anterior to the sternocleidomastoid. They are typically pulsatile, compressible and smooth, with mobility in the horizontal but not the vertical plane. Approximately 5% are malignant. Cystic hygromas are congenital lymphatic malformations situated at the root of the neck and are present at birth in 50% of neonates. Sternocleidomastoid tumours are usually found in the neonatal period and are located at the junction between the upper and middle thirds of the muscle. They tend to disappear with age. Laryngoceles are saccules that become expanded with air, often after straining. Dermoid cysts can be congenital or acquired. Congenital cysts are commonly located on the head or neck and acquired cysts are most commonly caused when a piece of skin is implanted into the dermis, secondary to trauma.

74 E: Greater cornu of the hyoid bone

Skeletal derivatives of the third branchial arch or 'thyrohyoid arch' include the inferior body and greater cornu of the hyoid bone. The remainder of the hyoid bone including the styloid process and stapes are derived from the second branchial arch or 'hyoid arch'. The incus and malleus are derivatives of the first branchial arch.

75 B: Peutz–Jehger – hamartoma

Peutz–Jehger disease is an autosomal dominant disorder characterised by the presence of hamartomatous polyps within the gastrointestinal tract as well as circumoral pigmentation. Examples of metaplasia include Barratt's oesophagus and squamous change of the cervix, bronchus or bladder. Examples of dysplasia include cervical intraepithelial neoplasia (CIN) and vulvar intraepithelial neoplasia (VIN). Paget's disease and FAP are examples of neoplastic disorders.

76 B: Hypercalcaemia

Thyroid surgery is associated with several complications. Hypothyroidism is an expected result and requires replacement with oral thyroxine. Haematoma formation can occur and, if it becomes enlarged, can compress the trachea, requiring urgent evacuation. Laryngeal oedema can be caused by trauma sustained during surgery and may make airway management difficult. There is a risk to the recurrent laryngeal and superior laryngeal nerves during thyroid surgery. Damage to the superior laryngeal nerve results in a monotonous voice because of paralysis of the cricothyroid muscle. Hypocalcaemia can result from inadvertent damage to the parathyroid glands and requires oral replacement.

77 C: Partially threaded cancellous screws

For intracapsular fracture fixation in the presence of good-quality bone, the best method of fixation is with cannulated screws. The majority of patients are elderly, with osteoporotic bone, so a hemiarthroplasty is performed. A dynamic hip screw is usually performed for extracapsular fractures.

78 D: Musculocutaneous

The musculocutaneous nerve pierces the coracobrachialis 5–8 cm distal to the coracoid process. This nerve gives branches to the coracobrachialis muscle, the biceps brachii and the brachialis muscles. The elbow joint is supplied by this nerve before it becomes the lateral cutaneous nerve of the forearm.

79 B: L4/5

Usually the L4/5 disc is involved followed closely by the L5/S1. Most herniations are posterolateral and patients present with symptoms of backache and sciatica. Acute central disc herniations can cause a cauda equina compression syndrome. In a classic syndrome the patient has pain at the backs of thighs and legs; numbness in the buttocks, perineum and soles of feet; weakness/paralysis of legs and feet; and dysfunction of the bladder and bowel.

80 D: A double-lumen endotracheal tube is contraindicated

Double-lumen endotracheal tubes are essential for any cardiothoracic or oesophageal procedure to allow control of individual lungs during surgery and to avoid damaging lungs while the chest is opened.

81 B: Systemic lupus erythematosus (SLE)

Pruritus ani is a common condition, and can be due to a variety of causes. Men are more commonly affected and symptoms worsen during hot weather and at night. Causes include skin diseases (eg eczema and psoriasis), general medical diseases (eg diabetes, myeloproliferative disorders, lymphoma and obstructive jaundice), perianal disease (eg anal fissure and Crohn's disease) and local irritants such as mucus and sweat. Often an 'itch/scratch' cycle is set up and so symptoms can persist even when the cause has been eradicated.

82 D: Split the cast and keep the arm elevated

The commonest cause of pain after a manipulation is because of swelling and a tight cast. It is important to keep the limb elevated to reduce the swelling and split the cast. Delay can lead to limb ischaemia and muscle damage resulting in ischaemic contractures. If a patient undergoes an open reduction and there are median nerve symptoms at presentation, then a carpal tunnel decompression can be done at the same time.

83 B: Cervical spine injury

Blind nasotracheal intubation is contraindicated in apnoea. Any nasotracheal intubation is contraindicated if a basal skull fracture is suspected from head or facial trauma. C-spine injury on its own is not a contraindication, especially in a breathing patient.

84 C: Radio-iodine treatment

First-line treatment for thyrotoxicosis disease is carbimazole. In certain individuals it has the unfortunate side effect of agranulocytosis and so propylthiouracil is used instead. This is also the drug of choice in pregnancy as it is protein-bound and therefore less likely to cross the placenta. Radio-iodine ablation is safe for patients in whom medical management has failed and who are not planning on becoming pregnant during treatment. Surgery for thyroid disorders is carried out for cosmesis, compression symptoms, retrosternal extension and carcinoma.

85 C: Vocal cord paralysis

Vocal cord paralysis only occurs with direct trauma to the cords or damage to the recurrent laryngeal nerves. A surgical cricothyroidotomy does not involve direct trauma to the cord or nerves because the incision occurs at the cricothyroid membrane.

86 B: Gastric juice – 2 litres

Average values of secreted fluids include:

- Mouth 1.5 litres
- Stomach 2–3 litres
- Gallbladder 500 ml
- Pancreas 1.5 litres
- Small bowel 1.5 litres
- Large bowel 100 ml excreted

87 A: Alpha$_1$-antitrypsin deficiency

Alpha1-antitrypsin deficiency causes emphysema, which results an increased compliance of the lung tissue. All of the other listed conditions decrease lung compliance.

88 D: 1650 ml

This scenario is demonstrating a class III haemorrhage in which there is tachycardia >120/min, a reduced blood pressure and urine output, and an increased respiratory rate >30 litres. Class III haemorrhage involves a blood loss of 1.5–2 litres.

89 E: 4950 ml

Volume replacement in the trauma setting uses the 3 for 1 replacement rule with crystalloids. Ideally, for class III haemorrhage, blood replacement should be given as soon as possible. In the meantime, the volume of crystalloid should be replaced with 3 litres for every litre of blood lost.

90 B: Clean-contaminated procedure

Laryngectomy is classed as a clean-contaminated procedure as it involves entering the airways and coming into contact with pathogens. Examples of procedures are listed below:

- Clean procedure – thyroidectomy
- Clean-contaminated procedure – cholecystectomy
- Contaminated procedure – right hemicolectomy
- Dirty procedure – perforated colon/faecal peritonitis.

91 C: The wings of the sphenoid form the posterior wall

The muscles involved in movement of the eye are lateral rectus, medial rectus, superior rectus, inferior rectus, superior oblique and inferior oblique. All, apart from inferior oblique, arise from a fibrous ring. Lateral rectus is supplied by CN

VI, superior oblique by CN IV and all the others by CN III. The orbit is made up of several bones with both wings of the sphenoid forming the posterior wall. The frontal bone forms the superior part, the lacrimal and ethmoid bones the medial part, the maxilla the inferior part and the zygoma the lateral part.

92 C: Is more effective than chlorhexidine against spores and fungi

Iodine solutions have a very broad-spectrum disinfecting activity, especially when compared with chlorhexidine. Unfortunately, iodine is easily deactivated when in contact with organic solutions such as bodily fluids. Chlorhexidine is less irritating to the skin and has a longer duration of action than iodine.

93 B: Radiotherapy alone

The majority of laryngeal cancers are squamous cell carcinomas. Staging and management is dependant on the location and extent of the tumour. In this case the tumour is limited to the vocal cord and there is no evidence of spread, making it a T1 tumour. This can be treated by either radiotherapy or endoscopic resection. In the case of this woman, who is a singer, radiotherapy is the preferred option as there is less risk of vocal cord damage.

94 D: Thicker wall of the ileum

	Jejunum	**Ileum**
Position	Upper left abdomen	Lower right abdomen
Extent	2/5	3/5
External feel and appearance	Thick, wide, vascular	Thin, narrow, pale
Peyer's patches	Few	Many
Vascular arcades	Few	Many
Vasa recti	Long	Short
Mesenteric fat	Less	More

95 C: Currents as high as 500 mA can be passed through the body at frequencies of 5 mHz

Monopolar diathermy uses a very-high-frequency alternating current at high voltages to cut and coagulate tissue using the patient as a circuit, where the active end acts as a current density channel. Cutting is accomplished by a continuous wave output of current whereas coagulation uses a pulsed output to help cool tissues while heating them and results in a coagulum rather than complete destruction.

96 B: The inferior thyroid artery is a branch of the external carotid artery

The thyroid is made up of two lobes connected by an isthmus that overlies the second and third tracheal rings. Occasionally there may be a pyramidal lobe. It obtains its blood supply from the superior thyroid artery (branch of the external carotid), which supplies the upper pole and the inferior thyroid artery (branch of the thyrocervical trunk of the subclavian artery), which supplies the lower pole and posterior part. In approximately 10% of the population there is an additional artery, the thyroid ima artery (arising from the arch of the aorta or brachiocephalic artery), which supplies the isthmus. It is drained by three veins: superior thyroid vein draining the upper pole, middle thyroid vein draining the lateral aspects and inferior thyroid vein draining the lower pole. Whereas the superior and middle veins drain into the internal jugular vein, the inferior thyroid veins drain into the brachiocephalic veins.

97 B: Intravenous lines may be placed in burnt skin provided no other site is accessible and good venous access is obtained

The priority in the management of burns is to remove the source of burns and then systematically resuscitate the victim, starting with airway, breathing and circulation. All burns are painful. Although full-thickness burns may have a central area of painless tissue because of burnt nerves, there is a transition area around the edges from surrounding normal skin and areas of lesser-degree burns, which will be very sensitive. Fluid replacement in burns uses a formula that does not incorporate the degree of burns as a factor, although percentage area burned and body weight are key factors.

98 D: Hypoglycaemia

Re-feeding syndrome occurs when previously malnourished patients are fed with high loads of carbohydrate, resulting in a rapid fall in phosphate, magnesium, potassium, and calcium levels, along with an increasing extracellular volume and subsequent hyponatraemia. Hypoglycaemia is not a key feature of the re-feeding syndrome although may be seen if the insulin response is oversensitive. Initial hyperglycaemia is the norm as a high-carbohydrate diet is given.

99 E: Mixed metabolic acidosis with metabolic alkalosis

It may be difficult to quantify exactly how much aspirin has been overdosed in this clinical scenario, but, a fair number is suspected as the patient is complaining of new-onset tinnitus. It is not unusual for patients to take an overdose and start vomiting a considerable amount. The initial aspirin absorption would result in an anion-gap metabolic acidosis. The resultant vomiting would cause a metabolic alkalosis, leading to the combined picture seen here, despite the blood gas results being fairly normal. Interpretation of blood gas results requires putting the entire clinical picture together. In aspirin overdose, a respiratory alkalosis may also been seen if the patient starts to hyperventilate, which is not uncommon.

100 D: Compensated respiratory acidosis

Most patients post-laparotomy for upper gastrointestinal surgery will have some ventilatory difficulties from the post-operative incision pain. This could result in a respiratory acidosis from hypoventilation, as indicated by the high P_{CO_2} value. A normal pH and high bicarbonate in this instance suggests a compensatory response.

101 A: Uncompensated metabolic acidosis

This diabetic patient has been starving for their procedure in the day-case unit. The blood gas results show a clear metabolic acidosis from the low pH, low bicarbonate, and normal P_{CO_2}. One must assume that this is due to diabetic ketoacidosis, which would result in an anion-gap metabolic acidosis because of the ketones present acting as unmeasured anions.

102 A: Proceed against the parents' wishes to an appendicectomy

An appendicectomy should be carried out if the patient agrees with the treatment and is competent to make that choice. In this case, she takes priority over her parents' wishes. For children under 16, they can consent to treatment if they are deemed competent to understand the procedure, risks and complications.

103 C: Extradural haematoma

Extradural haematomas usually follow a blow to the head in the region of the pterion, which is where the middle meningeal artery runs in the extradural space. This results in rupture of the artery and an extradural bleed. After an initial period of concussion, there is a lucid interval while the haematoma is expanding. At the point when the haematoma can no longer be accommodated, the intracranial pressure rises and coning can occur. Management is by formation of a burr hole to drain the haematoma.

104 D: The gene is located on the long arm of chromosome 5

FAP accounts for <1% of colorectal cancers and is characterised by the development of hundreds to thousands of polyps within the colon and rectum. It is inherited as an autosomal dominant condition, although some cases may arise as a de-novo mutation of the long arm of the chromosome 5 where the gene is located. Cancers develop in the fourth and fifth decades typically and this condition is associated with a 100% lifetime risk of developing cancer. Affected individuals are treated with a prophylactic total or subtotal colectomy.

105 E: C7 – cytolytic activity

Complement functions are as follows:

- **Opsonisation** – C3b
- **Chemotaxis** – C5a and C5, C6, C7
- **Anaphylatoxin** – C3a<C4a<C5a
- **Cytolysis** – C5b6789 complex.

106 E: MEN I – phaeochromocytoma

Multiple endocrine neoplasia (MEN) type I is an uncommon inherited disorder affecting the parathyroid, pituitary and pancreas. Occasionally, adrenal cortical disorders can also occur as part of the syndrome. Phaeochromocytomas are associated with MEN II.

107 C: *Neisseria meningitidis*

The spleen has a significant immune function and so this is therefore impaired following splenectomy. Specifically, there is a lack of splenic macrophages to clear opsonised micro-organisms and this can result in severe post-splenectomy sepsis. This most commonly affects younger patients in the first few months after splenectomy, although can occur several years later. The organisms that cause most concern are the encapsulated organisms such as *Streptococcus pneumoniae, Neisseria meningitidis* and *Haemophilus influenzae* B. People undergoing elective splenectomy should be immunised with the relevant vaccines, preferably at least 20 weeks prior to operation. They should also be started on a prophylactic dose of penicillin V.

108 B: Red pulp forms most of the splenic volume

White pulp consists of central arteries ensheathed by lymphoid nodules and lymphocytes. White pulp contains T lymphocytes located in the immediate the vicinity of the central artery. Most of the antibody synthesis in the spleen occurs in the white pulp. Red pulp forms most of the splenic volume and contains sinusoids, which trap defective red cells.

109 A: G0

The quiescent or G0 phase is the dormant phase of the cell cycle where no cell division takes place, although cells are still capable of undergoing mitosis. It is this phase of the cell cycle that is most resistant to chemotherapeutic agents. Most chemotherapeutic agents produce their lethal effect on cells that are actively replicating. Higher doses of chemotherapeutic agents are required to target cells in this phase of the cycle.

110 D: Use of all-metal instruments and cannula

Capacitance coupling occurs with the use of insulated instruments and combining plastic and metal ports with instruments when laparoscopic surgery is being performed. The combined energy is insulated as the metal–plastic–metal layering acts as a capacitor. Such coupling can be avoided by a high index of suspicion and vigilance over the use of port and instrument combinations. Use of all-similar ports avoids capacitance and coupling.

111 E: α- and β-adrenergic agonist

Dobutamine acts on both α1 and β1 adrenergic receptors as an agonist, although the racemic mixture contains some α1-antagonist activity as well. Dobutamine is used clinically for its β1 activity in increasing cardiac contractility in congestive cardiac failure due to non-ischaemic causes.

112 E: Vitamin B_3 (niacin)

Colonic flora comprise a huge population of both aerobic and anaerobic bacteria. They are involved in:

- Fermentation of indigestible carbohydrates and production of fatty acids that the colonic mucosa can use as an energy source
- Degradation of bilirubin to stercobilin, urobilin and urobilinogen
- Synthesis of vitamins B_1, B_2, B_{12} and vitamin K.

113 A: Both hypoxia and hypercapnia result in constriction of smaller alveolar vessels

Hypoxia and hypercapnia both cause constriction of the smaller alveolar vessel and thus divert blood to areas that are better oxygenated. This is in contrast to peripheral vessels, where the opposite response is seen and hypoxia causes vasodilatation. The ideal area for ventilation and perfusion matching ($V/Q=1$) within the lung occurs about two-thirds of the way up from the base of the lung.

114 B: It increases the GFR by simultaneous dilation of renal afferent arterioles and constriction of efferent arterioles

Atrial natriuretic peptide (ANP) is a 28-amino-acid peptide that is synthesised, stored and released by atrial cells in response to atrial distension, angiotensin II and sympathetic stimulation (β-adrenoceptor-mediated). Elevated levels of ANP are found during hypervolaemic states and congestive heart failure. ANP serves to increase the GFR and inhibit the tubular resorption of Na^+. The end result is an increase in sodium and water excretion.

115 C: Prolapse and haemorrhoidopexy (PPH)

This patient has presented with symptomatic and prolapsing piles. Treatment by injection and banding or conservative management is unlikely to deal ideally with the entire problem. The procedure for prolapse and haemorrhoidopexy (PPH) is the best option from the listed choices in this case. A Delorme procedure is the operation that employs the perineal approach to reduce a full-thickness bowel prolapse and is not indicated.

116 C: Left recurrent laryngeal nerve

The left recurrent laryngeal nerve can be damaged in thoracic surgery as it ascends from the vagus nerve and hooks around the ligamentum arteriosum to carry on cranially and supply the extrinsic muscles of the larynx. Damage to this nerve would result in a unilateral vocal cord palsy and hence hoarseness of voice.

117 C: Release of gastrin from the G cells in response to histamine stimulation

Gastrin is secreted from the G cells in response to ACh stimulation to act on the parietal cells and cause acid release. Histamine is released from the enterochromaffin cells in response to ACh to act directly on the parietal cells like gastrin. The three phases of gastric secretion include cephalic (30%), gastric (65%) and intestinal (5%) phases.

118 B: Pectineus

Pectineus is a medial rotator of the hip joint. It arises from the pectineal line of the pubis and a small area on the superior pubic ramus just below it and attaches to a vertical line below the lesser trochanter of the femur. The nerve supply is from the anterior division of the femoral nerve, although it may occasionally receive a twig from the obturator nerve as well.

119 A: Previous abdominal surgery scar

The commonest cause of small-bowel obstruction is adhesions within the peritoneal cavity. This usually results from previous abdominal surgery. The other causes listed are less common then adhesions and include an inguinal hernia, which may present as a lump in the groin above and medial to the pubic tubercle; or femoral hernia, which lies below and lateral to the pubic tubercle. Circumoral pigmentation is suggestive of Peutz–Jeghers syndrome which may cause an intussusception from hamartomatous polyps in the small bowel. A nodule at the umbilicus in combination with cachexia is suggestive of a Sister Joseph's nodule, which can indicate an internal malignancy.

120 E: Zollinger–Ellison syndrome

Zollinger–Ellison syndrome is caused by a gastrinoma, which results in excessive acid secretion due to high levels of gastrin. A course of PPI will not cure the ulcer as cessation of therapy will result in recurrence. The definitive treatment is by surgical excision of the gastrinoma. All of the other causes listed may be cured by a course of PPI.

121 D: Increase water retention by increasing distal nephron permeability to water

Osmoreceptors stimulate ADH release from the posterior pituitary in response to increases in extracellular fluid osmolality. ADH secretion is also stimulated by a decrease in blood pressure or decreased circulating volume. ADH serves to increase the water permeability in the distal tubule and collecting ducts in addition to increasing the arterial blood pressure by causing peripheral vasoconstriction.

122 D: Suxamethonium

Suxamethonium is an example of a depolarising muscle relaxant. It has a structure similar to acetylcholine, and acts in a similar way at the neuromuscular junction. Non-depolarising agents include gallamine and vecuronium, which have a slower onset but longer duration of action. Neostigmine is an agent used to reverse non-depolarising neuromuscular blockade. Propofol is an induction agent.

123 C: It is most commonly caused by atherosclerosis in younger patients

Renal artery stenosis is usually caused by a fibromuscular hyperplasia of the renal arteries rather than atherosclerosis in younger patients. Treatment options include surgery or dilation and stenting under angiographic control.

124 C: Urgent theatre for testicular exploration

This case presentation is highly suggestive of a testicular torsion. With the limited time in which to prevent testicular infarction, the management in this case without a doubt is urgent exploration of the testes in the operating theatre. Any investigation would delay the diagnosis and possibly lead to an unviable testis at surgery. Ideally these cases should be operated on as soon as possible but most definitely within 6 hours of onset. After this time irreversible changes can occur, and an orchidectomy should also be considered as a likely possibility.

125 D: Urethral catheterisation

Urethral strictures can be managed with urethral catheterisation. However, this is not a definitive treatment.

126 D: Quadrate lobe of the liver

Boundaries of the epiploic foramen of Winslow include:

- Anteriorly – free edge of the lesser omentum containing the porta hepatis
- Posteriorly – IVC
- Superiorly – caudate process of liver
- Inferiorly – first part of duodenum.

127 D: Posterior rectus sheath

The Pfannenstiel incision is a low-lying transverse incision commonly used in open gynaecological and obstetric procedures. Although the initial skin incision is transverse, the rectus muscle is opened vertically in the line of the linea alba. The skin and two layers of subcutaneous tissue (Camper's and Scarpa's fasciae) are incised as well as the linea alba and its overlying anterior rectus sheath to which it is fused. The peritoneum is the next encountered layer as the posterior rectus sheath is deficient below the level of the arcuate line, located roughly halfway between the pubis and umbilicus.

128 C: Fourth part of the duodenum

A standard right hemicolectomy can endanger the right ureter, right gonadal artery and vein and the second part of the duodenum. When this is made into an extended right hemicolectomy, the spleen can also be damaged as part of the mobilisation. The fourth part of the duodenum is relatively safe in this procedure as it lies near the ligament of Treitz.

129 B: Suprascapular nerve

Suprascapular nerve injury is a rare clinical syndrome, but may arise in volleyball players and those undergoing radical neck dissection for malignancy. The supraspinatus and infraspinatus muscles are affected and initiation of abduction is weakened.

130 B: 10

The **Glasgow coma scale** is a system used to record and monitor a patient's level of consciousness. There are a total of 15 points based on three categories:

- **Best motor response** (6 = obeys commands; 5 = localises to pain; 4 = withdraws from pain; 3 = abnormal flexion; 2 = abnormal extension; 1 = none)
- **Best verbal response** (5 = orientated; 4 = confused; 3 = inappropriate speech; 2 = incomprehensible sounds; 1 = none)
- **Best eye opening response** (4 = open spontaneously; 3 = open to speech; 2 = open to painful stimulus ; 1 = none).

A GCS of 8 is an important score as it is at this point that you consider a patient for intubation as they are unlikely to be able to protect their own airway.

131 D: Adductor pollicis

Adductor pollicis muscle is supplied by the ulnar nerve as well as most intrinsic muscles of the hand. Within the hand, the median nerve supplies the LOAF muscles, which include: lateral two lumbricals, opponens pollicis, abductor pollicis brevis and flexor pollicis brevis.

132 E: The trachea is lined by stratified squamous, non-keratinising epithelium

The trachea is lined by ciliated columnar epithelium and commences at the level of the cricoid cartilage (C6) and ends at the carina (T4/5), which is also the level of the second costal cartilage extending into the second rib.

133 C: Medial meniscus

Meniscal injuries classically arise when a large force is applied to the knee in a semi-flexed position. The medial cartilage is more commonly damaged than the lateral one due to anatomical factors of size, location and mobility. Cruciate injuries result from hyperextension of the knee and result in instability rather than locking (as found in meniscal tears).

134 D: HbF production is increased with the administration of erythropoietin (Epo)

Fetal haemoglobin (HbF), is made up of two α globin chains and two γ globin chains. This difference in globin structure makes HbF unable to react with 2,3-DPG and so it has a higher affinity for oxygen for a given Po_2. This ensures that oxygen is transferred from the maternal blood to the fetal blood, regardless of the Po_2 in the maternal blood. In comparison with the dissociation curve of adult haemoglobin, that of HbF is shifted to the left. It is also found in higher proportions in the blood of those individuals affected with sickle cell anaemia or thalassaemia such as in Arabian or African populations.

135 D: Tendon of obturator internus

The tendon of obturator internus and its corresponding nerve pass through the lesser sciatic foramen as well as the pudendal nerve and internal pudendal vessels. The other structures listed all pass through the greater sciatic foramen only.

PRACTICE PAPER 4: QUESTIONS

PRACTICE PAPER 4: QUESTIONS

1 Regarding the anatomy of the rectum:

- A The rectum begins after the termination of the sigmoid colon at the level of L5
- B The superior rectal artery is a branch of the internal iliac artery
- C The inferior rectal artery, which supplies the rectum, is a branch of the internal pudendal artery
- C The rectum has a mesentery
- E Lymphatic drainage is to the deep inguinal lymph nodes

2 You are assisting your consultant in performing an emergency Hartmann's procedure. Your consultant is operating in difficult territory as there is considerable inflammation following the perforation of a diverticulum and the anatomical planes are obscured. Great care is taken to prevent damage to structures surrounding the sigmoid colon. All of the following structures are at risk in this sigmoid colectomy, EXCEPT:

- A Left ureter
- B Hypogastric nerve plexus
- C Small bowel
- D Gonadal vessels
- E Superior mesenteric artery

3 The ovaries:

- A Are attached to the anterior aspect of the broad ligament
- B Receive their arterial supply from the aorta
- C Drain to the superficial inguinal nodes
- D Are not normally seen on ultrasound examination
- E Drain into the internal iliac veins

4 The following statements are true of gastric carcinoma in the UK, EXCEPT:

- A It is commoner in lower social classes
- B The site of cancer within the stomach moves more proximally with time
- C It is twice as common in men than in women
- D It is rising in incidence
- E It is found most commonly in people with blood group A

5 A 68-year-old man presents with a rectal tumour palpable at approximately 10 cm from the anal verge. CT confirms this and the biopsy shows it to be a rectal adenocarcinoma. The BEST surgical option would be:

- A A sigmoid colectomy
- B An abdominoperineal excision
- C An anterior resection
- D A left hemicolectomy
- E A subtotal colectomy

6 **All of the following structures are contained within the broad ligament, EXCEPT:**

- A Round ligament of the ovary
- B The ovarian artery
- C Round ligament of the uterus
- D The uterine artery
- E The ureters

7 **All of the following can be seen in the fasting state, EXCEPT:**

- A Enhanced ketogenesis in the liver
- B Enhanced lipolysis in adipose tissue
- C Stimulation of gluconeogenesis in the liver
- D Decreased pancreatic insulin output
- E Stimulation of gluconeogenesis in muscle via glucose-6-phosphate

8 **You have been asked to prescribe a course of erythromycin for a patient in order to improve the gut motility rather than as an antibiotic. Erythromycin-associated increases in gut motility are due to stimulation of which one of the following classes of receptors?**

- A Gastrin
- B Cholecystokinin
- C Secretin
- D Motilin
- E Enteroglucagon

9 Right-sided tumours of the large bowel present more frequently with which of the following characteristics when compared to left-sided tumours?

- A Large-bowel obstruction
- B Small-bowel obstruction
- C Blood mixed in with stools
- D Change in bowel habit
- E Iron deficiency anaemia

10 The following are all components of the Glasgow prognostic criteria in assessing an attack of acute pancreatitis, EXCEPT:

- A White cell count
- B Age
- C Serum albumin levels
- D Serum amylase levels
- E Serum glucose levels

11 Which one of the following statements is true regarding control of pancreatic exocrine secretion?

- A Secretion is inhibited by acetylcholine
- B Secretion is stimulated by dopamine
- C Secretion is inhibited by gastrin
- D Secretion is inhibited by cholecystokinin (CCK)
- E Secretion is stimulated by secretin

12 The glomerular filtration rate (GFR):

- A Increases in exercise
- B Decreases significantly in pregnancy
- C Decreases in the erect position
- D Is independent of the temperature of the surrounding environment
- E Does not change if the arterial blood pressure falls below 60 mmHg

13 A 23-year-old man presents to the Emergency Department with a 2-hour history of severe right abdominal colicky pain which radiates from the loin to the groin and is associated with microscopic haematuria on urine dipstick testing. A KUB study confirms your diagnosis of a right renal calculus lodged in the ureter. Which of the following statements is true with regard to renal calculi?

- A Phosphate stones are infection-induced
- B Hyperparathyrodism accounts for >50% of calcium-containing stones
- C A low calcium diet is important in preventing renal stone recurrence
- D Mixed calcium phosphate and calcium oxalate is the most common type of calcium-containing stone
- E Approximately 70% of people with calcium stones have hyperuricosuria

14 Which of the following micro-organisms is correctly paired with its description?

- A *Clostridium difficile* – Gram-negative cocci – aerobic
- B *Streptococcus faecalis* – Gram-positive cocci – aerobic
- C *Bacillus* species – Gram-negative bacilli – aerobic
- D *Actinomyces israelii* – Gram-positive bacilli – aerobic
- E *Escherichia coli* – Gram-negative bacilli – anaerobic

15 A 56-year-old man, who has recently had surgery for large-bowel obstruction secondary to a pelvic mass, has had an erect CXR brought to your attention. His surgery was 3 days ago and he now appears to have an ileus but is comfortable. Free air is apparent under his diaphragm. His abdomen is distended and he is tender in the midline. The free air is likely to be due to:

- A Perforated bowel
- B A normal finding 3 days post-laparotomy
- C An anastomotic breakdown
- D A diaphragmatic injury
- E Perforated ulcer

16 The following are criteria for consideration of dialysis, EXCEPT:

- A Intractable hyperkalaemia
- B Severe metabolic acidosis
- C Uraemic symptoms
- D Profuse pulmonary oedema
- E A high creatinine clearance

17 **A 31-year-old victim of a car crash is brought into the Emergency Department. It was noted that he complained of abdominal pain prior to collapsing into an unconscious state in the ambulance. He is haemodynamically unstable and as the FAST scanner is unavailable, a diagnostic peritoneal lavage (DPL) is performed. All of the following findings in the lavage fluid would result in a positive DPL test, EXCEPT:**

- A Positive Gram stain for bacteria
- B Red cells >50 000/mm^3
- C White cells >500/mm^3
- D Presence of food fibres
- E Presence of faeces

18 **A 53-year-old woman who has had a previous hysterectomy for benign disease presents with sudden-onset central colicky abdominal pain, nausea and vomiting and abdominal distension. She opened her bowels yesterday with the passage of flatus and a small volume of liquid brown stool. Erect CXR shows no free intraperitoenal air and the abdominal X-ray (AXR) is unremarkable, with some air seen in the rectum. Blood tests are unremarkable except for an amylase level of 356 IU/l. What is the most likely diagnosis?**

- A Small-bowel obstruction
- B Gallstone ileus
- C Gastroenteritis
- D Perforation of a peptic ulcer
- E Pancreatitis

19 Colonoscopy is indicated in all of the following people, EXCEPT:

- A A young brother of a patient with familial adenomatous polyposis (FAP)
- B A 52-year-old woman with unexplained iron deficiency anaemia
- C A 65-year-old patient with fresh PR bleeding from piles
- D A 45-year-old asymptomatic patient following removal of a hyperplastic polyp 1 year ago
- E A patient with curative resection of a caecal tumour by right hemicolectomy 2 years previously

20 Advantages of the use of bipolar diathermy over monopolar include all of the following during surgery, EXCEPT:

- A Lack of pacemaker interference
- B Not using the patient as part of an electrical circuit
- C Avoidance of patient plate burns
- D Avoidance of injuries from current channelling
- E Ability to cut as well as coagulate

21 **A 55-year-old patient is booked in to have a laparoscopic cholecystectomy. While discussing complications during the consent procedure you mention that there is a small chance of converting the procedure to an open one. In comparing laparoscopic cholecystectomy with open cholecystecomy, patients who undergo the laparoscopic approach have:**

- A Decreased rates of common bile duct (CBD) injuries
- B Longer hospital stay
- C Decreased vital capacity
- D Decreased serum catecholamines
- E Increased rate of post-operative pain

22 **A 57-year-old female patient received a living donor kidney from her brother 6 weeks ago. The kidney had good function and the serum creatinine was 97 μmol/l when she attended the day-case surgery unit to have her ureteric stent removed by means of a flexible cystoscope. A week after that her serum creatinine had increased to 356 μmol/l when she attended the follow-up clinic. Which of the following investigations will suggest the diagnosis?**

- A A kidney biopsy to confirm or exclude acute rejection
- B Angiography of the transplant renal artery to confirm or exclude renal artery stenosis
- C Send a sample of urine for culture and sensitivity
- D An urgent Doppler ultrasound scan
- E Initiate a pyrexia of unknown origin (PUO) screen

23 A 45-year-old woman had a cadaver kidney transplant 8 hours ago. She initially had good urine output, passing about 150–200 ml of urine per hour. She was anuric before the transplant. Approximately 30 minutes ago the urine output seemed to stop suddenly. What is the first thing you would do to manage the situation?

- A Phone and inform the consultant
- B Check the bladder catheter to make sure that it is not blocked by a thrombus
- C Request an urgent isotope scan to exclude renal artery thrombosis
- D Request an urgent Doppler ultrasound scan to exclude renovascular problems
- E Arrange for an urgent re-exploration of the transplant

24 A common complication following laparoscopic cholecystectomy is:

- A Bowel perforation
- B Capacitance coupling
- C Common bile duct injury
- D Shoulder-tip pain
- E Ileus

25 Which statement is true regarding the compartments of the lower leg?

- A The nerve within the anterior compartment is the deep peroneal nerve
- B Flexor hallucis longus lies within the anterior compartment
- C The posterior compartment is divided into deep and superficial parts by the interosseous membrane
- D Soleus is within the deep posterior compartment
- E The tibial nerve runs through the lateral compartment

26 A 57-year-old man who has been having peritoneal dialysis presented with severe abdominal pain with signs of peritonism. He has never had this problem before. Which of the following scenarios and actions best fits the current clinical situation?

- A He has a perforated hollow viscus and needs urgent laparotomy
- B He has peritonitis as a consequence of his peritoneal dialysis; the dialysis catheter needs to be removed urgently
- C The patient has peritonitis; a sample of the dialysate should be sent for culture and sensitivity and the patient should be started on first-line antibiotic therapy (eg intraperitoneal vancomycin)
- D The patient needs to have a CT scan to look for signs of bowel perforation
- E The patient needs reassurance and should be sent home for bedrest

27 A 23-year-old professional body-builder complains of localised pain in a swollen lower calf and plantar-flexion of right foot is found to be very weak. Which one of the following tendons has been injured in this case?

- A Tibialis anterior
- B Peroneus tertius
- C Calcaneal tendon
- D Flexor hallucis longus
- E Flexor digitorum longus

28 A cricket player feels a 'pop' in his calf as he is playing. His calf becomes tender and swollen. On examination, his doctor tells him that he has ruptured a tendon of a muscle that attaches to the calcaneus. Which one of the following is the tendon most likely to be injured?

- A Soleus
- B Plantaris
- C Gastrocnemius
- D Popliteus
- E Tibialis posterior

29 All of the following are recognised clinical features of Horner syndrome, EXCEPT:

- A Ptosis
- B Enophthalmos
- C Miosis
- D Unilateral anhidrosis
- E Argyll Robertson pupil

30 A 62-year-old man presents to the hospital with large-bowel obstruction. You decide to take this patient to the operating theatre after appropriate investigations and resuscitation. During laparotomy, a tumour is found in the transverse colon. Appropriate further management of this patient during surgery will include:

- A Transverse colectomy with defunctioning loop ileostomy
- B Transverse loop colostomy
- C Extended right hemicolectomy with defunctioning loop ileostomy
- D End-ileostomy
- E Left hemicolectomy with defunctioning loop ileostomy

31 A 27-year-old woman is undergoing a renal transplant from a cadaveric donor. Within minutes of the renal vessels being anastamosed, the kidney turns blue and becomes flaccid in nature. You diagnose hyperacute rejection on the basis that the histology shows deposition of immunoglobulins, complement and neutrophils in the vessel walls. The immunological basis for this type of rejection is based on:

- A Preformed donor antibodies directed against the host antigens
- B Preformed host antibodies directed against the donor antigens
- C Donor cytotoxic T lymphocytes directed against host antigens
- D Donor natural killer (NK) cells directed against host antigens
- E Host NK cells directed against donor antigens

32 During a posterior approach to the hip, you note that great care is taken to ensure that the sciatic nerve is not damaged. The following are all correct statements with regard to the sciatic nerve, EXCEPT:

- A Usually emerges from the greater sciatic foramen inferior to piriformis
- B Arises from the nerve roots L2–S1
- C Sciatic nerve injury results in weakness of knee flexion
- D The nerve usually divides into its two components at the superior border of the popliteal fossa
- E Runs in the same line as the posterior femoral cutaneous nerve

33 You arrange to take blood from a patient via a femoral stab. At which site could one expect to enter the femoral vein with a percutaneous needle?

- A Above the middle of the inguinal ligament
- B Lateral to the femoral arterial pulse
- C Medial to the pubic tubercle
- D Lateral to the pubic tubercle
- E Medial to the femoral arterial pulse

34 A Duke of Edinburgh expedition member experienced 'fallen arches' after walking long distances in unsupported shoes. The ligament that normally supports the inferior aspect of the head of the talus and which is primarily responsible for holding up the medial arch of the foot is the:

- A Spring ligament
- B Peroneus longus ligament
- C Deltoid ligament
- D Short plantar ligament
- E Long plantar ligament

35 A 49-year-old woman presents to the Emergency Department with severe left-sided abdominal pain, which becomes generalised, with fever. CT scan confirms perforated diverticulum, and she is prepared for theatre. Which of the following descriptions best describes the type of wound created by the required operation?

- A Clean wound
- B Clean-contaminated wound
- C Contaminated wound
- D Dirty wound
- E None of the above

36 A 31-year-old woman presents to you with recurrent abdominal pain and frequent bloody diarrhoea. You suspect inflammatory bowel disease and arrange for a colonoscopy with biopsy. Which one of the following features on biopsy would suggest ulcerative colitis rather than a diagnosis of Crohn's disease

- A Skip lesions
- B Rose-thorn ulceration
- C Presence of granulomas
- D Transmural (full-thickness) involvement
- E Presence of crypt abscesses

37 Which of the following structures located behind the medial malleolus lies most anteriorly?

- A Posterior tibial artery
- B Tibial nerve
- C Tendon of flexor hallucis longus
- D Tendon of flexor digitorum longus
- E Tendon of tibialis posterior

38 The following statements are true for squamous cell carcinoma (SCC) of the skin, EXCEPT:

- A Xeroderma pigmentosum is a recognised risk factor
- B SCC occurs in sun-exposed areas
- C SCC is called a Marjolin's ulcer when it occurs in chronic ulcers
- D Metastases are more common in SCC than in basal cell carcinoma
- E Psoralens appear to have a protective effect

39 All of the following may found as part of the MEN I (multiple endocrine neoplasia) syndrome, EXCEPT:

- A Gastrinoma
- B Adrenal cortical adenoma
- C Parathyroid hyperplasia
- D Pituitary adenoma
- E Phaeochromocytoma

40 A 20-year-old woman presents to the Breast Clinic with a firm painful 2 cm lump in the upper outer quadrant of the right breast. The lump is well-defined and extremely mobile. Your next step in managing this patient will be to:

- A Reassure and discharge if mammography is normal
- B Observe in outpatient clinics and further investigate if there are any changes
- C Perform an excision biopsy without the need for ultrasound
- D Perform an ultrasound and excision biopsy without fine-needle aspiration (FNA)
- E Perform an ultrasound and FNA

41 Which statement is true regarding the axilla?

- A Pectoralis major forms the posterior wall
- B Latissimus dorsi forms the lateral wall
- C The apex is bounded by the first rib, clavicle and scapula
- D Serratus anterior contributes to forming the posterior wall
- E The floor of the axilla is formed by the clavipectoral fascia

42 In the healthy full-term neonate, meconium should normally be passed:

- A Within 12 hours of birth
- B Within 24 hours of birth
- C Within 36 hours of birth
- D Within 48 hours of birth
- E Within the first 5 days

43 The most common cause of childhood subglottic stenosis is:

- A Congenital subglottic stenosis
- B Gastro-oesophageal reflux
- C Previous endotracheal tube intubation
- D Previous tracheostomy
- E Croup

44 Which of the following statements about the relations of the kidney and adrenal glands is FALSE?

- A The duodenum overlies the hilum of the right kidney
- B The adrenals lie within the renal fascia
- C The small intestine overlies the inferior pole of both kidneys
- D The hila of both kidneys lie at the approximate level of L3
- E There are five segmental branches from each renal artery

45 All of the following statements regarding FAP are true, EXCEPT:

- A Inheritance is autosomal dominant
- B The gene for FAP is carried on the short arm of chromosome 9
- C There is an association with congenital hypertrophy of the retinal pigment epithelium
- D All patients will eventually require a colectomy
- E Oesophagogastroduodenoscopy and sigmoidoscopy are always necessary in the post-operative surveillance period

46 Autologous blood transfusion is contraindicated in all of the following conditions, EXCEPT:

- A Hepatitis B
- B Severe hypertension
- C Steroid use
- D Unstable angina
- E Aortic stenosis

47 Which of the following are acceptable indications for performing an emergency room thoracotomy following chest trauma?

- A Haemothorax with an initial drainage of 1 l blood on chest tube drainage
- B Continuing haemothorax of at least 100 ml/hour on chest tube drainage
- C Presence of pulseless electrical activity following penetrating chest trauma
- D Asystole following blunt chest trauma
- E Worsening cardiac tamponade regardless of the nature of trauma

48 Overwhelming post-splenectomy sepsis is most commonly due to which of the following organisms?

- A *Escherichia coli*
- B *Neisseria meningitidis*
- C *Streptococcus pneumoniae*
- D *Haemophilus influenzae*
- E *Staphylococcus aureus*

49 **Which of the following thyroid malignancies occurs most frequently?**

- A Papillary carcinoma
- B Follicular carcinoma
- C Medullary carcinoma
- D Anaplastic carcinoma
- E Thyroid lymphoma

50 **Which one of the following statements about the abdominal aorta and its branches is TRUE?**

- A The inferior mesenteric artery lies at the level of L2
- B The gonadal arteries arise beneath the renal arteries
- C The common iliac artery divides into three branches
- D The median sacral artery arises at L3
- E There are five lumbar arteries

51 **All of the following are advantages of laparoscopic over open surgery, EXCEPT:**

- A Reduced hospital stay
- B Reduced operating time
- C Earlier return to work
- D Improved cosmesis
- E Shorter recovery time

52 Donated blood is routinely screened for all of the following infections, EXCEPT:

- A Hepatitis B
- B Hepatitis C
- C HIV 2
- D Syphilis
- E Cytomegalovirus (CMV)

53 All of the following cause a shift of the oxygen dissociation curve to the right, EXCEPT:

- A Increased temperature
- B Increased pH
- C Increased 2,3-DPG
- D Increased P_{CO_2}
- E Lack of local tissue perfusion

54 Select the one suture type that is not paired with its appropriate description:

- A Polypropylene (Prolene) – non-absorbable, synthetic, monofilament
- B Silk – non-absorbable, natural, multifilament
- C Polyester – absorbable, synthetic, multifilament
- D Polyglecaprine (PDS) – absorbable, synthetic, monofilament
- E Polyglactin (Vicryl) – absorbable, synthetic, multifilament

55 All of the following are prerequisites for screening tests to be valid, EXCEPT:

- A Natural history of the disease being screened for must be understood
- B Results must always be audited
- C Results of screening must always result in reduced morbidity and mortality
- D Test must also be used to detect early recurrence as well as primary pathology
- E Facilities for treatment MUST be made available

56 A 25-year-old girl is diagnosed with Cushing's disease secondary to an ACTH-secreting pituitary adenoma. Which of the following biochemical abnormalities would be expected on a blood test?

- A Hyponatraemia
- B Hypokalaemia
- C Hypoglycaemia
- D Hyperchloraemia
- E Hypocalcaemia

57 Which of the following electrolyte values is correctly associated with its intravenous fluid solutions?

- A 0.9% normal saline – Na^+ 147 mmol/l
- B 0.18% dextrose saline – Na^+ 25 mmol/l
- C Ringer's lactate – Na^+ 131 mmol/l
- D Hartmann's solution – Na^+ 131 mmol/l
- E 1.8% hypertonic saline – Na^+ 256 mmol/l

58 A 70-kg man (blood volume 5 litres) is involved in a road traffic accident and fractures his femur. On arrival at hospital he is confused and tachycardic at 130 bpm. Other measurements are BP 80/40 mmHg, respiratory rate 34 breaths/min, urine output 5 ml/hour. The most probable amount of blood loss is:

- A 750 ml
- B 1200 ml
- C 2500 ml
- D 500 ml
- E 1750 ml

59 Orchidopexy for undescended testes should be performed in children at which age?

- A Immediately at diagnosis
- B Between 3 and 6 months of age
- C Between 6 and 12 months of age
- D Between 12 and 15 months of age
- E Any time before the onset of puberty

60 The following physiological changes are seen in response to cardiogenic shock, EXCEPT:

- A Elevated JVP
- B Hypotension
- C Cool peripheries
- D Presence of a third heart sound
- E Decrease of the pulmonary capillary wedge pressure (PCWP)

61 All of the following are components of the Revised Trauma Scoring System, EXCEPT:

- A Heart rate
- B Respiratory rate
- C Systolic BP
- D Best verbal response to pain
- E Best motor response to pain

62 Which of the following is NOT a risk factor for breast cancer?

- A Affected sister
- B Li–Fraumeni syndrome
- C Multiparity
- D Obesity
- E Early menarche

63 The following are causes of metabolic acidosis with an increased anion gap, EXCEPT:

- A Rhabdomyolysis
- B Renal tubular acidosis
- C Chronic diarrhoea
- D Diabetic ketoacidosis
- E Salicylate overdose

64 The following are all risk factors for vascular disease, EXCEPT:

- A Homocystinaemia
- B Consumption of hard water
- C Familial dysbetalipoproteinaemia
- D Cigar smoking
- E Impaired glucose tolerance

65 An 18-year-old victim of a road traffic accident is brought into the Emergency Department unconscious. She makes incomprehensible sounds and opens her eyes to pain. On further examination, her right arm extends when a painful stimulus is applied; her left arm localises to the area of discomfort. Her GCS score is:

- A 8
- B 9
- C 10
- D 11
- E 12

66 **The diaphragm develops in utero with contributions from all of the following structures, EXCEPT the:**

- A Dorsal oesophageal mesentery
- B Peripheral rim derived from the body wall
- C Septum transversum
- D Vertebromuscular ridges
- E Pleuroperitoneal membranes

67 **A woman presents with a green discharge from her nipple. The most likely diagnosis is**

- A Carcinoma of the breast
- B Lactating breast
- C Duct ectasia
- D Breast abscess
- E Duct papilloma

68 **Which one of the following is an absolute contraindication to performing laparoscopic surgery?**

- A Pregnancy
- B BMI >40 kg/m^2
- C Previous abdominal surgery
- D Symptomatic chronic obstructive pulmonary disease
- E Presence of an uncorrected coagulopathy

69 The manubriosternal angle (angle of Louis) is the anatomical landmark of all of the following, EXCEPT:

- A Thoracic level T4
- B The level of the second rib and costal cartilage
- C The level of the tracheal bifurcation (carina)
- D The level of the commencement of the arch of the aorta
- E The level of the T4 dermatome

70 In a study of heavy alcohol drinkers and chronic pancreatitis, the odds ratio is stated to be 0.2 (odds of having pancreatitis in those who drink heavily). This means that:

- A For every five heavy drinkers, one will have chronic pancreatitis
- B For every five patients with pancreatitis, one will be a heavy alcohol drinker
- C For every six heavy drinkers, one will have chronic pancreatitis
- D For every six patients with pancreatitis, one will be a heavy alcohol drinker
- E It is difficult to draw a conclusion and more data are needed

71 Which of the following is an appropriate clearance margin for removal of a squamous cell carcinoma of the skin?

- A 1–2 cm
- B 5 cm
- C 0.5 cm
- D 3–4 cm
- E 2 mm

72 **Psammoma bodies are typically found in which of the following thyroid cancers?**

- A Papillary
- B Follicular
- C Medullary
- D Anaplastic
- E Lymphoma

73 **Flow within a vessel is directly affected by all of the following factors, EXCEPT:**

- A Radius of the vessel wall
- B Blood haematocrit
- C Length of the vessel
- D Vessel wall tension
- E Cardiac failure

74 **Risk factors for bladder transitional cell carcinoma include all of the following, EXCEPT:**

- A Smoking
- B Cyclophosphamide
- C Pelvic irradiation
- D Exposure to benzidine
- E Exposure to schistosomiasis

75 **A 44-year-old woman undergoes resection of the terminal ileum for treatment of symptomatic Crohn's disease. She is at increased risk of which of the following diseases following surgery?**

- A Appendicitis
- B Gastritis
- C Cholecystitis
- D Hepatitis
- E Pancreatitis

76 **Which of the following associations of hypersensitivity reactions with its corresponding disease is correct?**

- A Type I – allergic contact dermatitis
- B Type II – pernicious anaemia
- C Type III – hyperacute renal graft rejection
- D Type IV – autoimmune haemolytic anaemia
- E Type V – Goodpasture syndrome

77 **Cerebral blood flow is increased in all of the following conditions, EXCEPT during:**

- A Systemic hypocarbia
- B Seizures
- C Systemic hypoxia
- D Chronic anaemia
- E Hypertension

78 **Which one of the following disorders will cause hypercalcaemia?**

- A Hypothyroidism
- B Hyperthyroidism
- C Myositis ossificans
- D Carcinoid syndrome
- E Acute pancreatitis

79 **Absolute contraindications to DPL following major abdominal trauma include which one of the following?**

- A Pregnancy
- B Morbid obesity
- C Evisceration of bowel
- D Abdominal scarring from previous surgery
- E Suspected internal bleeding

80 **All of the following may be found in the transurethral resection (TUR) syndrome, EXCEPT:**

- A Hyponatraemia
- B Tachycardia
- C Confusion
- D Nausea
- E Hyperammonaemia

81 Which one of the following statements is correct regarding the movements of breathing?

- A Expiration is primarily due to active contraction of the internal intercostals
- B Movement of ribs 2–7 is a 'pump handle' type of action, which increases the anterior–posterior diameter of the thorax
- C Movement of ribs 8–12 increases the vertical diameter of the thorax
- D The first rib moves laterally during inspiration
- E Contraction of the diaphragm aids expiration

82 A 50-kg woman sustains full-thickness burns to 40% of her body. Her fluid replacement for the next 8 hours will be:

- A 1600 ml
- B 2800 ml
- C 4000 ml
- D 6600 ml
- E 8000 ml

83 All of the following factors impair wound healing, EXCEPT:

- A Jaundice
- B Hypoglycaemia
- C Poor tissue oxygenation
- D Zinc deficiency
- E Presence of infection

84 A GP calls you for advice regarding an 80-year-old man who has a loud bruit in the right side of his neck. Outpatient Doppler investigations have revealed a 55% stenosis of the internal carotid artery. Appropriate advice on management of this man would include:

- A Antiplatelet agents with lifestyle advice and treatment to control vascular risk factors
- B Urgent referral to a vascular surgeon
- C Elective endarterectomy
- D Elective bypass grafting
- E Observation alone as the patient is asymptomatic

85 A patient requires removal of sebaceous cyst from his scalp under local anaesthesia. Which preparation is most appropriate?

- A Lidocaine and adrenaline 5 mg/kg
- B Prilocaine 2 mg/kg
- C Bupivicaine 6 mg/kg
- D Lidocaine 5 mg/kg
- E Bupivicaine and adrenaline 2 mg/kg

86 A 50-year-old woman complains of a cramping pain in her buttocks, which occurs after walking 50 yards and is relieved by resting. You organise an angiogram to assess the pelvic and lower limb vasculature. Stenosis of which of the following vessels is suspected clinically?

- A Common iliac artery
- B Iliolumbar artery
- C External iliac artery
- D Superficial femoral artery
- E Profunda femoris artery

87 Thoracic outlet syndrome classically presents with all of the following, EXCEPT:

- A Neck and shoulder pain
- B Digital gangrene due to ischaemia
- C Weakened radial pulse on arm elevation
- D Wasting of the thenar eminence
- E Paraesthesia along the ulnar border of the forearm

88 Which of the following statements is FALSE regarding laryngeal carcinoma?

- A Distant metastases are found in 20% of patients at presentation
- B Squamous cell carcinoma of the larynx represents approximately 1% of malignancies in men
- C Hoarseness is the commonest presenting symptom
- D Verrucous carcinoma is a form of squamous cell carcinoma
- E The glottis has virtually no lymphatic drainage

89 A man is involved in a road traffic accident and injures his left leg. Following the injury he finds himself unable to extend the left knee and notices loss of sensation along the medial side of the lower leg up to the big toe. The likely nerve injured is:

- A Sciatic nerve
- B Tibial nerve
- C Femoral nerve
- D Common peroneal nerve
- E Superficial peroneal nerve

90 A 43-year-old man presents to the clinic with a slowly growing, painless firm mass antero-inferior to the left ear. He has no lymph nodes palpable. His facial movements are normal. The most likely diagnosis in this case is:

- A Warthin's tumour
- B Salivary calculi
- C Mumps infection
- D Pleomorphic adenoma
- E Adenoid cystic carcinoma

91 All of the following may be found in cardiac tamponade, EXCEPT:

- A Widened pulse pressure
- B Distended neck veins
- C Hypotension
- D Kussmaul's sign
- E Pulsus paradoxus

92 A 75-year-old man is brought into the Emergency Department with a 1-hour history of sudden-onset severe chest pain radiating to the back, which occurred at rest. He has a history of rheumatoid arthritis, severe asthma and hypertension. The heart rate is 105/min, BP is 170/95 mmHg and CXR shows a widened mediastinum. Appropriate management of this patient includes all of the following, EXCEPT:

- A Insertion of large-bore intravenous lines and fluid resuscitation
- B CT scan of the chest with contrast
- C Initiation of intravenous β blocker therapy
- D Urgent referral to a cardiac surgeon
- E Analgesia and medical management if a type B thoracic aortic dissection is found on investigation

93 A patient is referred to you in clinic with bilateral inguinal hernias. He is otherwise well. You advise:

- A Bilateral open repair
- B Unilateral open repair followed by the smaller hernia repaired at a later date
- C Bilateral laparoscopic repair
- D Watch and wait for now
- E A truss

94 A 33-year-old man presents with a month's history of foul-smelling creamy left ear discharge with some hearing loss and mild otalgia. On examination, there is a dark crusting mass overlying the pars flaccida. Rinne's test is negative on the left, and Weber's localises to the left. The diagnosis is:

- A Otitis externa
- B Cholesteatoma
- C Canal exostoses
- D Suppurative otitis media
- E Glomus jugulare

95 All of the following statements are true of solitary thyroid nodules, EXCEPT:

- A They are more prevalent in women
- B In the adult population, more than 90% are benign
- C They should be surgically removed in all patients
- D Fewer than 20% of cold nodules are malignant
- E The risk of a hot nodule being malignant is very small

96 The following signs may be present in a tension pneumothorax, EXCEPT with:

- A Hyper-resonance to percussion on the affected side
- B Increased elevated jugular venous pressure (JVP) on the opposite side
- C Tracheal shift to the affected side
- D Displaced apex beat
- E Absent breath sounds on the affected side

97 Which one of the following statements about the anatomy of the heart is FALSE?

- A The anterior cardiac veins drain into the right atrium
- B The fossa ovalis may remain patent in 10% of normal subjects
- C The sinus venosus forms part of the ventricular walls
- D The sinoatrial node lies in the upper end of the crista terminalis
- E The aorta is derived from the truncus arteriosus

98 The intercostal neurovascular bundle, which runs in the subcostal groove of the ribs, is located anatomically between which of the following layers?

- A Between skin and subcutaneous tissues
- B Between subcutaneous tissues and the external intercostals
- C Between external intercostals and internal intercostals
- D Between internal intercostals and innermost intercostals
- E Between the innermost intercostals and the pleura

99 Which of the following structures passing through the diaphragm are correctly associated with their corresponding vertebral levels?

- A T8 – oesophagus with vagus nerves
- B T8 – aorta with the thoracic duct
- C T10 – inferior vena cava (IVC) with the right phrenic nerve
- D T10 – oesophagus with vagus nerves
- E T10 – aorta with the thoracic duct

100 Which of the following is NOT used in the management of an impacted food bolus in the oesophagus?

- A Barium swallow
- B Flexible nasendoscopy
- C Buscopan
- D Rigid oesophagoscopy
- E Glucagon

101 Which one of the following statements about the great vessels is TRUE?

- A The left brachiocephalic artery divides to form the left common carotid artery and left subclavian artery
- B The right subclavian vein and right internal jugular vein join to form the right brachiocephalic trunk
- C The left internal jugular vein drains directly into the SVC
- D The right common carotid artery arises directly from the aortic arch
- E The IVC joins the SVC before draining into the right atrium

102 The following arteries are all directly involved in the blood supply to the stomach, EXCEPT:

- A Right gastric artery
- B Left gastric artery
- C Gastroduodenal artery
- D Short gastric arteries
- E Left gastroepiploic artery

103 A man is stabbed in the arm during a fight. On examination, he finds himself unable to extend his wrist, although his elbow movement is intact. The injury is most likely to involve:

- A The radial nerve in the axilla
- B The median nerve as it passes between heads of pronator teres
- C The ulnar nerve as it passes behind the median epicondyle
- D The radial nerve in the spiral groove
- E The median nerve as it arises from the lateral and medial cords of the brachial plexus

104 The following layers are encountered when a standard muscle-splitting Lanz incision is made for appendicectomy, EXCEPT:

- A Camper's fascia
- B External oblique aponeurosis
- C Internal oblique muscle
- D Rectus sheath
- E Transversalis fascia

105 The initial drug of choice in the treatment of acute tonsillitis is:

- A Penicillin V
- B Ampicillin
- C Cefuroxime
- D Erythromycin
- E Metronidazole

106 Which of the following is true of the brachioradialis muscle?

- A It originates from the lateral aspect of the supracondylar ridge of the radius
- B It is the main muscle involved in the supinator reflex
- C It attaches to the ulnar styloid process
- D It is supplied by the deep branch of the radial nerve
- E It often contains a nerve supply from a branch of the musculocutaneous nerve

107 The lateral compartment of the leg is supplied by which of the following nerves?

- A Tibial nerve
- B Common peroneal nerve
- C Lateral popliteal nerve
- D Deep peroneal nerve
- E Superficial peroneal nerve

108 Following pelvic surgery, a patient reports numbness along the medial thigh as well as weakness of hip adduction. Which nerve is most likely to have been injured during the operation?

- A Obturator
- B Femoral
- C Inferior gluteal
- D Superior gluteal
- E Sciatic

109 The afferent limb of the cremaster reflex is provided by which of the following nerves?

- A Genital branch of the genitofemoral nerve
- B Femoral branch of the genitofemoral nerve
- C Pudendal nerve
- D Iliohypogastric nerve
- E Ilio-inguinal nerve

110 A young boy has been stabbed in the right forearm. He now has difficulty in flexing his wrist and pronating the forearm along with loss of sensation over the lateral fingers on the palmar surface. Which of the following nerves has been injured?

- A Deep branch of radial nerve
- B Median nerve
- C Ulnar nerve
- D Superficial branch of radial nerve
- E Median palmar nerve

111 All of the listed vessels contribute to Little's area in epistaxis, EXCEPT:

- A Sphenopalatine artery
- B Superior labial artery
- C Ascending pharyngeal artery
- D Ophthalmic artery
- E Anterior ethmoidal artery

112 The characteristic features of a Colles' fracture include the following, EXCEPT:

- A Dinner fork deformity
- B Radial displacement
- C Occurring within 2.5 cm of wrist joint
- D Subluxation of carpus
- E Angulation in opposite direction to Smith's fracture

113 Which of the following statements about the femoral canal is FALSE?

- A It contains a lymph node called Cloquet's node
- B The femoral nerve lies laterally within the canal
- C The femoral sheath is derived from extraperitoneal, intra-abdominal fascia
- D It serves as a pathway for lower limb lymphatics
- E It is approximately 0.5 cm wide

114 A 37-year-old man presents to the Emergency Department complaining of a painful, swollen and warm knee. There is no history of trauma. He feels unwell and his temperature is 38.5 °C. He is unable to mobilise because of the pain. All of the following are correct steps in the management of this patient in the Emergency Department, EXCEPT:

- A An urgent full blood count with erythrocyte sedimentation rate (ESR) and C-reactive protein (CRP)
- B High-dose intravenous antibiotics
- C Knee X-ray
- D Analgesia
- E Blood cultures

115 Which statement regarding the parotid gland is TRUE?

- A Tumours of the gland can result in sensory loss of the affected side of the face
- B The parotid duct pierces buccinator opposite the second lower molar tooth
- C The retromandibular vein passes through the gland
- D The external carotid artery lies deep to the gland
- E The gland overlies the anterior belly of the digastric muscle

116 The coronary sinus typically receives drainage from all of the following cardiac veins, EXCEPT the:

- A Great cardiac vein
- B Anterior cardiac vein
- C Middle cardiac vein
- D Small cardiac vein
- E Posterior cardiac vein

117 The earliest pathological changes in bone during acute haematogenous osteomyelitis of childhood occur in the:

- A Metaphyseal-physeal junction
- B Diaphysis
- C Metaphyseal-diaphyseal junction
- D Epiphysis
- E Subperiosteal portion of the metaphysis

118 With regard to humeral supracondylar fractures:

- A They most commonly occur in the elderly population
- B The distal fragment is usually tilted forwards
- C They should always be observed in theatre during daylight hours
- D They require vigilant observation for signs of brachial artery damage
- E Reduction is helped by elbow extension with pressure applied behind the olecranon

119 Raised serum amylase may be seen in all of the following conditions, EXCEPT:

- A Perforated duodenal ulcer
- B Parotiditis
- C Ruptured abdominal aortic aneurysm (AAA)
- D Intestinal obstruction
- E Hyperparathyroidism

120 You wish to proceed with organ donation from a patient with a severe spinal cord and head injury and suspected brainstem death. All of the following criteria may be used in the diagnosis of brainstem death following injury, EXCEPT:

- A Absence of the pupillary light reflex
- B Absence of the corneal reflex
- C Absence of the gag and cough reflex
- D Absence of limb spinal reflexes
- E Absence of motor cranial nerve function

121 Complications of massive blood transfusion include all of the following, EXCEPT:

- A Hypothermia
- B Hyperthermia
- C Hyperkalaemia
- D Hypercalcaemia
- E Metabolic acidosis

122 Which of the following statements about the larynx is TRUE?

- A The top of the thyroid cartilage lies at the level of C3
- B The cricoid cartilage is a derivative of the sixth arch
- C All the intrinsic muscles except cricothyroid are supplied by the superior laryngeal nerve
- D The hyoid bone lies at the level of C2
- E The posterior cricoarytenoids close the vocal cords together

123 A 50-year-old man is admitted to the hospital to undergo an anterior resection for carcinoma of the rectum. He has a long history of asthma and has been taking 5 mg prednisolone for the previous 3 months since his last discharge from hospital after an acute attack. Which of the following steroid replacement regimens is ideal in this patient?

- A 50 mg hydrocortisone IV pre-operatively only
- B 50 mg hydrocortisone IV pre-operatively and 6-hourly for the first 24 hours
- C 100 mg hydrocortisone IV pre-operatively and then 50 mg 6-hourly for at least the first 48 hours
- D 100 mg hydrocortisone IV pre-operatively and then 100 mg 6-hourly for at least the first 48 hours
- E 100 mg hydrocortisone IV pre-operatively and then 100 mg 6-hourly for at least the first 72 hours

124 Which statement is true regarding the surface anatomy of the abdomen?

- A The gallbladder lies at the level of the 10th costal cartilage in the midclavicular line
- B The neck of the pancreas lies at L2
- C The superior pole of the kidney lies at the level of the 9th rib posteriorly
- D The transpyloric plane of Addison lies halfway between the suprasternal notch and the iliac crests
- E The spleen lies over the 9th, 10th and 11th ribs posteriorly

125 Evidence-based treatments with proved efficacy in managing ARDS (acute respiratory distress syndrome) include all of the following, EXCEPT:

- A Early steroid administration
- B Prone position ventilation
- C Activated protein C
- D Inverse ratio ventilation
- E Inhaled nitric oxide

126 Breast cancer is more commonly found in women who:

- A Are multiparous
- B Had an early menarche
- C Live in a developing country
- D Had an early menopause
- E Had their first pregnancy at an early age

127 **A 67-year-old woman is admitted to the hospital for a total hip replacement. Her past medical history includes a single myocardial infarction (MI), which occurred 2 years ago, stable angina controlled with tablets, hypertension, insulin-dependent diabetes and a previous renal transplant. Her ASA class is:**

- A ASA 1
- B ASA 2
- C ASA 3
- D ASA 4
- E ASA 5

128 **A 42-year-old man presents to the Emergency Department with a profusely bleeding scalp laceration acquired during a fall. You decide that he needs to have the laceration sutured under local anaesthetic. He has a past history of severe alcoholic cirrhosis and mild asthma. Which one of the following local anaesthetic agents is potentially toxic in this patient?**

- A Cocaine
- B Lidocaine
- C Procaine
- D Benzocaine
- E Tetracaine

129 A 34-year-old woman is admitted to the Neurosurgical Unit with a large subarachnoid haemorrhage following rupture of a berry aneurysm. Appropriate management includes all of the following, EXCEPT:

- A Early mobilisation
- B Intravenous fluid rehydration
- C Cerebral angiography within 24 hours of admission
- D Initiation of nimodipine therapy
- E Surgical clipping of the aneurysm following failed coiling

130 Which one of the following statements about the diaphragm is FALSE?

- A It attaches to the xiphoid
- B The left crus arises from L1–2
- C The left phrenic nerve pierces the diaphragm together with the IVC at the level of T8
- D The aorta pierces the diaphragm at T12
- E It arises from the lower six costal cartilages laterally

131 Which one of the following types of renal stones is radiolucent on kidney, ureter and bladder (KUB) films?

- A Calcium stones
- B Struvite stones
- C Urate stones
- D Cystine stones
- E Oxalate stones

132 All of the following viruses have been directly linked to cancer pathogenesis, EXCEPT:

- A Herpes simplex virus
- B Hepatitis B virus
- C Human papilloma virus
- D Human lymphocyte T cell lymphotropic virus (HTLV–1)
- E Epstein–Barr virus

133 All of the following primary sites metastasise classically with osteolytic lesions, EXCEPT:

- A Kidney
- B Prostate
- C Breast
- D Lung
- E Thyroid

134 Which one the following is correctly a component of the definition of SIRS (systemic inflammatory response syndrome)?

- A Heart rate >100/min
- B Temperature <35 °C or >38 °C
- C Respiratory rate >25/min
- D Partial pressure of carbon dioxide (P_{CO_2}) <4.3 kPa
- E White cell count (WCC) >4×10^9/l or or >11×10^9/l or >10% immature forms

135 Which one of the following features of bowel ischaemia suggests a high mortality?

- A Haemorrhagic free fluid at laparoscopy
- B Low oxygen saturation on blood gas analysis
- C Presence of atrial fibrillation
- D Serum lactate >4 mmol/l
- E WCC $>20 \times 10^9$/l

PRACTICE PAPER 4: ANSWERS AND TEACHING NOTES

1
2
3 B
4 D
5 C
6 E
7 E
8 D
9 E
10 D
11 C ? X
12 B ? X
13 A ?
14 C ? X
15 B
16 E ?
17 E ? X
18 A
19 D
20 A X
21 D ?
22 A X
23 B
24 B ? X
25 A
26 D X
27 E
28 C X
29 E
30 C
31 B ?

32 B
33 E
34 E ? X
35 C ? X
36 C ? X
37 C ? X
38 E
39 B X
40 E X
41 D ? X
42 B ?
43 E ? X
44 D
45 E ? X
46 D ? X
47 D ? X
48 C
49 A
50 B
51 B ?
52 E
53 B ?
54 E X
55 D ?
56 B E
57 C X
58 E
59 D
60 D ? X
61 D ? X
62 D X
63 C ?
64 B
65 10 X

66 B ? X
67 C ?
68 E
69 E
70 A ? X
71 A
72 A
73 C X
74 B — X
75 B X
76 A ? C X
77 B ? X
78 B
79 C
80 E X
81 E ? X
82 C
83 B
84 A
85 D ? X
86 A
87 E X
88 B X
89 C
90 D
91 A ?
92 D ? X
93 A ? X
94 B ?
95 C
96 C

97 D ? X
98 D ?
99 D
100 A ?
101 B
102 E X
103 D
104 D
105 D X
106 E X
107 E
108 A
109 B ?
110 B
111 E ? X
112 E X
113 BA
114 B
115 B X
116 D X
117 C ? X
118 D
119 E ?
120 E ? X
121 D
122 D ? X
123 E ?
124 E ?
125 D ? X
126 B
127 E
128 A X
129 C X
130 C ?

131 C
132 A
133 B
134 D ?
135 C X
+36
23

PRACTICE PAPER 4: ANSWERS AND TEACHING NOTES

1 C: The inferior rectal artery, which supplies the rectum, is a branch of the internal pudendal artery

The rectum continues on from the sigmoid colon and starts at the level of S3 at the rectosigmoid junction. The rectum is supplied mainly by the superior rectal artery, which is a branch of the inferior mesenteric artery. The other two arteries, the middle and inferior rectal arteries, are branches of the internal iliac artery and the internal pudendal artery respectively. The rectum has no mesentery, although it does have peritoneal covering, which might be referred to as the 'mesorectum'. The lymphatic drainage follows the arterial supply and lymph drains into the inferior mesenteric nodes or the internal iliac nodes.

2 E: Superior mesenteric artery

The other structures are very much at risk during a sigmoid colectomy but the SMA is located some distance from sigmoid colon. The inferior mesenteric artery can be cut or intentionally ligated as necessary.

3 B: Receive their arterial supply from the aorta

The ovaries are attached to the posterior surface if the broad ligament by the mesovarium and are normally seen on ultrasound. The arterial supply is via the ovarian arteries, which arise from the aorta at the level of L1. Venous drainage on the left is to the left renal vein and on the right to the inferior vena cava (IVC). Lymph drainage is to the para-aortic nodes.

4 D: It is rising in incidence

Gastric cancer has declined in incidence over the last century. It is twice as common in men and commoner in lower social classes, Japanese people, and persons with blood group A. Other risk factors include dietary nitrosamines, pernicious anaemia, post-gastrectomy, atrophic gastritis, hypogamma-globulinaemia, and presence of *Helicobacter pylori*. Interestingly, over the last half century, the site of gastric cancer has moved more proximally.

5 C: An anterior resection

Anterior resections are performed for rectal cancers which can be excised adequately with a sufficient anorectal margin distally. For the very distal rectal tumours or anal tumours, an abdominoperineal resection must be undertaken with an end-stoma.

Sigmoid colectomies can be used for treatment of sigmoid tumours or excision of an area of diverticular disease, and left hemicolectomies for left colonic tumours.

6 E: The ureters

The broad ligaments are double folds of peritoneum that extend across the pelvic cavity from the lateral margins of the uterus to the lateral pelvic walls. Within the broad ligaments are contained:

- The round ligaments of the ovaries and uterus
- The ovarian and uterine blood vessels, lymphatics and nerves
- The fallopian tubes in its upper free border on either side.

The ureters pass anteriorly, just under the broad ligament and are not contained within it.

7 E: Stimulation of gluconeogenesis in muscle via glucose-6-phosphate

The **fasting state** serves to maintain energy sources by mobilising reserve energy stores within the body. The physiological changes include changes in the:

- **Liver:**
  - Increased glycogen degradation
  - Increased gluconeogenesis
  - Increased ketogenesis
  - Increased fatty acid oxidation
- **Fat:**
  - Increased lipolysis
  - Increased β oxidation of fatty acids
  - Decreased uptake of lipids
- **Muscle:**
  - Decreased glucose uptake by muscles
  - Uptake of fatty acids and ketone bodies
  - Proteolysis for gluconeogenesis
- **Pancreas:**
  - Decreased insulin secretion
  - Increased glucagon secretion.

8 D: Motilin

Erythromycin belongs to the macrolide group of antibiotics. The macrolides can stimulate motilin-like receptors which serve to initiate the migrating motor complexes within the gastrointestinal tract. There is direct stimulation of smooth muscle as well as excitation of nerves, which increase peristalsis within the gastrointestinal tract.

9 E: Iron deficiency anaemia

Right-sided tumours more frequently present with iron deficiency, as their symptoms may be masked simply by their location within the gastrointestinal tract. An obstructive presentation is less likely than left-sided tumours because the colonic contents are virtually liquid as they enter the ileocaecal junction and hence pass through even tight malignant strictures on the right side. For a similar stenosis on the left side, a faecal bolus may impact and present with obstruction. Also, blood is more noticeable on the stools with left-sided tumours as is a change in bowel habit.

10 D: Serum amylase levels

Glasgow (Imrie) scoring system for acute pancreatitis includes:
one point for each of the following: age >55; WBC >15 × 10^9; glucose >10 mmol/l; urea >16 mmol/l; PaO_2 <8 kPa; calcium <2 mmol/l; albumin <32 g/l; LDH >600 units/l, ALT >100 iu/l. Any score >3 constitutes a severe attack of acute pancreatitis.

11 E: Secretion is stimulated by secretin

Pancreatic exocrine secretion is stimulated by:

- Acetylcholine via vagal innervation
- Cholecystokinin – secreted by intestinal mucosa
- Secretin – secreted by the duodenum and jejunum on passage of an acid food bolus
- Gastrin.

Dopamine is not involved in pancreatic secretion. Pancreatic juice is secreted into the dudodenum via the pancreatic duct, which opens into the gastrointestinal tract at the same site as the common bile duct. It is made up of a number of enzymes, secreted by the acinar cells of the pancreas, including pancreatic amylase (which breaks down carbohydrates to dextrins and polysaccharides), pancreatic lipase (which breaks down neutral fat to glycerol and fatty acids), ribonuclease, deoxyribonuclease (involved in the breakdown of nucleic acids and free mononucleotides) and a variety of proteolytic enzymes (trypsin, chymotrypsin, elastase and carboxypeptidase), which break down proteins into small peptides and amino acids.

Secretion from the exocrine pancreas is regulated by both neural and endocrine controls. Like the stomach, the pancreas is innervated by the vagus nerve, which applies a low-level stimulus to secretion; secretions are scanty and rich in enzymes and are secreted reflexly in the 'cephalic' phase of pancreatic secretion when food is thought about or chewed. However, the most important stimuli for pancreatic secretion come from three hormones secreted by the enteric endocrine system, cholecystokinin, secretin and gastrin.

Cholecystokinin: This hormone is synthesized and secreted by enteric endocrine cells located in the duodenum. Its secretion is strongly stimulated by the presence of partially digested proteins and fats in the small intestine. As chyme floods into the small intestine, CCK is released into the bloodstream by the duodenal cells and is responsible for stimulating secretion of pancreatic enzymes from the pancreatic acinar cells.

Secretin: This hormone is also a product of endocrinocytes located in the epithelium of the proximal small intestine. Secretin is released in response to acid in the duodenum, which occurs when acid-laden chyme from the stomach flows through the pylorus. The predominant effect of secretin on the pancreas is to stimulate duct cells to secrete water and bicarbonate. As soon as this occurs, the enyzmes secreted by the acinar cells are flushed out of the pancreas, through the pancreatic duct into the duodenum.

Gastrin: This hormone, which is very similar to cholecystokinin, is secreted in large amounts by the stomach in response to gastric distension and irritation. In addition to stimulating acid secretion by the parietal cell, gastrin stimulates pancreatic acinar cells to secrete digestive enzymes.

12 C: Decreases in the erect position

The GFR and the pressures within the glomerular capillaries are largely independent of changes in systemic arterial pressure due to autoregulation of blood flow in healthy kidneys. Final urine production is largely controlled by tubular reabsorption of water from the filtrate. Autoregulation is one of the many mechanisms keeping the GFR in check. Sympathetic nerve activity, angiotensin II, antidiuretic hormone (ADH) and natriuretic peptide hormones all play a role in regulating GFR under different physiological conditions. Blood within the efferent glomerular arteriole contains a higher concentration of plasma proteins and red blood cells as there is a loss of plasma volume to form glomerular filtrate.

A rise in oncotic pressure within the glomerular capillaries will lead to an increase in the GFR, but in healthy individuals the oncotic pressure would never rise to this level because of the relatively small amount of filtrate formed in humans. GFR decreases in exercise, as blood is diverted to the exercising muscles. There is a 20% increase in GFR in pregnancy. On standing erect, activation of the sympatho-adrenal system leads to vasoconstriction of the afferent arteriole, which leads to a fall in pressure in the glomerular capillary. A cold environment leads to a fall in the GFR, due to activation of sympatho-adrenal renal vasoconstriction. Glomerular filtration ceases in severe hypotension and anuria will result.

13 A: Phosphate stones are infection-induced

Calcium stones are the most common, comprising 75% of all renal calculi. Calcium oxalate is the most common cause of a calcium-containing stone (50%); calcium phosphate stones comprise 5% of stones. Research has shown no evidence to support the use of a diet low in calcium to prevent recurrence of renal stones. Around 15% of patients with a calcium-containing stone also present with hyperuricosuria. Hyperparathyroidism only accounts for 5–7% of renal calculi. Phosphate stones are found in alkaline urine, especially if it is infected with urea-splitting organisms such as *Proteus* and some staphylococci.

14 B: *Streptococcus faecalis* – Gram-positive cocci – aerobic

Bacteria can be classified in terms of their shape (eg rods or cocci) and the colour they become on Gram-staining (pink = positive, blue = negative). They can also be classified according to whether they are aerobes or anaerobes. In the example, all are incorrectly paired apart from B. The correct descriptions are: *C. difficile* – Gram-positive rod, anaerobic; *Bacillus* species – Gram-positive rod, aerobic; *Actinomyces israelii* – Gram-positive, anaerobic; *E. coli* – Gram-positive bacillus (facultative anaerobe).

15 B: A normal finding 3 days post-laparotomy

The presence of free intraperitoneal air is common following any intra-abdominal surgery, whether open or laparoscopic. Other causes include perforation of a viscus, the presence of gas-forming organisms, or even following waterskiing in women, where air enters via the genital tracts. Free air takes a few days to resolve provided the original pathology or procedure has been dealt with, and absorption is usually complete within 5 days.

16 E: A high creatinine clearance

Options A, B and D are relative indications for dialysis. The presence of uraemic symptoms (C) is an absolute indication for dialysis. A low creatinine clearance and not a high one is a relative indication for dialysis.

17 B: Red cells >50 000/mm^3

A DPL is an extension of the abdominal examination and is performed rapidly in haemodynamically unstable patients by instilling warm saline into the abdominal cavity via a small abdominal incision under local anaesthetic. The fluid is retrieved and examined for various features.

A positive result is obtained if any of the following are observed in the lavage fluid:

- Positive Gram stain for bacteria
- Red cells >100 000 /mm^3
- White cells >500/mm^3
- Presence of food fibres
- Presence of faeces.

An absolute contraindication to DPL is any need for an urgent laparotomy. Relative contraindications to DPL include coagulopathy, cirrhosis, morbid obesity and previous abdominal scarring. In pregnancy DPL should be performed above the umbilicus.

Complications of DPL include:

- Bleeding
- Infection (wound) or peritonitis
- Perforation of bladder or bowel
- Other organ injury.

18 A: Small-bowel obstruction

The diagnosis is small-bowel obstruction until proved otherwise. The history of central colicky abdominal pain, vomiting and abdominal distension, with a previous history of abdominal surgery should always prompt this as the main working diagnosis. The fact that her bowels opened yesterday does not exclude a small-bowel obstruction and certainly in the early period of the obstruction the bowel distal to the obstruction can empty itself of gas and faeces. The presence of a normal AXR also does not exclude small-bowel obstruction as the bowel loops might be filled with fluid and might not demonstrate the classic 'ladder' pattern of gas-filled bowel loops. Gallstone ileus also causes small-bowel obstruction, but there is usually air seen within the biliary tree – it is still possible in this case, but generally it is much less likely.

19 D: A 45-year-old asymptomatic patient following removal of a hyperplastic polyp 1 year ago

Hyperplastic polyps generally do not require any colonoscopic follow-up as they are benign lesions. Certainly in an asymptomatic 45-year-old, a repeat colonoscopy is not warranted 1 year later. Other indications for colonoscopy include the investigation of PR bleeding, change in bowel habit, unexplained iron deficiency anaemia, follow-up after cancer surgery, and for a strong family history.

20 E: Ability to cut as well as coagulate

Bipolar diathermy uses the principle of high-current channelling, which occurs between the two tips of the diathermy forceps to coagulate tissue only. Cutting is accomplished by the use of monopolar diathermy, in which the patient is used as part of a circuit, and can be complicated by diathermy plate burns, pacemaker interference, and current channelling in the digits or peripheries.

21 D: Decreased serum catecholamines

Advantages of laparoscopic surgery over the open approach include:

- Less post-operative pain
- Shorter hospital stay
- Earlier return to work
- Improved cosmesis
- Decreased stress response
- Fewer wound complications.

Disadvantages include:

- Longer operating time (in some cases)
- Respiratory and cardiac stress following pneumoperitoneum
- Longer learning curve for procedures
- Higher rate of CBD injuries in cholecystecomies using the laparoscopic approach in some cases (not significant).

22 D: An urgent Doppler ultrasound scan

A Doppler ultrasound scan will show hydronephrosis if the cause is a ureteric stricture which has been masked by the presence of the ureteric stent. A lymphocoele, which can distort and obstruct the ureter, can also be visualised. Suspicion of renal artery stenosis can be raised if the flow through the renal artery is increased. A kidney biopsy would be performed after the ultrasound scan if in the first instance there is no evidence of hydronephrosis, lymphocoele or renal artery stenosis; alternatively, an angiogram could be done to confirm renal artery stenosis. A urine culture and PUO screen would not address the problem.

23 B: Check the bladder catheter to make sure that it is not blocked by a thrombus

Do the simple manoeuvre first. A Doppler ultrasound scan might be required to confirm or exclude problems with the vascular anastomoses. Acute tubular necrosis due to re-perfusion injury could also be the cause, but there is usually a suggestive history of a period of ischaemia in the donor prior to kidney retrieval. An isotope scan usually clinches the diagnosis.

24 D: Shoulder-tip pain

Shoulder-tip pain is a common sequela of laparoscopic surgery. This occurs as the diaphragm undergoes irritation from the excess gas in the peritoneal cavity. The referred pain travels along the phrenic nerve route and is referred to the shoulder tip quite commonly. The other listed complications are recognised but uncommon.

25 A: The nerve within the anterior compartment is the deep peroneal nerve

The lower leg is divided into three compartments: anterior, posterior and lateral. The interosseous membrane running between the tibia and fibula divides the anterior and posterior compartments, while the anterior and posterior fascial septa, which both attach to the fibula, enclose the lateral compartment. The posterior compartment is further divided into deep and superficial compartments by the transverse fascia. The deep compartment contains tibialis posterior, flexor digitorum longus, flexor hallucis longus and popliteus, and the superficial compartment contains gastrocnemius, soleus and plantaris. It also contains the tibial nerve. The anterior compartment contains tibialis anterior, extensor digitorum longus, extensor hallucis longus and the deep peroneal nerve. The lateral compartment contains peroneus longus and brevis and the superficial peroneal nerve.

26 C: The patient has peritonitis; a sample of the dialysate should be sent for culture and sensitivity and the patient should be started on first-line antibiotic therapy (eg intraperitoneal vancomycin)

The peritoneal dialysis catheter might need to be removed if the patient has not responded after 3–5 days of treatment.

27 C: Calcaneal tendon

The calcaneal tendon or Achilles' tendon is the thickest and strongest tendon of the body. The gastrocnemius and soleus insert on the calcaneus via this tendon. These muscles are important plantar-flexors of the foot. The other listed tendons which were not damaged include:

- Tibialis anterior – inverts and dorsiflexes the foot
- Peroneus tertius – everts the foot
- Flexor hallucis longus – flexes the big toe
- Flexor digitorum longus – flexes toes 2–4.

28 B: Plantaris

Plantaris is a very small muscle in the posterior compartment of the leg and is innervated by the tibial nerve, like the other muscles of this compartment. It has a very long and thin tendon that attaches directly to the calcaneus, unlike the gastrocnemius and soleus, which insert on the calcaneus via the calcaneal tendon. These muscles are important plantar-flexors of the foot, so it is likely that the tendon connected to these muscles has been damaged. Popliteus is a muscle on the posterior knee which allows rotation medially and unlocks to initiate flexion of the knee. Tibialis posterior is also a muscle in the posterior compartment that plantar-flexes and inverts the foot.

29 E: Argyll Robertson pupil

An Argyll-Robertson pupil is a small, irregular pupil that does not react to light but does react to accommodation. It is seen in cases of tertiary syphilis. Horner syndrome is characterised by the presence of ptosis, miosis, enophthalmos and anhidrosis.

30 C: Extended right hemicolectomy with defunctioning loop ileostomy

Transverse colon tumours are best treated with an extended right hemicolectomy and a defunctioning loop ileostomy to protect the anastomosis, as oedamatous bowel from the obstruction may weaken the join. Transverse colectomies are inferior to extended right hemicolectomies: studies have revealed that a more complete lymph node dissection can occur when taking the right colic nodes as part of the right hemicolectomy as well as making a superior anastomosis from the ileo-colic join as opposed to the colo-colic join.

31 B: Preformed host antibodies directed against the donor antigens

The clinical scenario presented here is that of a hyperacute rejection. This type of rejection occurs on table immediately during the transplant itself after vascularisation of the kidney has been achieved, and is immunologically due to preformed host antibodies directed against the donor antigens.

32 B: Arises from the nerve roots L2–S1

The sciatic nerve is the largest nerve in the body, formed by the nerve fibres of anterior primary rami of the fourth lumbar to third sacral spinal nerves. It is the most lateral structure emerging through the greater sciatic foramen and emerges inferior to the piriformis muscle in the majority of people. In roughly 12% of people, however, the sciatic nerve divides before exiting the greater sciatic foramen and the common peroneal branch pierces piriformis. In about 0.5% of people the common fibular branch passes superior to the muscle, where it is more susceptible to injury from gluteal injections. The nerve usually divides into its two components at the superior border of the popliteal fossa. Damage to the sciatic nerve in the buttock will result in loss of knee flexion as well as loss of all power below the level of the knee joint as both the tibial and common peroneal nerves will be affected. The posterior femoral cutaneous nerve runs downwards in the same line as the sciatic nerve but is superficial to biceps femoris.

33 E: Medial to the femoral arterial pulse

The structures in the femoral triangle from lateral to medial are the femoral nerve, artery, vein and canal (the latter is not in the femoral sheath, unlike the others). The femoral pulse can be palpated at the midinguinal point, halfway between the anterior superior iliac spine and the pubic symphysis. The vein would be found medial to the arterial pulse. Damage of the femoral nerve in this procedure can lead to loss of sensation on the anterior part of the thigh and unopposed flexion of the knee.

34 A: Spring ligament

The arches of the foot are maintained by the shape of the interlocking bones, the ligaments of the foot, and muscle action. The spring ligament, which passes from the sustentaculum tali of the calcaneus forwards to the tuberosity of the navicular bone supports the inferior aspect of the head of the talus. The deltoid ligament is on the medial aspect of the ankle and stabilises the ankle joint during eversion, preventing the ankle joint from dislocating. The short plantar ligament is deep to the long plantar ligament and stretches from the plantar surface of the calcaneus to the cuboid. The long plantar ligament arises from the plantar surface of the calcaneus, forms a tunnel with the peroneus longus tendon with the cuboid, and is inserted into the bases of the three lateral metatarsals. The long plantar ligament is generally important in maintaining all the arches of the foot, but the spring ligament is specifically associated with the medial arch and the head of the talus.

35 D: Dirty wound

Wounds can be classified according to the risk of wound contamination. Clean operations are those that are carried out through sterile uninfected skin, where the gastrointestinal, genitourinary and respiratory tracts are not breached; clean-contaminated is when there is breaching of a hollow viscus other than the colon; contaminated is when contamination of the wound has occurred, eg from a bite or opening of the colon; finally, dirty operations are those in which the operation is carried out in the presence of pus or a perforated viscus. The example used in the question – a perforated diverticulum – would most likely require a Hartmann's operation and would be classified as dirty.

36 E: Presence of crypt abscesses

The presence of crypt abscess on biopsy is suggestive of ulcerative colitis. Crohn's disease shows the presence of skip lesions with thickening of the bowel wall, including encroachment onto mesenteric fat. A linear mucosal ulceration is also seen on macroscopic appearance, leading to a 'cobblestone' pattern of islands of surviving mucosa. Ulcerative colitis reveals an inflamed and ulcerated mucosal pattern that exhibits contact bleeding and is continuous from the rectum proximally. Fistulae may occur in Crohn's but not in ulcerative colitis.

37 E: Tendon of tibialis posterior

The medial malleolus is formed by the lower end of the tibia, in contrast to the lateral malleolus, which is a part of the fibula. Important structures pass behind the medial malleolus in the area sometimes referred to as the 'tarsal tunnel'. These structures are bounded by the flexor retinaculum of the ankle joint, which connects the medial malleolus to the calcaneus. The structures in the tarsal tunnel are (from anterior to posterior):

- Tendon of tibialis posterior
- Tendon of flexor digitorum longus
- Posterior tibial artery with its venae commitantes
- Tibial nerve
- Tendon of flexor hallucis longus.

38 E: Psoralens appear to have a protective effect

Psoralens and psaloren plus ultraviolet A (PUVA) treatment increase the risk of developing squamous cell carcinoma (SCC) of the skin. Other risk factors include frequent exposure to sunlight over many years, fair skin, blonde hair, blue eyes, family history, sensitive skin, chronic ulcers, actinic keratoses, radiation, arsenic/coal/tar exposure, immunosuppression, tobacco use, xeroderma pigmentosum, and previous SCC of the skin.

39 E: Phaeochromocytoma

Phaeochromocytomas are found as part of the MEN II syndrome. MEN I comprises parathyroid, pituitary, and pancreatic neoplasms. Occasionally, adrenal cortical adenomas also occur as part of the MEN I syndrome.

40 D: Perform an ultrasound and excision biopsy without fine-needle aspiration (FNA)

A young woman presenting with a well-defined mobile breast lump is clinically presenting with a fibroadenoma. Although this may be left alone as it is a benign condition, ideally a histological diagnosis should be obtained for completeness. This is best done by excising the lump and will also provide reassurance and peace of mind to the patient that the lump has been removed. An FNA might be inconclusive and a histological diagnosis is better than a cytological one. An ultrasound is done at the same time to further assess the lump architecture and look for other co-existing lumps that could be removed at the same time.

41 C: The apex is bounded by the first rib, clavicle and scapula

The axilla is a space shaped like a pyramid which has anterior, posterior and medial walls. The anterior wall is formed by pectoralis major and minor; the posterior wall is formed by subscapularis, latissimus dorsi and teres major and the medial wall is formed by serratus anterior and the ribs. The floor is formed by axillary fascia. The apex is formed by the first rib, clavicle and scapula.

42 B: Within 24 hours of birth

The first stool is passed within 24 hours of birth in 99% of healthy full-term infants and within 48 hours in all healthy full-term infants. Failure of a full-term newborn to pass meconium within the first 24 hours should raise a suspicion of intestinal obstruction. Lower intestinal obstruction may be associated with disorders such as Hirschsprung's disease, anorectal malformations, meconium plug syndrome, small left colon syndrome, hypoganglionosis, and neuronal intestinal dysplasia.

43 C: Previous endotracheal tube intubation

Subglottic stenosis is acquired in 95% of cases, and 90% of these are due to previous intubation. Only 5% of stenoses are due to congenital causes. The most important risk factor is duration of intubation. Other causes include trauma, post-surgical trauma, such as previous cricothyroidotomy or high tracheostomy. Gastro-oesophageal reflux may worsen pre-existent subglottic stenosis, or be a factor in its own right in patients with no previous history of endotracheal intubation or laryngotracheal trauma. Croup causes subglottic swelling and will be worse in patients with pre-existent subglottic stenosis.

44 D: The hila of both kidneys lie at the approximate level of L3

The adrenals lie within the renal fascia and receive their blood supply from the suprarenal arteries, branches of the renal arteries and branches of the inferior phrenic arteries. The kidneys are retroperitoneal organs and lie at the L2 level. The duodenum lies over the hilum of the right kidney and the small intestine lies over the inferior pole of both kidneys. Renal arteries divide into five segmental arteries, with four passing anterior to the renal pelvis and one passing posteriorly.

45 B: The gene for FAP is carried on the short arm of chromosome 9

FAP is an autosomal dominant condition leading to adenomatous polyps in the large bowel from the second decade onwards. The gene for FAP is carried on the long arm of chromosome 5. FAP is associated with congenital hypertrophy of the retinal pigment epithelium and gastroduodenal polyps, hence the need for lifelong OGD [AQ] even after a mandatory prophylactic colectomy has been performed.

46 C: Steroid use

Autologous blood transfusion is the use of a patient's own blood for transfusion. It may be collected in advance of surgery, immediately prior to surgery or from blood lost intraoperatively. Contraindications for this type of transfusion include active infection, severe hypertension, unstable angina and aortic stenosis.

47 C: Presence of pulseless electrical activity following penetrating chest trauma

Emergency room thoracotomy should be performed only by a qualified surgeon. The indications are for penetrating trauma only where the patient undergoes a witnessed arrest that is not asystole. Initial drainage of >1.5 l of blood or continued drainage of >200 ml/hour are also indications for thoracotomy, it usually can be done in theatres while the patient is resuscitated en route. Pericardiocentesis can be performed for pericardial tamponade in the initial setting.

48 C: *Streptococcus pneumoniae*

Overwhelming post-splenectomy sepsis is due to infection with encapsulated organisms, the most common being *Streptococcus pneumoniae*. Patients are also at risk from *Haemophilus influenzae* and *Neisseria meningitidis* infections but to a lesser extent than from streptococcal infections.

49 A: Papillary carcinoma

Papillary carcinomas are the most frequent of all the thyroid malignancies, comprising 60–80% of all thyroid malignancies. Follicular carcinomas (10–18%), medullary carcinomas (5–10%), thyroid lymphomas (<2%) and anaplastic carcinomas (5–15%) occur less commonly.

50 B: The gonadal arteries arise beneath the renal arteries

The abdominal aorta passes through the crura of the diaphragm at the level of T12 and descends to L4, where it divides into left and right common iliacs and a median sacral artery. It gives off three unpaired visceral branches (coeliac trunk at T12, superior mesenteric artery at L1 and inferior mesenteric artery at L3). There are three paired visceral branches (suprarenal vessels, renal arteries and gonadal arteries), five paired parietal branches (to the diaphragm) and four paired lumbar arteries (to the posterior abdominal wall).

51 B: Reduced operating time

Laparoscopic surgery has its advantages over open surgery, with improved cosmesis leading to an earlier recovery and shorter post-operative hospital stay, reduced pain, and an earlier return to work after surgery. The operating time is variable, but in most procedures it is longer than the open time.

52 E: Cytomegalovirus (CMV)

Blood from donors in the UK is not routinely screened for CMV unless it is used for donation in special groups such as neonates and immunosuppressed patients. Screening does occur for syphilis (*Treponema*), HIV, hepatitis B and hepatitis C.

53 B: Increased pH

A right shift in the oxygen dissociation curve decreases oxygen affinity, allowing oxygen to be released only at higher partial pressures. This is known as the Bohr effect and the mechanism serves to increase oxygen extraction. Causes of right shift include acidosis, increased temperature and increased levels of 2,3-DPG in the blood.

54 C: Polyester – absorbable, synthetic, multifilament

Different sutures have particular properties, which make them useful for different purposes. They can be classified into absorbable vs non-absorbable; monofilament vs multifilament and synthetic vs natural. Absorbable sutures are used for the closure of tissues that heal quickly, whereas non-absorbable sutures are used for those that take longer. Monofilament sutures glide through tissues more smoothly than multifilament sutures and are therefore useful in vascular surgery, whereas braided sutures give knots more 'hold'.

55 D: Test must also be used to detect early recurrence as well as primary pathology

Screening tests are becoming popular in the UK, with most health strategies aimed at prevention and early detection as opposed to cure of disease. For a national screening programme to be valid, certain prerequisites must be fulfilled. These include disease and test criteria as follows:

Disease criteria:

- Common disease
- Important health problem
- Should have a long premorbid latent period
- Should be asymptomatic
- Should be detectable at an early stage
- Should be treatable by defined means in a cost-effective way at the time of detection.

Test criteria:

- Highly sensitive and specific
- Non-invasive
- Must be able to be audited
- Cost-effective and acceptable to patients
- The test or its results should be without harm to the patient.

Screening tests are not designed to detect early recurrence from primary disease.

56 B: Hypokalaemia

Cushing's disease will cause a hypokalaemia, along with hypernatraemia and hyperglycaemia due to the excess cortisol secreted from the adrenal cortex or endogenous sources.

57 D: Hartmann's solution – Na^+ 131 mmol/l

- Hartman's solution contains 131 mmol/l of Na^+
- 0.9% normal saline contains 154 mmol/l of Na^+
- 0.18% saline contains 30 mmol/l
- Ringer's lactate contains 147 mmol/l Na^+.

58 E: 1750 ml

Loss of blood volume is associated with physiological responses, mainly mediated by the sympathetic nervous system, which aim to maintain blood pressure and hence blood supply to vital organs. Haemorrhagic shock can be divided into four classes depending on the amount of blood lost. Each class is associated with particular parameters that help in the estimation of blood loss.

- **Class I** is loss of 0–15% of circulating volume and there are no obvious changes, apart from the patient perhaps feeling uncomfortable and restless.

- **Class II** (15–30% loss) is associated with a rise in pulse rate to >100, reduced urine output to 20–30 ml per hour, raised respiratory rate of 20–30 breaths per minute. Blood pressure is normal but pulse pressure is reduced.
- **Class III** (30–40% loss) is associated with a tachycardia of >120 bpm, reduction in both pulse pressure an blood pressure and reduction in urine output to 10–20 ml per minute.

With **class IV** (>40% blood loss) the patient becomes anxious and might be confused. There is a tachycardia of >130 bpm, blood pressure and pulse pressure are low and the patient is anuric. Respiratory rate is >40 breaths per minute.

59 D: Between 12 and 15 months of age

Undescended testes should undergo further examination and orchidopexy between 12 and 15 months of age. There is evidence of early damage to sperm-producing germ cells as well as an increased risk of carcinoma in later life for undescended testes.

60 E: Decrease of the pulmonary capillary wedge pressure (PCWP)

Cardiogenic shock is a major complication of a variety of acute and chronic disorders that impair the ability of the heart to maintain adequate tissue perfusion. This most commonly follows acute myocardial infarctions. Haemodynamic criteria include sustained hypotension, reduced cardiac index, and an elevated pulmonary capillary wedge pressure (PCWP). Bedside signs may include cool peripheries, gallop rhythm, elevated JVP, low pulse pressure and distant heart sounds.

61 A: Heart rate

Components of the Revised Trauma Scoring System include respiratory rate, systolic BP and Glasgow Coma Scale score, but not heart rate.

62 C: Multiparity

Genetic factors are an important consideration in breast cancer as the *BRCA 1* and *2* genes are implicated in 2% of cases. It may also be associated with genetic syndromes such as Li–Fraumeni syndrome. Other risk factors include advanced age (risk rises linearly with age), hyperplasia with atypia of breast tissue, nulliparity, early menarche/late menopause and obesity.

63 C: Chronic diarrhoea

The normal anion gap is 10–16 mmol/l. It is calculated by subtracting the difference between the cations (Na^+ and K^+) and anions (HCO_3^- and Cl^-). It reflects the presence of unmeasured anions in the serum and will be raised in the presence of lactate, ketones, or other ingested agents such as aspirin in overdose. Chronic diarrhoea results in a loss of bicarbonate, although this is matched by a compensatory increase in serum Cl^- so that the anion gap remains normal.

64 B: Consumption of hard water

Drinking hard water has been shown to have a protective effect in preventing vascular disease and the converse is true for soft water, which is a risk factor. High levels of blood homocysteine and hyperlipidaemia are other risk factors for vascular disease.

65 B: 9

Eyes open to pain = 2

Localises pain = 5

Makes incomprehensible sounds = 2

Therefore GCS = 9

66 D: Vertebromuscular ridges

The diaphragm develops in utero, receiving contributions from the four following structures:

- Dorsal oesophageal mesentery
- Peripheral rim derived from the body wall
- Septum transversum
- Pleuroperitoneal membranes.

It develops cranially and acquires its cervical nerve supply from the phrenic nerve (C3, 4, 5), and migrates caudally to lie between the thorax and abdomen.

67 C: Duct ectasia

Duct ectasia is dilatation and inflammation of the mammary ducts and commonly affects middle-aged women. It usually presents with tenderness, erythema and a green/brown nipple discharge. Discharge can be physiological in lactation, pregnancy, and following mechanical stimulation. Bloodstained discharge is a worrying sign and might indicate carcinoma or duct papilloma. Breast abscess does not tend to present with nipple discharge. It usually presents with pain, fever, swelling and erythema.

68 E: Presence of an uncorrected coagulopathy

The presence of an uncorrected coagulopathy is a contraindication to any surgical procedure. A BMI >40 kg/m^2, pregnancy, previous abdominal surgery, and other systemic disorders are relative contraindications, although recently surgeons have taken on board such cases without problem. A BMI >40 kg/m^2 is the norm for most laparoscopic bariatric surgeons.

69 E: The level of the T4 dermatome

The manubriosternal angle of Louis marks the level of the second costal cartilage and rib. It is situated at about the level of T4/T5 and is anatomically related to the level of the tracheal bifurcation and the commencement of the aortic arch. The T4 dermatome is classically marked by the inter-nipple line.

70 C: For every six heavy drinkers, one will have chronic pancreatitis

The odds in heavy drinkers of having chronic pancreatitis is quoted as 0.2 or 1/5. This means that for every one heavy drinker with the disease, five heavy drinkers will not (ie 1 out of every 6 heavy drinkers will be affected).

71 A: 1–2 cm

Squamous cell carcinoma is a malignant tumour of epidermal keratinocytes and is most commonly found on areas of the body that have been exposed to the sun. Surgery should achieve a 1–2 cm clearance margin. This is in contrast to the management of basal cell carcinoma (0.5 cm clearance margin) and malignant melanoma, which is based on clinical appearance (impalpable – 1 cm; palpable – 2 cm; nodular – 3 cm).

72 A: Papillary

Pathologically, a psammoma body is a round collection of calcium seen on microscopy. The term is derived from the Greek word *psammos* meaning 'sand'. They are theoretically supposed to originate from a single necrotic cell in which layers of calcium salts are deposited. Psammoma bodies may be found in papillary thyroid, endometrial and ovarian adenocarcinomas, meningiomas and mesotheliomas.

73 D: Vessel wall tension

Poiseuille's law states that the flow within a vessel is directly proportional to the radius to the power of 4 and inversely proportional to the viscosity of the blood (including haematocrit) and length of the vessel. Flow will also be affected in cardiac pump failure, but not directly by vessel wall tension.

74 E: Exposure to schistosomiasis

Schistosomiasis is a risk factor for squamous and not transitional cell carcinoma of the bladder, which occurs more commonly in clinical practice. Other risk factors for transitional cell carcinoma include smoking, irradiation, drugs such as cyclophosphamide, exposure to chemical substances such as benzidine and β-naphthylamine dyes used in textile, printing, and rubber industries.

75 C: Cholecystitis

Terminal ileal resection due to Crohn's disease leads to loss of bile salt reabsorption, so these patients have an increased cholesterol secretion and a lowered bile acid secretion, which lead to cholesterol supersaturation and the formation of gallstones.

76 B: Type II – pernicious anaemia

Hypersensitivity type I – immediate hypersensitivity or allergy

Hypersensitivity type II – antibody to cell-bound antigen (cytotoxic)

Hypersensitivity type III – immune complex reaction

Hypersensitivity type IV – delayed hypersensitivity

Hypersensitivity type V – IgG Ab stimulatory effect

77 A: Systemic hypocarbia

Cerebral blood flow is increased in seizures, systemic hypoxia and hypercarbia, chronic anaemia and hypertension. Hypocarbia causes cerebral vasoconstriction and reduced blood flow.

78 B: Hyperthyroidism

Hyperthyroidism is a recognised cause of hypercalcaemia. This is thought to be due to a direct effect of the thyroid hormone primarily on bone metabolism, although, the exact mechanism is still unclear.

79 C: Evisceration of bowel

The only absolute contraindication to DPL is the need for laparotomy. Of the listed conditions, only evisceration of bowel necessitates laparotomy. The other conditions listed are relative contraindications.

80 B: Tachycardia

TUR syndrome results from hypervolaemia due to excessive absorption of irrigation fluid during transurethral resections. A dilutional hyponatraemia results, with bradycardia and hypotension. Confusion and hyperammonaemia may be seen if metabolism of absorbed glycine from the irrigation fluid occurs. Management of this condition includes stopping the irrigation fluid, administering diuretics, and possibly twice-normal saline as well. It is advisable to seek senior advice early on in this situation.

81 B: Movement of ribs 2–7 is a 'pump handle' type of action, which increases the anterior–posterior diameter of the thorax

During inspiration the thorax expands, causing the pleural pressure to drop, resulting in air entry. The upper ribs (2–7) move with a 'pump handle' action, therefore increasing the AP diameter of the thorax. The lower ribs (8–12) move with a 'bucket handle' type of action which increases the lateral diameter. Movement of the ribs is brought about by contraction of the internal and external intercostal muscles. Expiration is a passive process due to elastic recoil of the lungs. The first rib is immobile. Contraction of the diaphragm causes it to flatten and therefore increases the vertical diameter of the thorax during inspiration.

82 C: 4000 ml

The ATLS guideline for fluid resuscitation in burns states that, ideally, 2–4 ml/kg/% burns should be given in the first 24 hours. Half of this should be given in the first 8 hours. The higher fluid volume of 4 ml/kg/% burns should be used for full-thickness burns as there is less of a skin barrier. Also, the aim is to minimise renal failure from myoglobinuria and keep the kidney well flushed.

83 B: Hypoglycaemia

Local factors that impair wound healing include poor blood supply, haematoma, infection, early movement, foreign bodies, radiation and denervation. Systemic factors include malnutrition and zinc/vitamin C deficiency, drugs, neoplasia, diabetes, older age, jaundice and uraemia. Hyperglycaemia from diabetes as opposed to hypoglycaemia would impair wound healing.

84 A: Antiplatelet agents with lifestyle advice and treatment to control vascular risk factor

Asymptomatic carotid artery stenosis which is <70% stenosed should be managed conservatively with antiplatelet agents such as aspirin and changes in lifestyle measures, along with risk-reduction strategies.

85 A: Lidocaine and adrenaline 5 mg/kg

Different local anaesthetics have different maximal recommended doses. Exceeding these can result in toxicity, which presents as perioral tingling, paraesthesia, anxiety and drowsiness, and may progress to coma and cardiovascular collapse. Use of adrenaline together with a local anaesthetic slows the systemic absorption and therefore prolongs duration of action and increases the maximum recommended dose. Lidocaine is commonly used for minor operations; bupivicaine has a longer duration of action and is used in epidural and spinal anaesthesia. Prilocaine is used in regional nerve blocks. Maximum recommended doses are: lidocaine 3 mg/kg, bupivicaine 2 mg/kg and prilocaine 6 mg/kg. The corresponding doses for preparations containing adrenaline are 5 mg, 3 mg and 6 mg, respectively.

86 A: Common iliac artery

Buttock claudication should alert the clinician to suspect a stenosis of either the internal iliac artery or common iliac artery. External iliac artery or profunda femoris stenosis would cause thigh claudication. Superficial femoral artery (SFA) stenosis classically causes calf claudication.

Buttock claudication and impotence in males should raise the suspicion of Leriche's syndrome, which is due to internal iliac stenosis.

87 D: Wasting of the thenar eminence

The commonly affected roots in thoracic outlet syndrome include the C8 and T1 roots, resulting in wasting of hypothenar muscles as well as the medial forearm. Although there are reported cases of median nerve involvement in severe cases, this is not classic of the syndrome generally.

88 A: Distant metastases are found in 20% of patients at presentation

Squamous cell carcinoma of the larynx represents approximately 1% of malignancies in men. It is five times commoner in men than in women. Smoking tobacco and drinking alcohol predispose towards carcinoma. Hoarseness is the commonest and may be the only presenting symptom. Stridor and dyspnoea are late symptoms. Verrucous carcinoma is a variant of well-differentiated squamous cell carcinoma. Tumours affecting just the glottis have minimal risk of metastases as there is virtually no glottic lymphatic drainage. Metastases normally imply spread into adjacent sites such as the subglottis or supraglottis.

89 C: Femoral nerve

The femoral nerve is formed from nerve roots L2–L4 and is the nerve of the anterior thigh; it supplies psoas, iliacus, tensor fascia lata, sartorius and quadriceps femoris. It also supplies sensation to a strip of skin on the medial side of the lower leg as far as the big toe. Damage to this nerve therefore results in sensory loss in this area of skin and also loss of knee extension.

90 D: Pleomorphic adenoma

The parotid is affected by 80% of all salivary tumours; 80% of parotid tumours are benign; and 80% of benign tumours in the parotid gland are pleomorphic adenomas. Gender incidence is equal and it occurs most commonly in the fifth decade. Management involves superficial parotidectomy; recurrence is possible. Warthin's tumour (papillary cystadenoma) is a benign tumour seen in elderly men in their seventh decade. Adenoid cystic carcinoma is the commonest malignant tumour, commonly in minor glands. Patients often complain of facial pain and may present with facial paresis. Mumps infection often causes bilateral parotitis in young patients. Salivary calculi are commonest in submandibular glands, because of their higher concentrations of mucus. Swelling and pain occur on eating.

91 A: Widened pulse pressure

Cardiac tamponade is a medical emergency where fluid or blood accumulate within the pericardial space and compress the heart, resulting in failure of the cardiac pump. This is similar to a tension pneumothorax and can present with sudden collapse or deterioration in cardiac function. Signs include muffled heart sounds on auscultation, hypotension, narrowed pulse pressure, low-voltage ECG complexes, raised JVP, Kussmaul's sign and pulsus paradoxus. An urgent pericardiocentesis should relieve the pressure from within the enclosed pericardial space.

92 C: Initiation of intravenous β-blocker therapy

Ideally, the management of a thoracic dissection should be to resuscitate the patient as soon as possible and to decide on a management plan. Investigations are ideal when the patient is stable. Most type B dissections are medically managed with control of hypertension, but in this case the patient suffers from severe asthma, so intravenous β-blocker therapy is contraindicated. Other antihypertensive measures should be used in the meantime and a cardiac surgeon should be involved in the decision-making process as soon as possible.

93 C: Bilateral laparoscopic repair

NICE guidelines suggest the use of laparoscopic surgery for the treatment of bilateral inguinal hernias. In centres where this is not performed, the open approach must be employed, although, given the choice, the laparoscopic surgeon should be advised.

94 B: Cholesteatoma

A cholesteatoma is a three-dimensional epidermal structure made of keratinising squamous cells, exhibiting independent growth, replacing middle ear mucosa and reabsorbing underlying bone. It is due to implanted epithelium. It produces a discharge, often foul and creamy. Deafness can be conductive from ossicular erosion, or sensory via toxin production. Attic crusting, marginal perforations, or debris containing retraction pockets are the principal signs. A rounded, pearly-white mass is diagnostic. Otitis externa affects just the external canal. Canal exostoses are external canal hyperostoses. Suppurative otitis media presents with an erythematous bulging tympanic membrane. Glomus jugulare is a rare hypervascular tumour that arises within the jugular foramen of the temporal bone.

95 C: They should be surgically removed in all patients

Nodules detected by thyroid scans are classified as cold, hot or warm: 85% of thyroid nodules are cold, 10% are warm and 5% are hot. Also remember that 85% of cold nodules are benign, 90% of warm nodules are benign and 95% of hot nodules are benign. They are about four times commoner in women. Not all thyroid nodules require excision, especially if they are asymptomatic and can be treated conservatively.

96 C: Tracheal shift to the affected side

A tension pneumothorax presents with acute dyspnoea and occasionally chest pain. This may lead to sudden collapse, and an urgent pleural decompression is required to prevent cardiorespiratory compromise. The signs include decreased breath sounds and hyper-resonance to percussion on the affected side, along with a tracheal shift to the opposite side. Displacement of the apex beat may occur with mediastinal shift, and the JVP would be raised bilaterally as the thoracic pressure is increased.

97 C: The sinus venosus forms part of the ventricular walls

The heart is formed from a primitive heart tube, which develops five swellings: truncus arteriosus (forms aorta and pulmonary trunk and infundibulum of ventricles); bulbus cordis; ventricle; atrium; and sinus venosus (forms the smooth-walled part of the atrial walls). Inside the right atrium this smooth part and a rough area (true atrium) are separated by a ridge called the crista terminalis. The sinoatrial node is situated at the top of this. Anterior cardiac veins drain directly into the right atrium. The fossa ovalis is the obliterated foramen ovale, which allows the passage of blood from the right to the left atrium in the fetus, therefore bypassing the lungs. It remains patent in 10% of the population.

98 D: Between internal intercostals and innermost intercostals

The intercostal neurovascular bundle runs in the subcostal groove under each rib and consists of a vein, artery and nerve (running superiorly to inferiorly). This bundle is located between the internal and innermost intercostals muscular layers.

99 D: T10 – oesophagus with vagus nerves

The following structures pass through the main openings in the diaphragm:

- T8 – IVC and right phrenic nerve
- T10 – oesophagus with right and left vagus nerves, left gastric artery and vein, and lymphatics
- T12 – aorta, thoracic duct and azygos vein.

100 A: Barium swallow

Impaction of foreign bodies depends on their size and shape. Aerodigestive tract abnormalities make impaction more likely. Assessment is initially via plain lateral and anteroposterior neck and chest radiographs. Flexible nasendoscopy may demonstrate impaction at the cricopharyngeus. Barium swallow is not used as it coats the mucosa, making oesophagoscopy and identification of a foreign body difficult. Intravenous Buscopan and diazepam is often used first line. Studies have shown glucagon to aid in oesophageal sphincter relaxation. Failure to pass conservatively will require removal via rigid oesophagoscopy under general anaesthesia.

101 B: The right subclavian vein and the right internal jugular vein join to form the right subclavian trunk

The subclavian vein and internal jugular veins join on each side forming the brachiocephalic veins, which then drain into the SCV. However, although there is a right brachiocephalic artery (which arises from the arch of the aorta and gives rises to the right subclavian artery and right common carotid artery), there is no corresponding left brachiocephalic artery, and the left subclavian artery and common carotid artery arise directly from the arch of the aorta. The SCV and IVC drain separately into the right atrium.

102 C: Gastroduodenal artery

The blood supply to the stomach is entirely derived from the coeliac axis. The following arteries directly supply the stomach:

- Short gastric arteries – fundus
- Right and left gastric arteries – lesser curvature
- Right and left gastroepiploic arteries – greater curvature.

The gastroduodenal artery runs behind the first part of the oesophagus and divides into the right gastroepiploic and superior pancreaticoduodenal arteries.

103 D: The radial nerve in the spiral groove

The radial nerve arises from the posterior cord of the brachial plexus and passes along the posterior aspect of the humerus in the spiral groove, where it is vulnerable to damage from a fractured humerus. It then pierces the lateral intermuscular septum and divides into the posterior interosseous nerve and the superficial radial nerve at the level of the lateral epicondyle. Damage to the nerve in the spiral groove causes wrist drop but not loss of elbow extension because the nerves supplying the triceps muscle are given off more proximal to this. For there also to be loss of elbow extension, damage would have to be at the level of the axilla.

104 D: Rectus sheath

The Lanz incision incises through the skin, subcutaneous tissue, external oblique aponeurosis, internal oblique muscle (split), transversus abdominis, extraperitoneal fat, and peritoneum. The rectus muscle and sheath are encountered if the incision is too medially placed, but should not be encountered in a standard Lanz incision.

105 A: Penicillin V

Acute tonsillitis is caused by viral infections in up to 50% of cases. Penicillin V is the drug of choice as most bacterial tonsillitis is caused by penicillin-sensitive group A β-haemolytic streptococci. Ampicillin should never be used in acute tonsillitis as this causes generalised maculopapular rash in patients with wrongly diagnosed infectious mononucleosis. Erythromycin is given to patients allergic to penicillin.

106 B: It is the main muscle involved in the supinator reflex

The brachioradialis muscle is the main muscle involved in the so-called 'supinator' reflex. It arises from the upper two-thirds of the lateral supracondylar ridge of the humerus and inserts into the radial styloid process. It is supplied by the main radial nerve and is involved in flexion of the elbow in a semi-prone position.

107 E: Superficial peroneal nerve

The lateral compartment of the leg comprises the peroneus longus and brevis muscles, both of which evert the ankle at the subtalar joint. They are both supplied by the superficial peroneal nerve.

108 A: Obturator

The adductors of the hip are supplied by the obturator nerve, which arises from the anterior primary rami of L2, L3 and L4. The skin overlying the medial compartment of the thigh is also supplied by this nerve. Damage is not a common occurrence, but can occur with deep pelvic dissection, especially deep and medial to the inferior aspect of the psoas muscle.

109 B: Femoral branch of the genitofemoral nerve

The cremasteric reflex is mediated by the two branches of the genitofemoral nerve. The afferent limb of this reflex is mediated by the femoral branch of the genitofemoral nerve and the efferent limb by the genital branch.

110 B: Median nerve

The median nerve can be injured in stab wounds to the anterior cubital fossa along with the brachial artery. Damage to this nerve at the elbow results in loss of pronation, weakness of wrist flexion with deviation, and loss of sensation on the lateral palm and radial three and a half digits.

111 C: Ascending pharyngeal artery

Little's area (also known as Kiesselbach's plexus) is implicated in anterior epistaxis. It is located over the anterior nasal septum and is formed by anastamoses between the sphenopalatine, greater palatine, superior labial and anterior ethmoidal arteries (the last is a branch of the ophthalmic artery). These are branches of both the external and internal carotids. The ascending pharyngeal artery anastomoses with the posterior nasal and sphenopalatine vessels over the posterior middle turbinate in an area known as Woodruff's plexus. This area is implicated in posterior epistaxis.

112 D: Subluxation of carpus

Dinner fork deformity, radial displacement, and a fracture within 2.5 cm of the wrist joint are characteristic of a Colles' fracture, as well as radial shortening. There is commonly an associated ulnar styloid fracture. Carpal subluxation usually occurs when there is a Barton's fracture (intra-articular fracture through the dorsal or volar lip of the distal radius). Smith's fracture is an extra-articular fracture with volar displacement.

113 B: The femoral nerve lies laterally within the canal

The femoral canal is a space, approximately 0.5 cm in diameter, which lies between the medial aspect of the femoral sheath and the wall of the femoral vein. It allows the passage of lower limb lymphatics and allows for expansion of the femoral vessels. It also contains fat and Cloquet's node.

114 B: High-dose intravenous antibiotics

The clinical picture is of septic arthritis. The correct management of this presentation should be a thorough history and examination. A full blood count and inflammatory markers should be obtained to ascertain the extent of sepsis and because they are helpful for suture monitoring. Blood cultures can be positive, especially when taken during a period of pyrexia. The knee should be aspirated with an aseptic technique in clean surroundings, ie in theatre and NOT the Emergency Department. Only after the samples for microbiology have been obtained can the patient be given antibiotics. Knee X-rays will rule out bony pathology and can act as a baseline if there is joint destruction in the future.

115 C: The retromandibular vein passes through the gland

The parotid gland lies between the mastoid process and the sternocleidomastoid muscle posteriorly and the ramus of the mandible anteriorly. The upper pole lies between the cartilaginous part of the auditory tube and the capsule of the temporomandibular joint. The lower pole lies below and behind the angle of the mandible. The parotid duct emerges from the anterior border of the gland and pierces buccinator at the level of the second upper molar tooth to enter the mouth. Structures that pass through the parotid gland are the external carotid artery (which divides within the gland into its terminal branches), retromandibular vein and facial nerve. Tumours can therefore cause a facial palsy due to nerve infiltration.

116 B: Anterior cardiac vein

The anterior cardiac veins drain directly into the anterior aspect of the right atrium. The other listed veins drain directly into the coronary sinus. The posterior cardiac vein may occasionally join the great cardiac vein instead of direct drainage into the sinus.

117 A: Metaphyseal-physeal junction

The vascularity in the region of the metaphyseal-physeal junction is the greatest and therefore this area is affected first in osteomyelitis. Infection spreads to the subperiosteal and diaphyseal areas afterwards. The epiphysis is affected early in the presence of septic arthritis.

118 D: They require vigilant observation for signs of brachial artery damage

Supracondylar fractures are commoner in children. Falling onto an outstretched hand hyperextends the child's elbow, leading the distal fragment to tilt posteriorly. The anteriorly tilted proximal fragment can damage the brachial artery. Patients with such supracondylar fractures should be taken to theatre as soon as possible as delay leads to excessive swelling and difficulty in reduction. Reduction is performed by flexing the elbow and applying pressure behind the olecranon.

119 E: Hyperparathyroidism

Raised serum amylase is classically seen in acute pancreatitis.

Other causes include:

- **Congenital:**
  - congenital hyperamylasaemia
- **Acquired:**
  - infection, eg mumps

- Neoplasm, eg pancreatic carcinoma
- Vascular, eg mesenteric ischaemia
- Inflammatory, eg hepatitis, post-ERCP (endoscopic retrograde cholangiopancreatography), peritonitis
- Trauma, eg burns, perforated duodenal ulcer, intestinal obstruction or perforation
- Drugs, eg opiates
- Metabolic, eg renal failure, renal transplant, diabetic ketoacidosis, macroamylasaemia.

120 D: Absence of limb spinal reflexes

To proceed with organ donation in a brainstem-dead donor, the tests of brainstem death must be verified by two separate senior physicians after exclusion of endocrine, metabolic, therapeutic and hypothermic abnormalities which could mask the examination. The test is in two sections, one to assess the lack of respiratory drive, and the second to establish brainstem inadequacy.

Lack of respiratory drive following hypercarbia:

The subject is pre-oxygenated with 100% oxygen and then disconnected from the ventilator for 10 minutes. The P_{CO_2} is allowed to rise and a level of >6.5 kPa should stimulate respiration in a normal but not in a brainstem-dead individual.

Brainstem tests:

- Absent pupillary and corneal reflexes
- Absent cranial nerve functioning
- Absent gag and cough reflexes
- Cold caloric test to demonstrate lack of vestibulo-ocular reflexes.

Spinal reflexes are not relevant in brainstem death testing as they may very well be present in brain-dead individuals if the spinal cord has not sustained any injuries.

121 D: Hypercalcaemia

Massive blood transfusion is defined as a transfusion equivalent to the patient's blood volume administered within 24 hours. Complications of massive blood transfusion include volume overload, thrombocytopenia, coagulopathy, hypothermia, hypocalcaemia, and hyperkalaemia. Hypocalcaemia occurs due to the chelation of calcium by the citrate in the additive solution in stored blood.

122 B: The cricoid cartilage is a derivative of the sixth arch

The larynx is made up of cartilages and associated ligaments, which move from the action of the laryngeal muscles. The four main cartilages are the thyroid cartilage (found at the level of C4 and a fourth arch derivative), arytenoid cartilage, cricoid cartilage (found at the level of C6 and a sixth arch derivative) and the epiglottis. All of the intrinsic muscles of the larynx except cricothyroid are supplied by the recurrent laryngeal nerve. Cricothyroid is supplied by the superior laryngeal nerve. The actions of the intrinsic muscles open the cords (posterior cricoarytenoids), close the larynx during swallowing (lateral cricoarytenoids) and alter the tension of the cords to change pitch during speech (thyroarytenoids and cricothyroids).

123 E: 100 mg hydrocortisone IV pre-operatively and then 100 mg 6-hourly for at least the first 72 hours

Patients on steroids undergoing surgery require peri-operative steroid replacement in order to prevent an addisonian crisis. This is dependent on the level of surgery and includes:

- **Minor surgery:** 50 mg IV hydrocortisone pre-operatively with continuation of oral steroids immediately after resuming oral intake
- **Intermediate:** 50 mg hydrocortisone IV pre-operatively and 6-hourly for the first 24 hours and then switch to oral.
- **Major surgery:** 100 mg hydrocortisone IV pre-operatively and then 100 mg 6-hourly for at least the first 72 hours.

124 E: The spleen lies over the 9th, 10th and 11th ribs posteriorly

Important surface landmarks in the abdomen include: liver, from the nipple line to the 10th rib; gallbladder, at 9th costal cartilage midclavicular line; kidney, superior pole at the level of the 12th rib posteriorly; pancreas, at L1; spleen, overlying the 9th, 10th and 11th ribs posteriorly. The transpyloric plane of Addison lies midway between the suprasternal notch and the pubis at the level of L1.

125 A: Early steroid administration

There is still much debate about the use of early steroid therapy in the management of ARDS. Proven treatment strategies at present include, but are not limited to: prone position ventilation, activated protein C administration in sepsis, inverse ratio ventilation, inhaled nitric oxide use, management of the initial disease, nutritional support and early goal-directed therapy, mechanical ventilation with small tidal volumes and permissive hypercarbia, and strict control of fluid resuscitation.

126 B: Had an early menarche

Risk factors for breast cancer include female sex, older age, early menarche and late menopause, nulliparity, late first birth age, family history of breast cancer, atypical breast hyperplasia, and geographical location.

127 C: ASA 3

ASA 1 – normal healthy individual

ASA 2 – patient with mild systemic disease

ASA 3 – patient with severe systemic disease that limits activity but is not incapacitating

ASA 4 – incapacitating systemic disease that is constantly life-threatening

ASA 5 – moribund, not expected to survive 24 hours with or without surgery

This patient has activity-limiting severe systemic disease, but not regarded as constantly life-threatening enough to be classed as ASA 4. If this patient came in with an emergency condition, the acute problem could strain the pre-existing systemic diseases enough to lead to a reclassification as ASA 4.

128 B: Lidocaine

Amide-type local anaesthetics such as lidocaine undergo hydrolysis by microsomal enzymes in the liver. The metabolism of such types of anaesthetics can be affected by severe liver dysfunction and they are best avoided in such cases. Ester-type local anaesthetics are mainly hydrolysed by pseudocholinesterases.

129 A: Early mobilisation

Subarachnoid haemorrhage represents a neurosurgical emergency. It can be caused by trauma or occur spontaneously occur when a berry aneurysm ruptures, leading to haemorrhage. Management includes early referral to a neurosurgical unit for bedrest, intravenous fluids, nimodipine therapy, cerebral angiography and coiling of the aneurysm. Other alternatives include clipping of the aneurysm base at open surgery and insertion of a ventricular drain to allow any blood to drain out and prevent a hydrocephalus from forming.

130 C: The left phrenic nerve pierces the diaphragm together with the IVC at the level of T8

The diaphragm arises from the six lower costal cartilages laterally, xiphoid anteriorly, arcuate ligaments and crura posteriorly. The left crus arises from the lumbar vertebrae L1–2 and the right one arises from L1–3. The following structures pierce the diaphragm: at T8 – left phrenic nerve and IVC; at T10 – oesophagus and vagi; at T12 – aorta and thoracic duct. It is also pierced by the splanchnic nerves and sympathetic chain.

131 C: Urate stones

Over 90% of renal calculi are radio-opaque. Urate or uric acid stones arise in acidic urine and are generally hard, light-brown stones, which are smooth on the surface with facets.

132 A: Herpes simplex virus

Herpes simplex virus has not yet been identified as a cancer-causing virus. It is associated with high-risk infectious groups who may also carry the hepatitis, HIV, and human papilloma viruses, all of which are linked to known malignancies.

133 B: Prostate

The commonest of tumours to metastasise to bone include kidney, prostate, breast, lung, and thyroid tumours. Most of these form osteolytic bony metastases with the exception of prostate cancers which cause a sclerotic lesion, most commonly in the lumbar spine, as the venous drainage via Batson's plexus is connected.

134 D: Partial pressure of carbon dioxide (P_{CO_2}) <4.3 kPa

SIRS is the syndrome resulting from the body's reaction to a critical illness. Defining criteria include:

Temperature >38 °C or <36 °C

Heart rate >90/min

Respiratory rate >20/min or P_{CO_2} <4.3 kPa

WCC $>12 \times 10^9$/l or $<4 \times 10^9$/l, or >10% immature forms.

135 D: Serum lactate >4 mmol/l

A serum lactate level of >4 mmol/l is associated with a 50% mortality rate in any disease and should be taken very seriously. Haemorrhagic free fluid found at surgery indicates bowel infarction and should prompt a search for dead bowel with a view to resection. Atrial fibrillation, low oxygen saturation and high white cell counts are all indicators of systemic disease. However, if the original disease process is treated in addition to adequate oxygen and fluid resuscitation, then these parameters should resolve themselves.

Index

Topics have been indexed by question number.